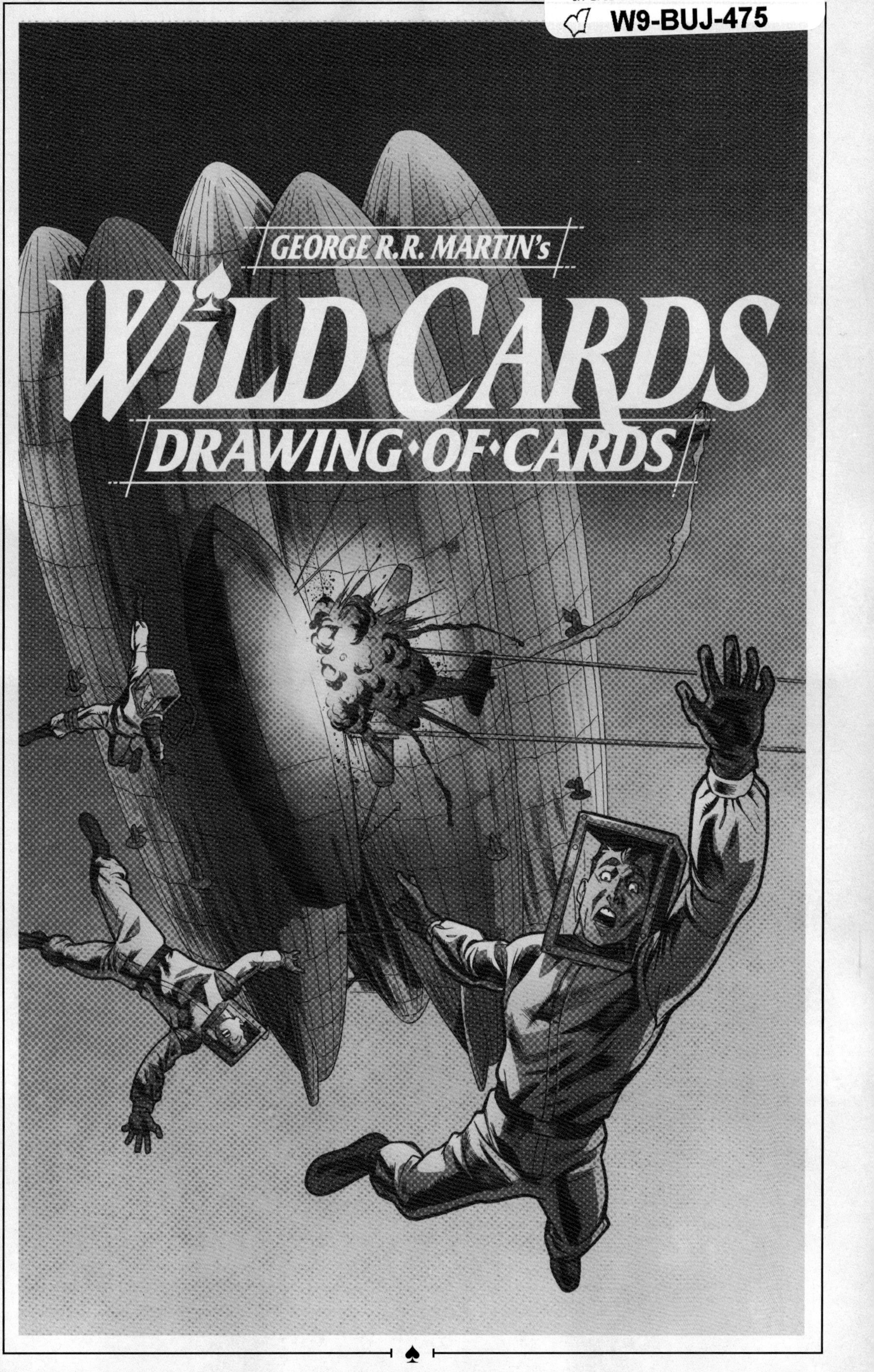
GEORGE R.R. MARTIN's
WILD CARDS
DRAWING·OF·CARDS

COLLECTION EDITOR .... *Jennifer Grünwald*

ASSISTANT EDITOR .... *Daniel Kirchhoffer*

ASSISTANT MANAGING EDITOR......... *Maia Loy*

ASSOCIATE MANAGER, TALENT RELATIONS ......
.... *Lisa Montalbano*

VP, PRODUCTION & SPECIAL PROJECTS ....
.... *Jeff Youngquist*

BOOK DESIGNER .... *Jay Bowen*

SVP PRINT, SALES & MARKETING ....
.... *David Gabriel*

EDITOR IN CHIEF .... *C.B. Cebulski*

WILD CARDS: THE DRAWING OF CARDS. Contains material originally published in magazine form as WILD CARDS: THE DRAWING OF CARDS (2022) #1-4. First printing 2022. ISBN 978-1-302-92504-8. Published by MARVEL WORLDWIDE, INC., a subsidiary of MARVEL ENTERTAINMENT, LLC. OFFICE OF PUBLICATION: 1290 Avenue of the Americas, New York, NY 10104. © 2022 The Wild Cards Trust. No similarity between any of the names, characters, persons, and/or institutions in this book with those of any living or dead person or institution is intended, and any such similarity which may exist is purely coincidental. Marvel, its characters, and its logos are © and TM Marvel Characters, Inc. **Printed in the U.S.A.** KEVIN FEIGE, Chief Creative Officer; DAN BUCKLEY, President, Marvel Entertainment; DAVID BOGART, Associate Publisher & SVP of Talent Affairs; TOM BREVOORT, VP, Executive Editor; NICK LOWE, Executive Editor, VP of Content, Digital Publishing; DAVID GABRIEL, VP of Print & Digital Publishing; SVEN LARSEN, VP of Licensed Publishing; MARK ANNUNZIATO, VP of Planning & Forecasting; JEFF YOUNGQUIST, VP of Production & Special Projects; ALEX MORALES, Director of Publishing Operations; DAN EDINGTON, Director of Editorial Operations; RICKEY PURDIN, Director of Talent Relations; JENNIFER GRÜNWALD, Director of Production & Special Projects; SUSAN CRESPI, Production Manager; STAN LEE, Chairman Emeritus. For information regarding advertising in Marvel Comics or on Marvel.com, please contact Vit DeBellis, Custom Solutions & Integrated Advertising Manager, at vdebellis@marvel.com. For Marvel subscription inquiries, please call 888-511-5480. **Manufactured between 11/11/2022 and 12/13/2022 by SEAWAY PRINTING, GREEN BAY, WI, USA.**

10 9 8 7 6 5 4 3 2 1

This book contains excerpts from *Now and Then: An Original Wild Cards Graphic Novel* and *George R. R. Martin Presents Wild Cards: Sins of the Father.*

Now and Then: An Original Wild Cards Graphic Novel is a work of fiction. Names, characters, places, and incidents are the products of the authors' imaginations or are used fictitiously. Any resemblance to actual events, locales, or persons, living or dead, is entirely coincidental. Copyright © 2022 by Wild Cards Trust. All rights reserved. Published in the United States by Bantam Books, an imprint of Random House, a division of Penguin Random House LLC, New York. BANTAM BOOKS is a registered trademark and the B colophon is a trademark of Penguin Random House LLC. ISBN 978-0-8041-7708-5

George R. R. Martin Presents Wild Cards: Sins of the Father is a work of fiction. Names, characters, places, and incidents are the products of the authors' imaginations or are used fictitiously. Any resemblance to actual events, locales, or persons, living or dead, is entirely coincidental. Copyright © 2023 by Wild Cards Trust. All rights reserved. Published in the United States by Bantam Books, an imprint of Random House, a division of Penguin Random House LLC, New York. BANTAM BOOKS is a registered trademark and the B colophon is a trademark of Penguin Random House LLC. ISBN 978-0-8041-7710-8

GEORGE R.R. MARTIN's

WILD CARDS
DRAWING·OF·CARDS

WORLD WAR II HAS ENDED, AND THE WORLD IS BEGINNING ITS RECOVERY FROM THE DEVASTATING CONFLICT. EVEN FOR THE VICTORS, THE AFTERMATH IS NO CAKEWALK, AS **ROBERT TOMLIN**--THE WAR HERO KNOWN AS **JET BOY**--IS DISCOVERING.

HIS TIME AS A REAL-LIFE PULP HERO IN A JET PLANE ON THE FRONT LINES AT AN END, HE HAS RETURNED HOME TO A WORLD HE BARELY REMEMBERS... AND ONE ABOUT TO CHANGE EVEN MORE THAN HE COULD IMAGINE.

WRITER.. **Paul Cornell**

PENCILERS.. **Mike Hawthorne** (#1-2) & **Enid Balám** (#3-4)

INKERS... **Adriano Di Benedetto** (#1-2) & **Lee Townsend** (#3-4)

COLORIST................ **Ruth Redmond**

LETTERER................. **VC's Cory Petit**

COVER ART..................................... **Steve Morris**

ASSOCIATE EDITORS .... **Annalise Bissa** & **Lauren Amaro**

EDITOR .... **Jordan D. White**

ADAPTED FROM STORIES BY .... **Howard Waldrop**, **George R.R. Martin** & **Roger Zelazny**

WITH ADDITIONAL MATERIAL BY .... **Kevin Andrew Murphy** & **Melinda M. Snodgrass**

FROM THE MOSAIC NOVEL *WILD CARDS*, EDITED BY....... **George R.R. Martin**

WILD CARDS CREATED BY THE WRITERS OF ..... **the Wild Cards Consortium**

WILD CARDS CONSULTANT......................... **Raya Golden**

♠

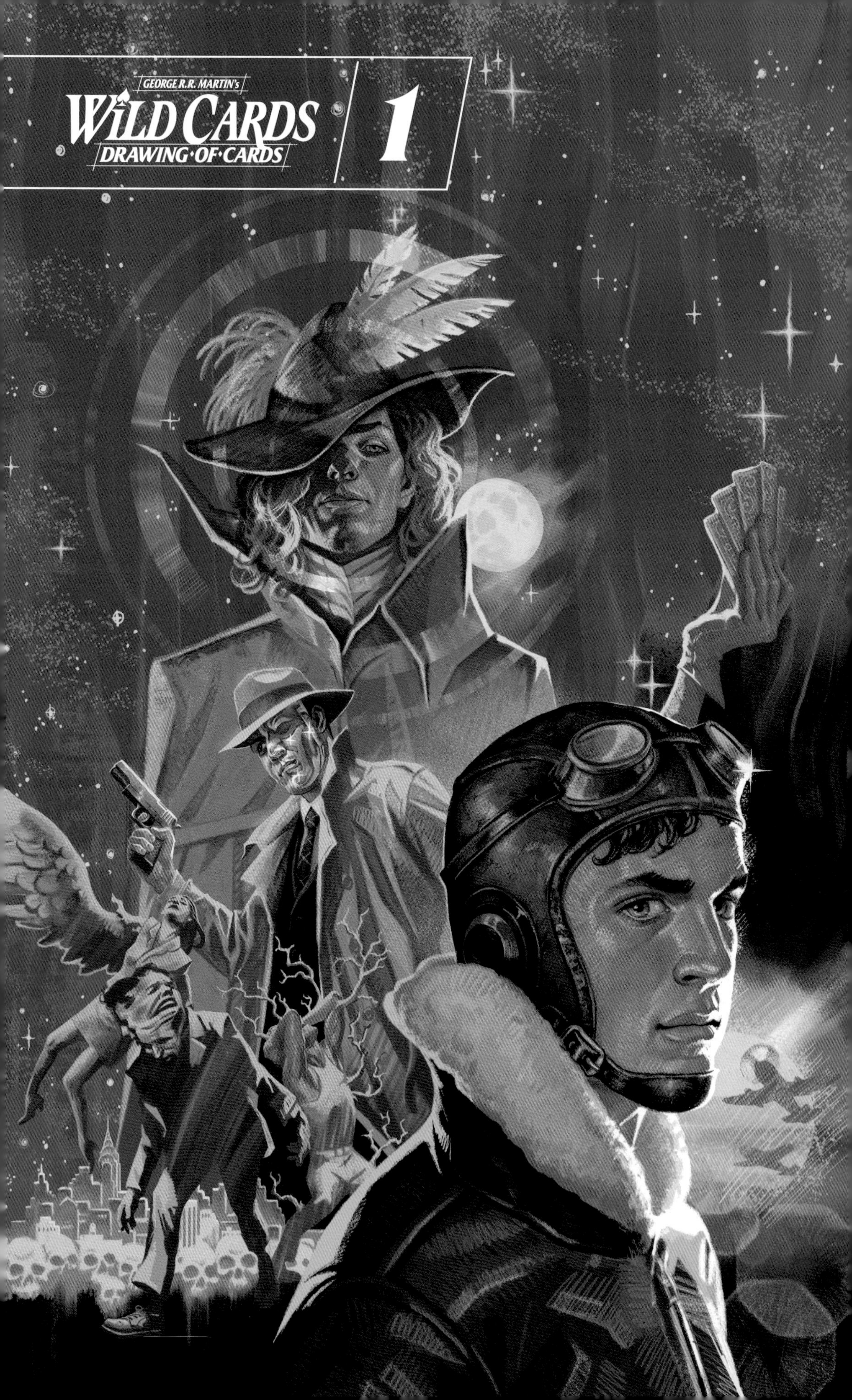
GEORGE R.R. MARTIN's
WILD CARDS
DRAWING·OF·CARDS
1

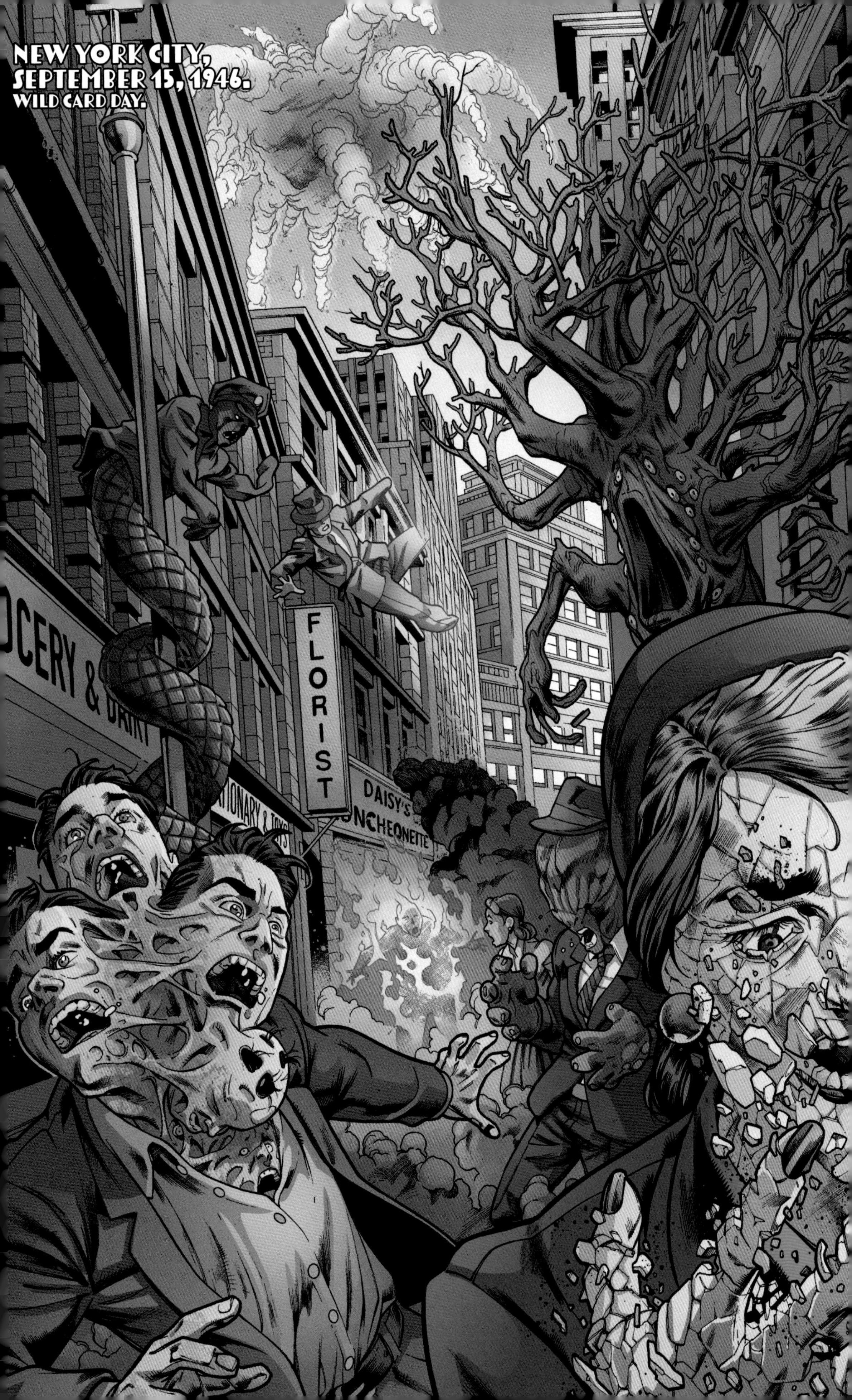
NEW YORK CITY,
SEPTEMBER 15, 1946.
WILD CARD DAY.
FLORIST
DAISY'S

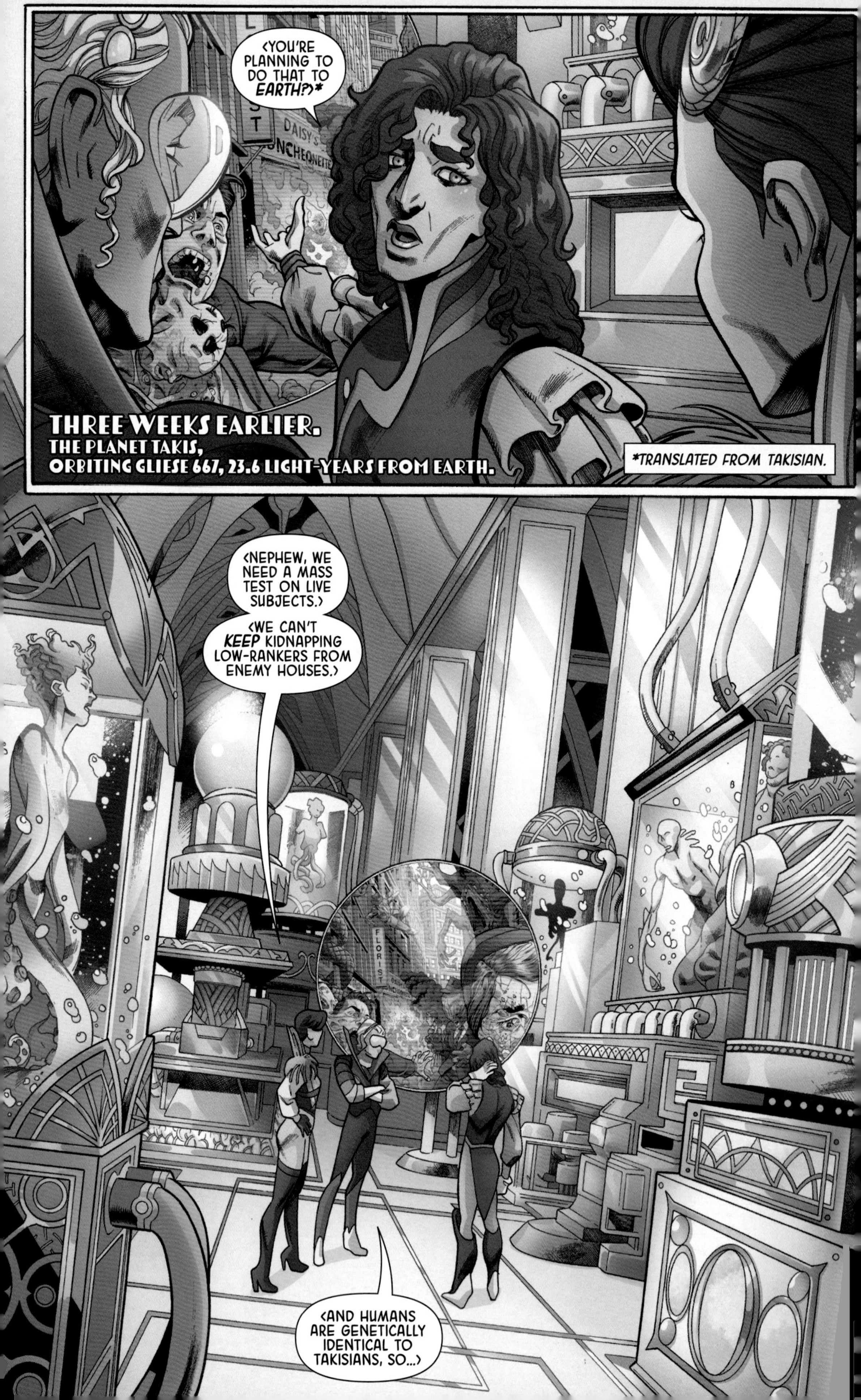

<YOU'RE PLANNING TO DO THAT TO EARTH?>*
DAISY'S
THREE WEEKS EARLIER.
THE PLANET TAKIS,
ORBITING GLIESE 667, 23.6 LIGHT-YEARS FROM EARTH.
*TRANSLATED FROM TAKISIAN.
<NEPHEW, WE NEED A MASS TEST ON LIVE SUBJECTS.>
<WE CAN'T KEEP KIDNAPPING LOW-RANKERS FROM ENEMY HOUSES.>
FLORIST
<AND HUMANS ARE GENETICALLY IDENTICAL TO TAKISIANS, SO...>

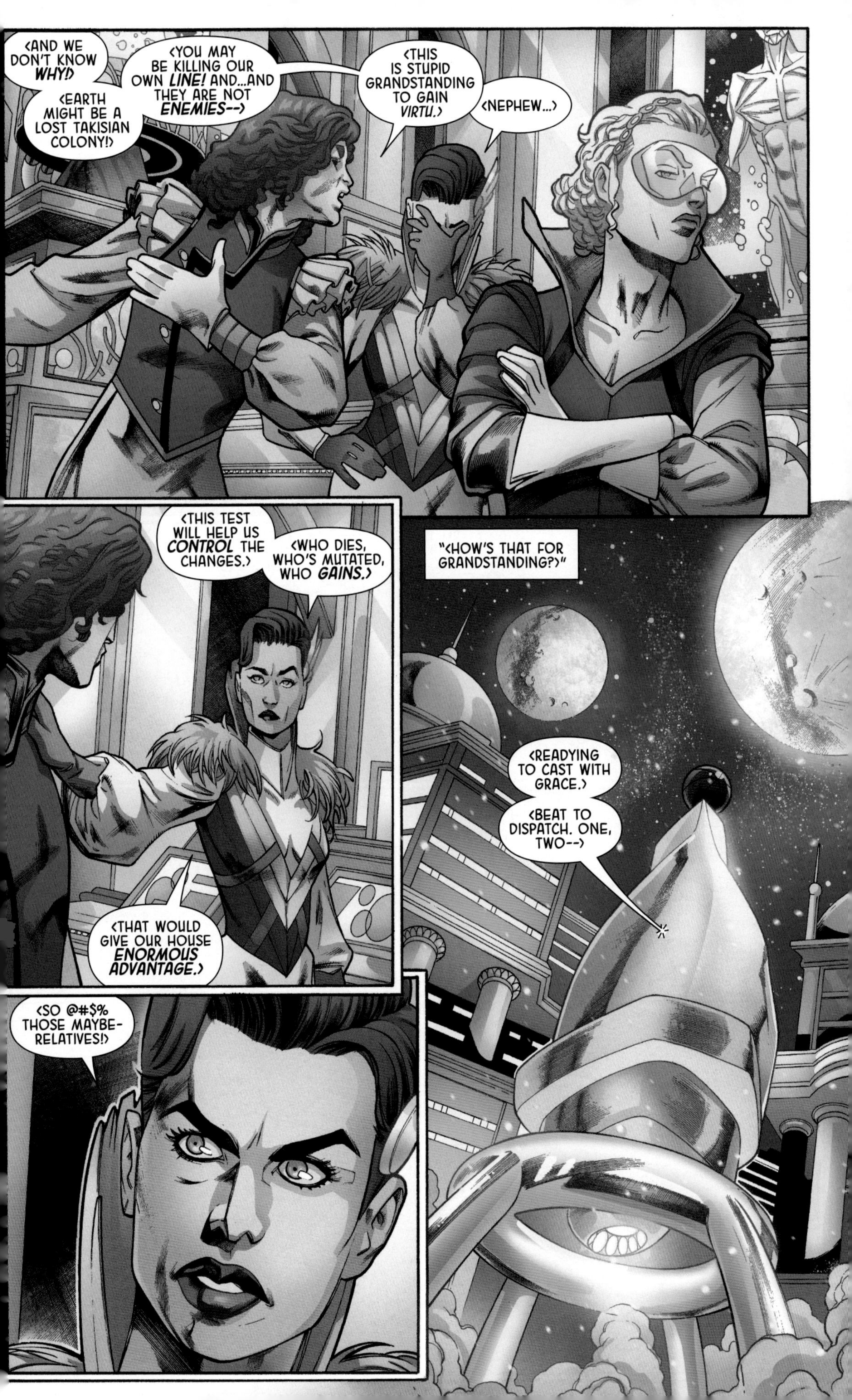

<AND WE DON'T KNOW WHY!>
<EARTH MIGHT BE A LOST TAKISIAN COLONY!>
<YOU MAY BE KILLING OUR OWN LINE! AND...AND THEY ARE NOT ENEMIES-->
<THIS IS STUPID GRANDSTANDING TO GAIN VIRTU.>
<NEPHEW...>
<THIS TEST WILL HELP US CONTROL THE CHANGES.>
<WHO DIES, WHO'S MUTATED, WHO GAINS.>
<THAT WOULD GIVE OUR HOUSE ENORMOUS ADVANTAGE.>
<SO @#$% THOSE MAYBE-RELATIVES!>
"<HOW'S THAT FOR GRANDSTANDING?>"
<READYING TO CAST WITH GRACE.>
<BEAT TO DISPATCH. ONE, TWO-->

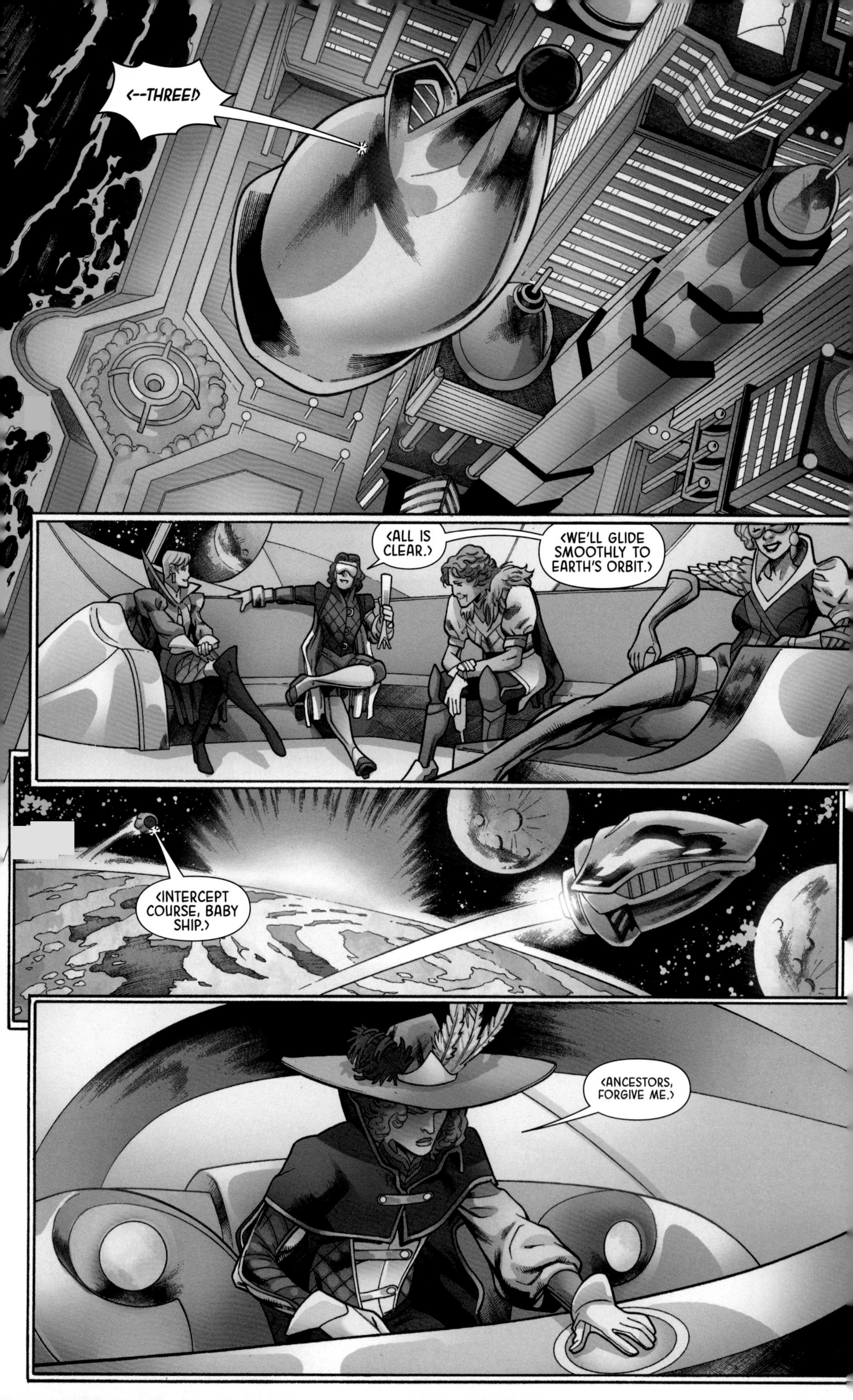
<--THREE!>
<ALL IS CLEAR.>
<WE'LL GLIDE SMOOTHLY TO EARTH'S ORBIT.>
<INTERCEPT COURSE, BABY SHIP.>
<ANCESTORS, FORGIVE ME.>

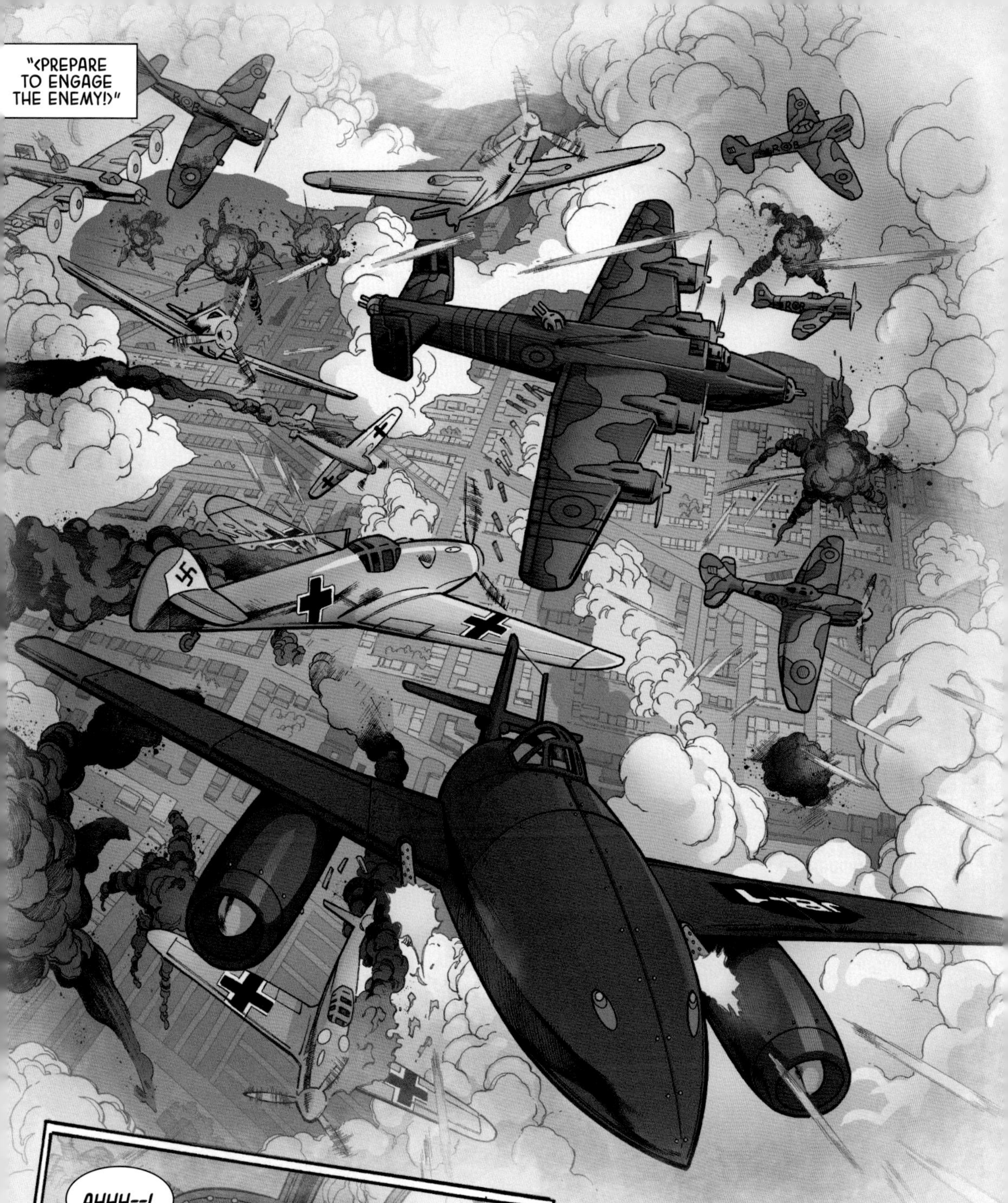
"‹PREPARE TO ENGAGE THE ENEMY!›"

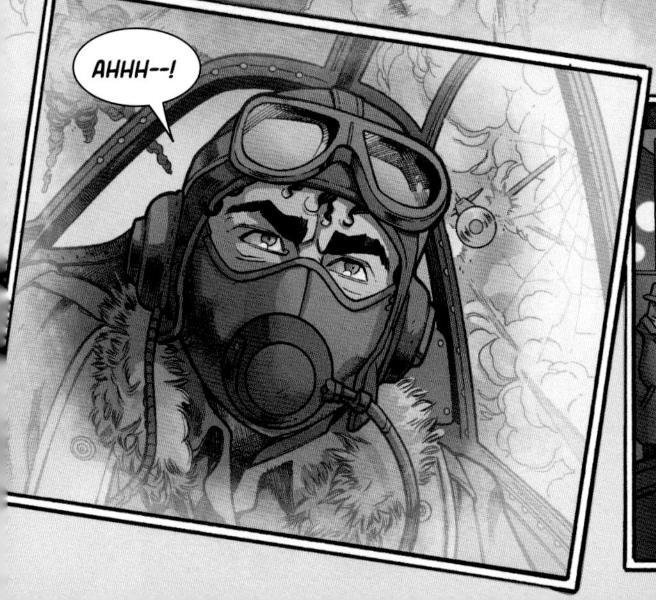
AHHH--!

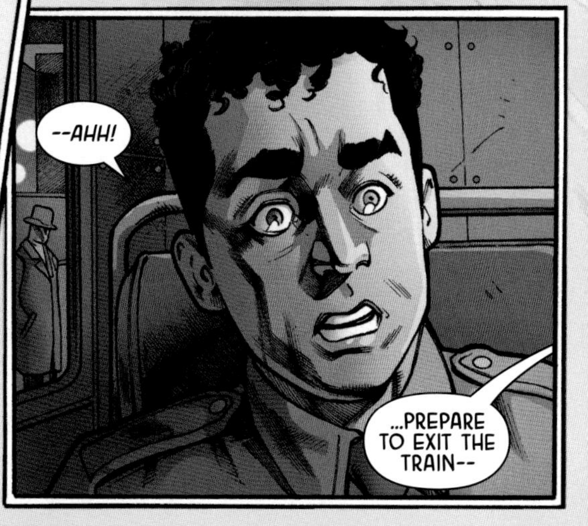
--AHH!
...PREPARE TO EXIT THE TRAIN--

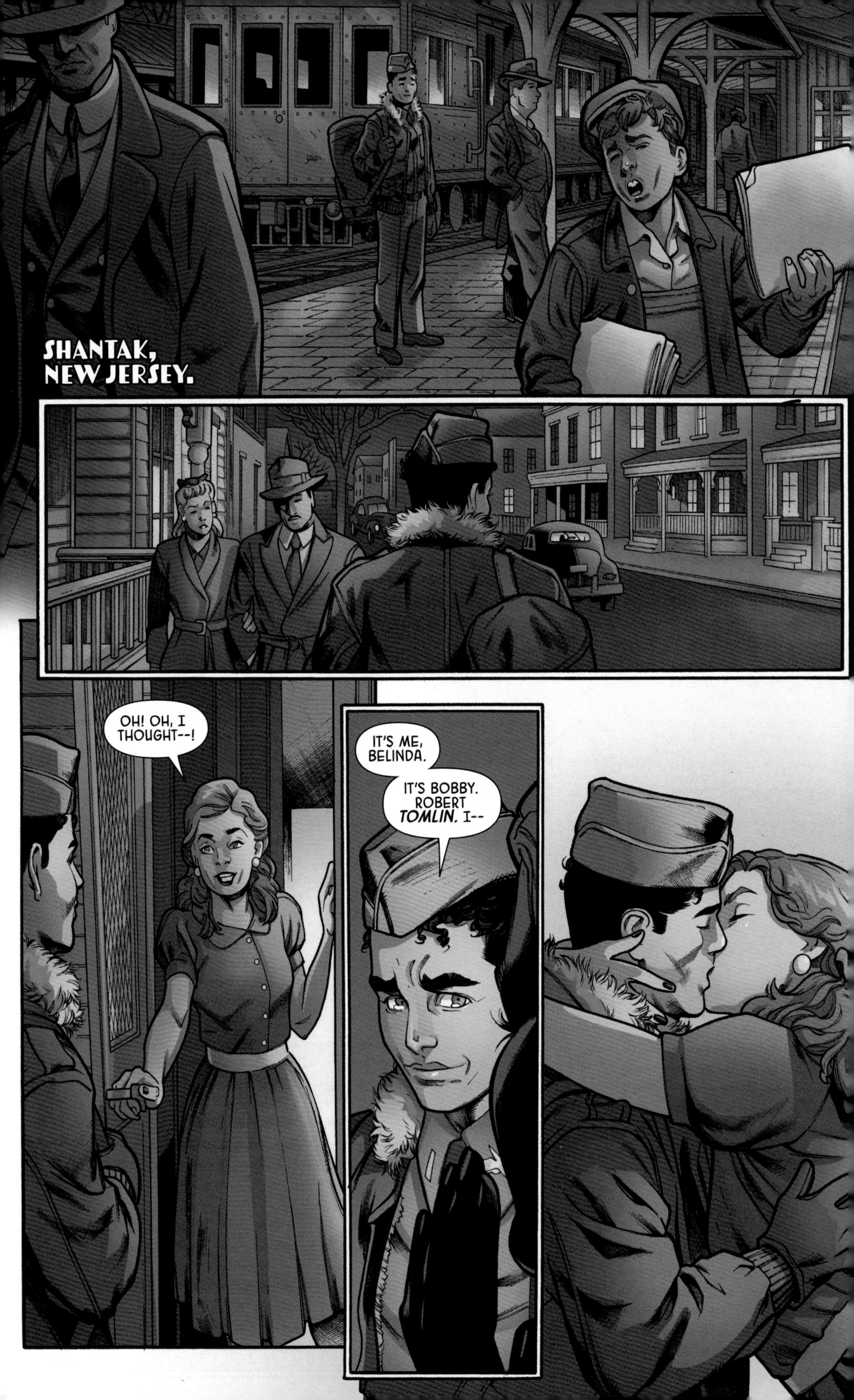
SHANTAK,
NEW JERSEY.
OH! OH, I THOUGHT--!
IT'S ME, BELINDA.
IT'S BOBBY. ROBERT *TOMLIN.* I--

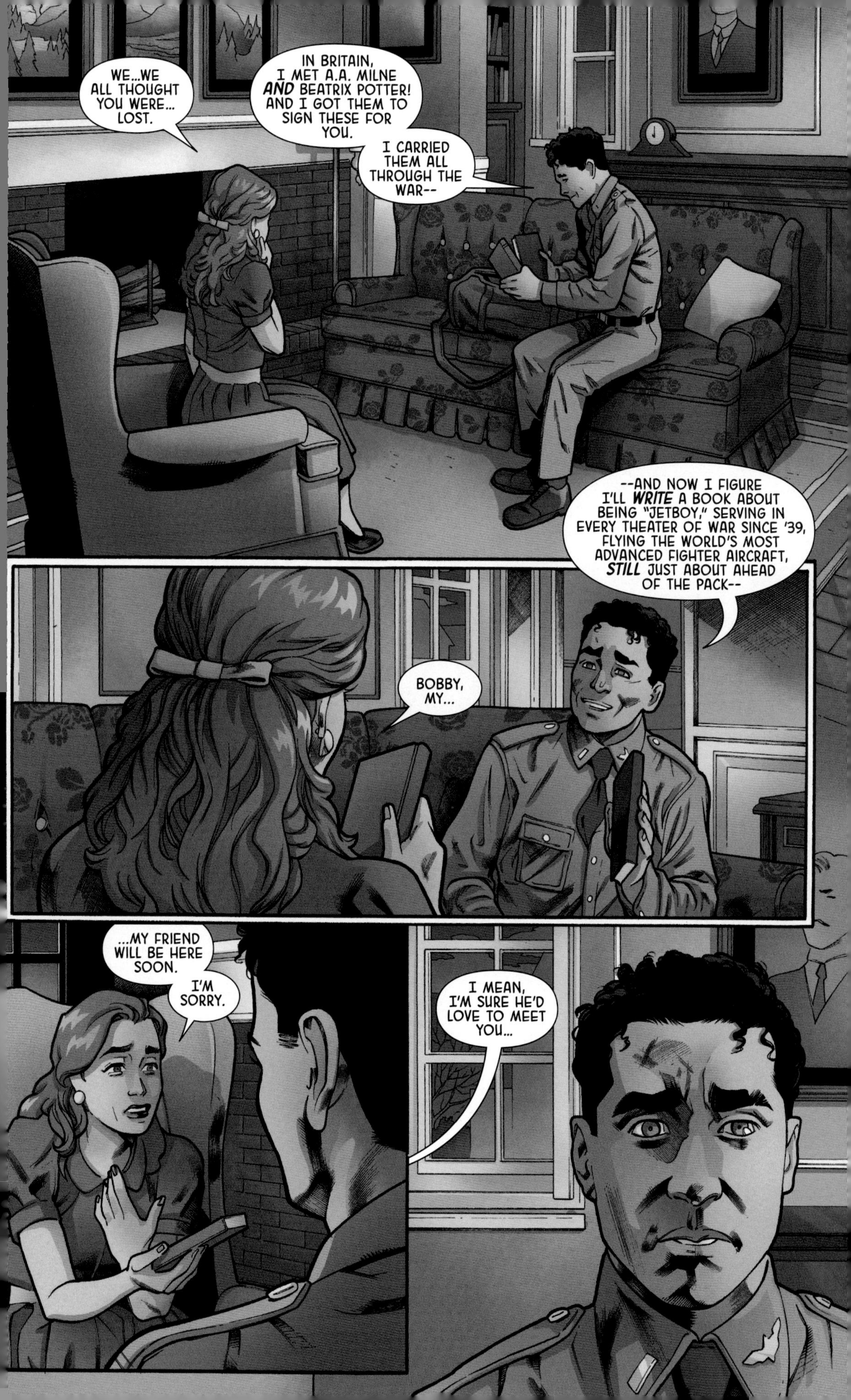
WE...WE ALL THOUGHT YOU WERE... LOST.
IN BRITAIN, I MET A.A. MILNE **AND** BEATRIX POTTER! AND I GOT THEM TO SIGN THESE FOR YOU.
I CARRIED THEM ALL THROUGH THE WAR--
--AND NOW I FIGURE I'LL **WRITE** A BOOK ABOUT BEING "JETBOY," SERVING IN EVERY THEATER OF WAR SINCE '39, FLYING THE WORLD'S MOST ADVANCED FIGHTER AIRCRAFT, **STILL** JUST ABOUT AHEAD OF THE PACK--
BOBBY, MY...
...MY FRIEND WILL BE HERE SOON.
I'M SORRY.
I MEAN, I'M SURE HE'D LOVE TO MEET YOU...

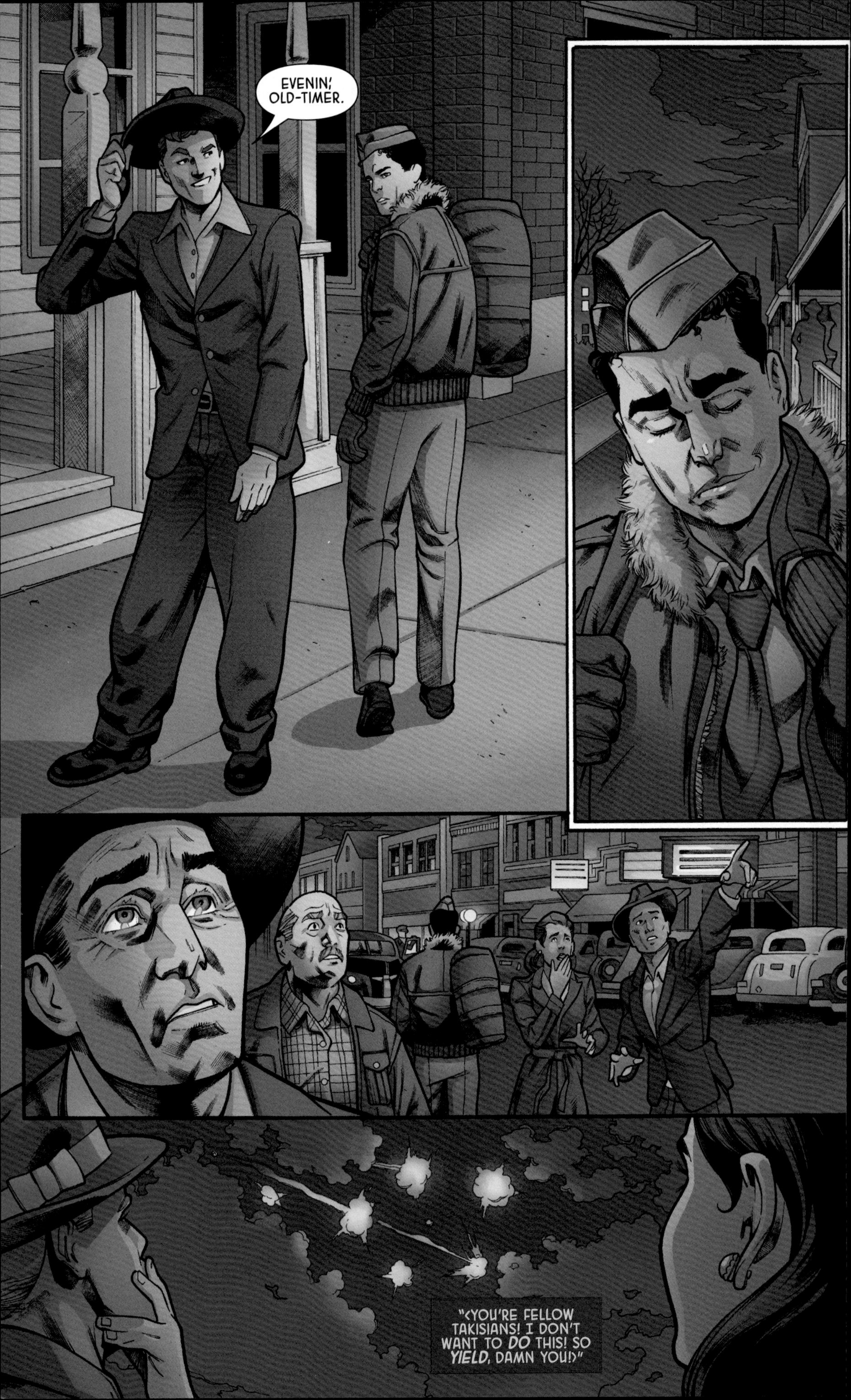
EVENIN', OLD-TIMER.
"<YOU'RE FELLOW TAKISIANS! I DON'T WANT TO *DO* THIS! SO *YIELD*, DAMN YOU!>"

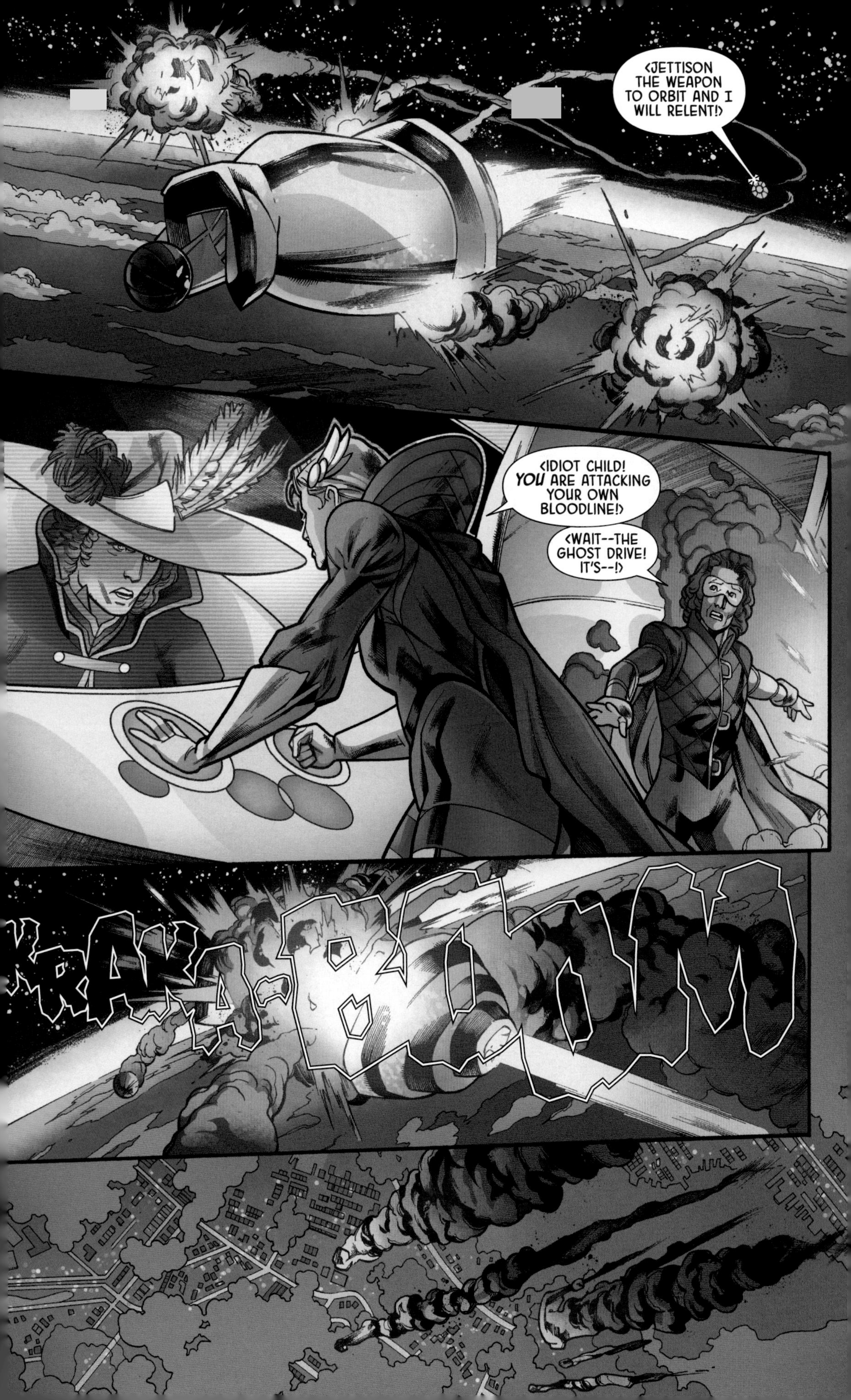
‹JETTISON THE WEAPON TO ORBIT AND I WILL RELENT!›
‹IDIOT CHILD! *YOU* ARE ATTACKING YOUR OWN BLOODLINE!›
‹WAIT--THE GHOST DRIVE! IT'S--!›
KRAKA-BOOM

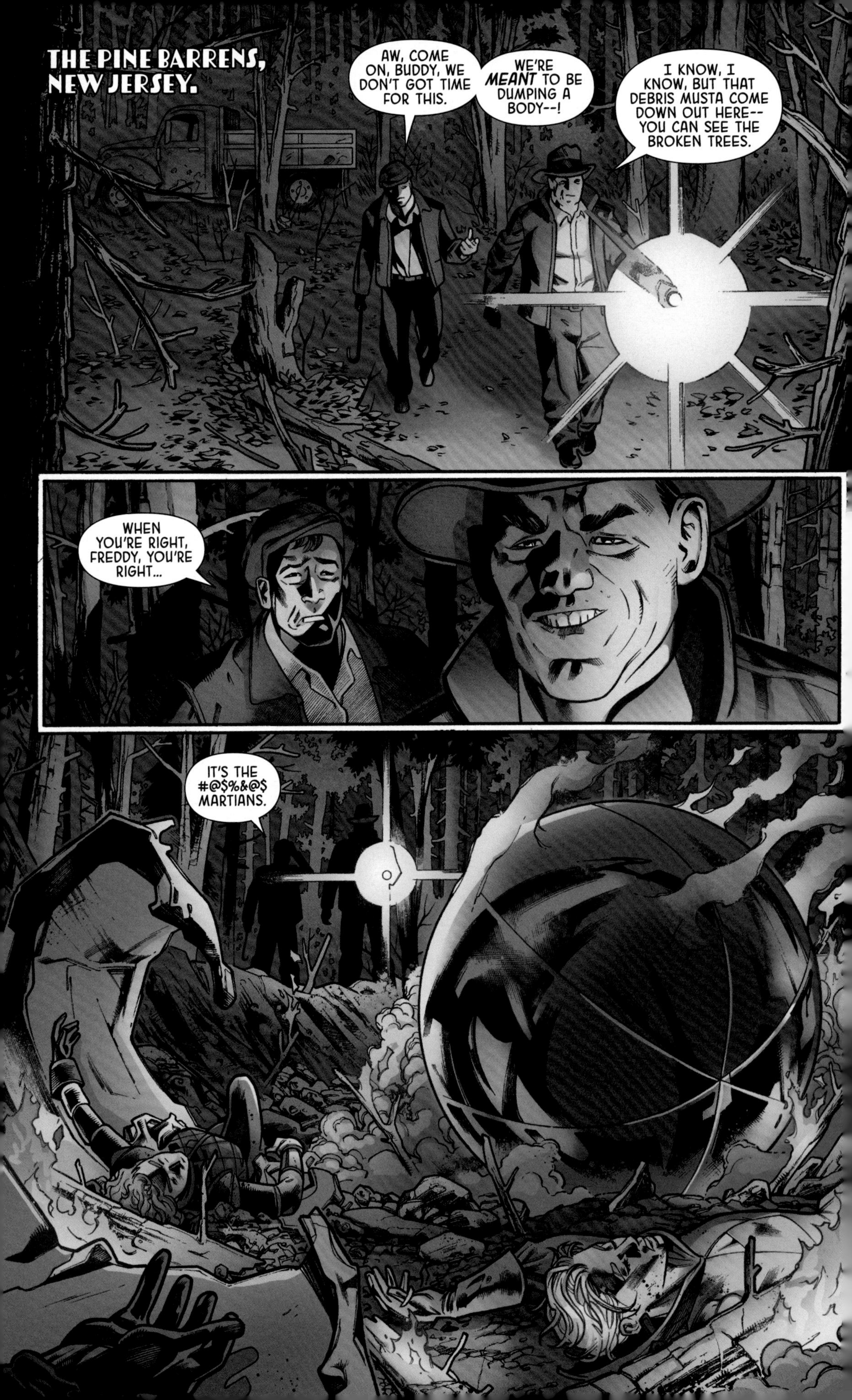
THE PINE BARRENS, NEW JERSEY.
AW, COME ON, BUDDY, WE DON'T GOT TIME FOR THIS.
WE'RE *MEANT* TO BE DUMPING A BODY--!
I KNOW, I KNOW, BUT THAT DEBRIS MUSTA COME DOWN OUT HERE-- YOU CAN SEE THE BROKEN TREES.
WHEN YOU'RE RIGHT, FREDDY, YOU'RE RIGHT...
IT'S THE #@$%&@$ MARTIANS.

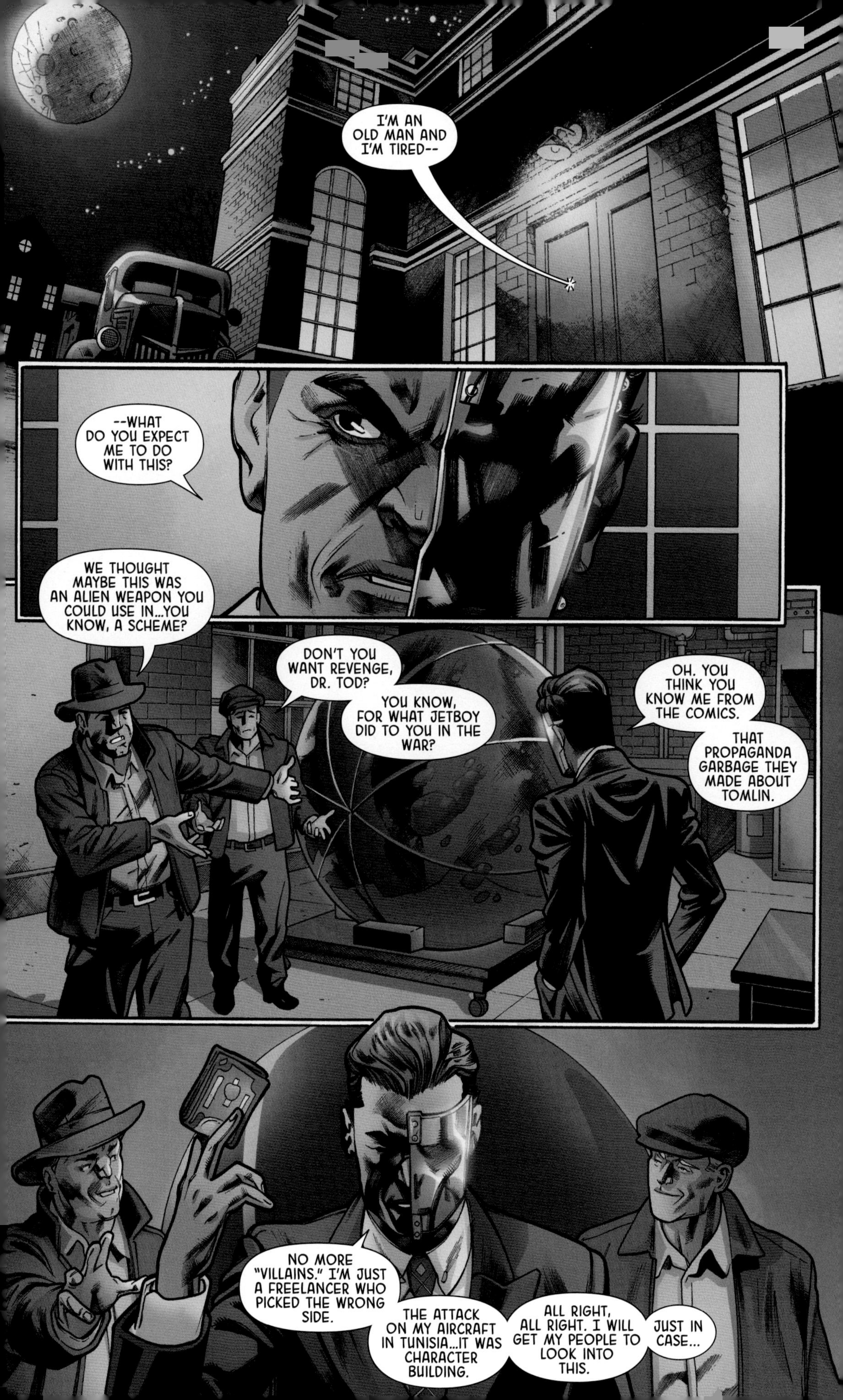

I'M AN OLD MAN AND I'M TIRED--
--WHAT DO YOU EXPECT ME TO DO WITH THIS?
WE THOUGHT MAYBE THIS WAS AN ALIEN WEAPON YOU COULD USE IN...YOU KNOW, A SCHEME?
DON'T YOU WANT REVENGE, DR. TOD?
YOU KNOW, FOR WHAT JETBOY DID TO YOU IN THE WAR?
OH. YOU THINK YOU KNOW ME FROM THE COMICS.
THAT PROPAGANDA GARBAGE THEY MADE ABOUT TOMLIN.
NO MORE "VILLAINS." I'M JUST A FREELANCER WHO PICKED THE WRONG SIDE.
THE ATTACK ON MY AIRCRAFT IN TUNISIA...IT WAS CHARACTER BUILDING.
ALL RIGHT, ALL RIGHT. I WILL GET MY PEOPLE TO LOOK INTO THIS.
JUST IN CASE...

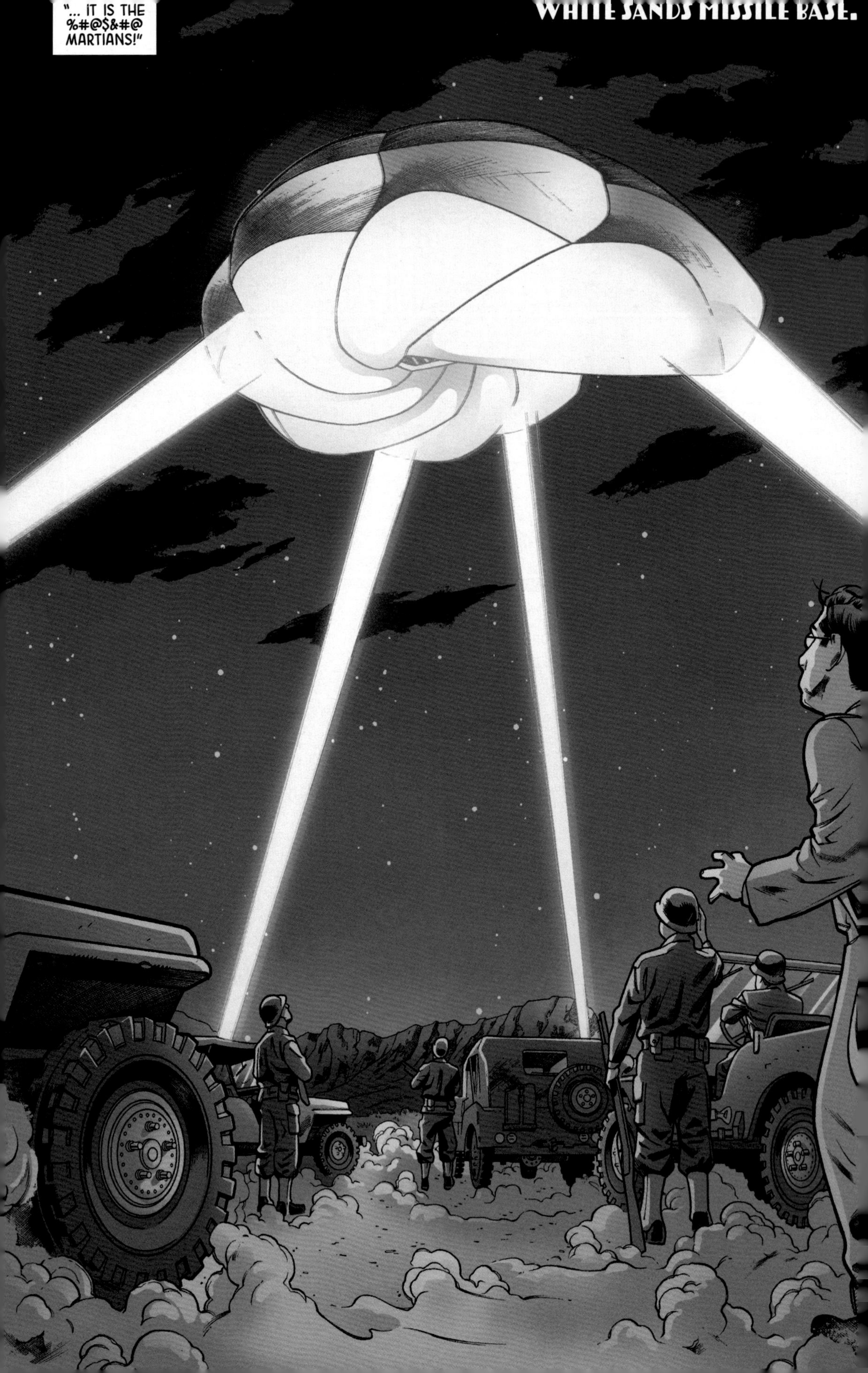
"... IT IS THE %#@$&#@ MARTIANS!"
WHITE SANDS MISSILE BASE.

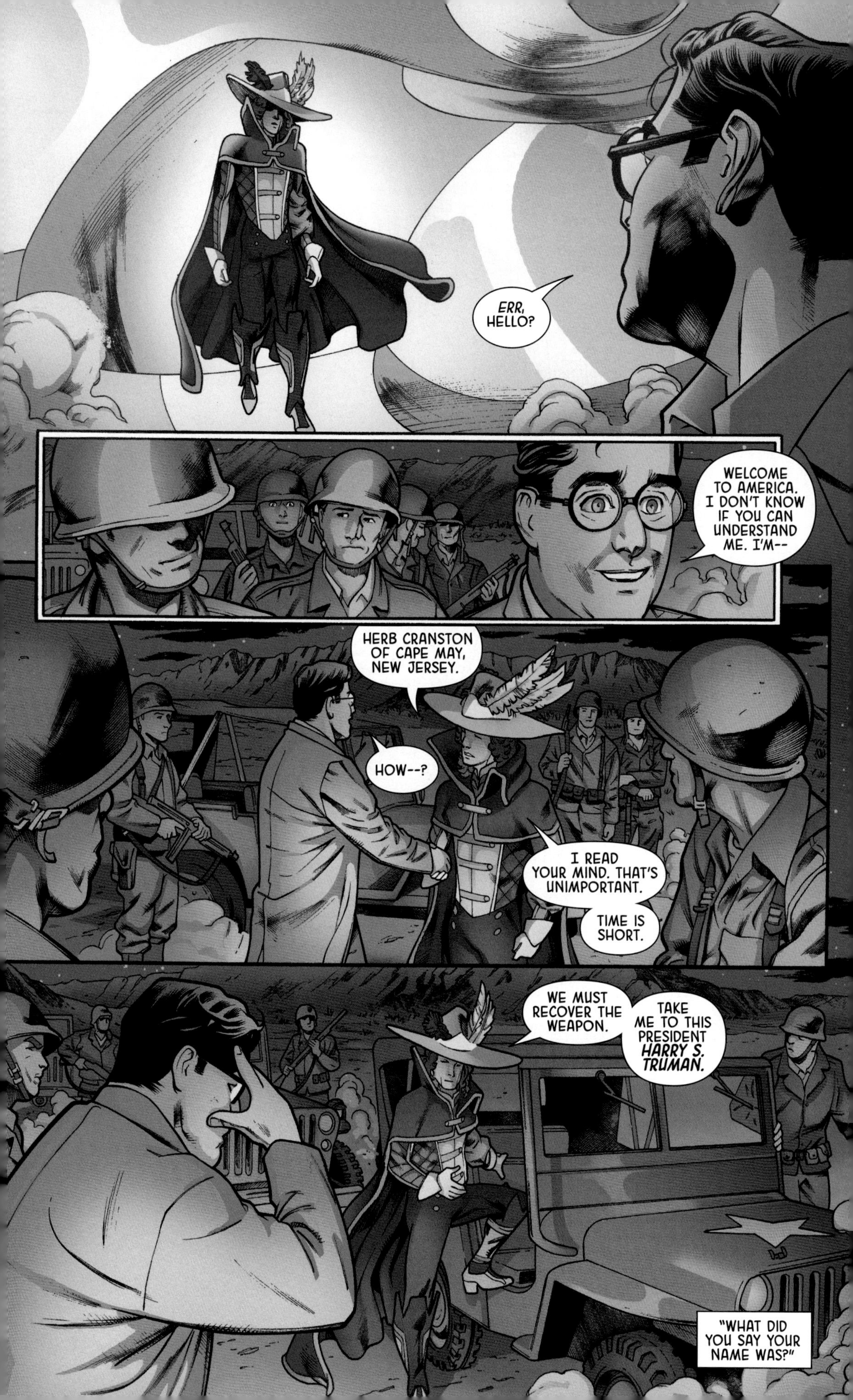

ERR, HELLO?
WELCOME TO AMERICA. I DON'T KNOW IF YOU CAN UNDERSTAND ME. I'M--
HERB CRANSTON OF CAPE MAY, NEW JERSEY.
HOW--?
I READ YOUR MIND. THAT'S UNIMPORTANT.
TIME IS SHORT.
WE MUST RECOVER THE WEAPON.
TAKE ME TO THIS PRESIDENT ***HARRY S. TRUMAN.***
"WHAT DID YOU SAY YOUR NAME WAS?"

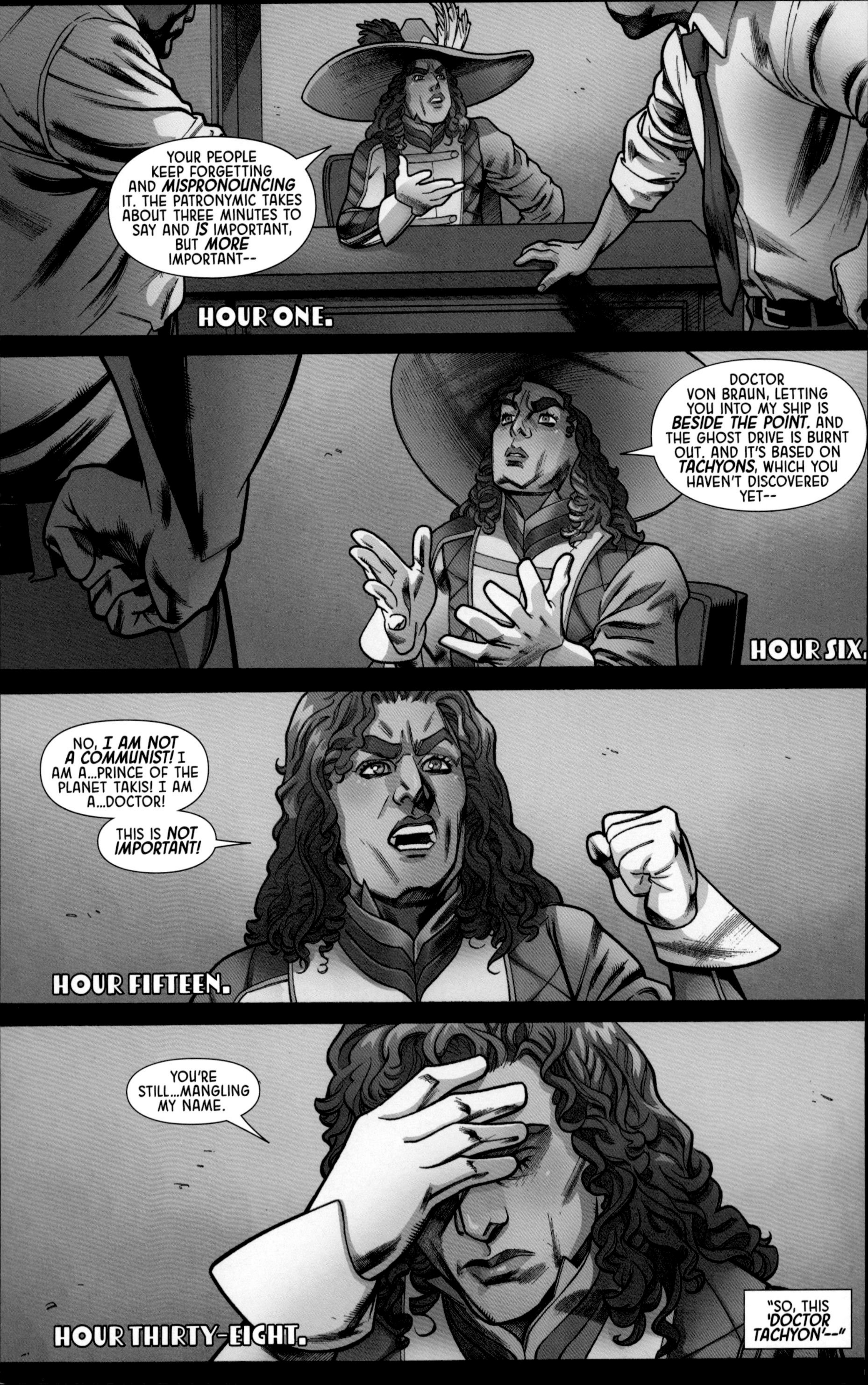

YOUR PEOPLE KEEP FORGETTING AND MISPRONOUNCING IT. THE PATRONYMIC TAKES ABOUT THREE MINUTES TO SAY AND IS IMPORTANT, BUT MORE IMPORTANT--
HOUR ONE.
DOCTOR VON BRAUN, LETTING YOU INTO MY SHIP IS BESIDE THE POINT. AND THE GHOST DRIVE IS BURNT OUT. AND IT'S BASED ON TACHYONS, WHICH YOU HAVEN'T DISCOVERED YET--
HOUR SIX.
NO, I AM NOT A COMMUNIST! I AM A...PRINCE OF THE PLANET TAKIS! I AM A...DOCTOR!
THIS IS NOT IMPORTANT!
HOUR FIFTEEN.
YOU'RE STILL...MANGLING MY NAME.
HOUR THIRTY-EIGHT.
"SO, THIS 'DOCTOR TACHYON'--"

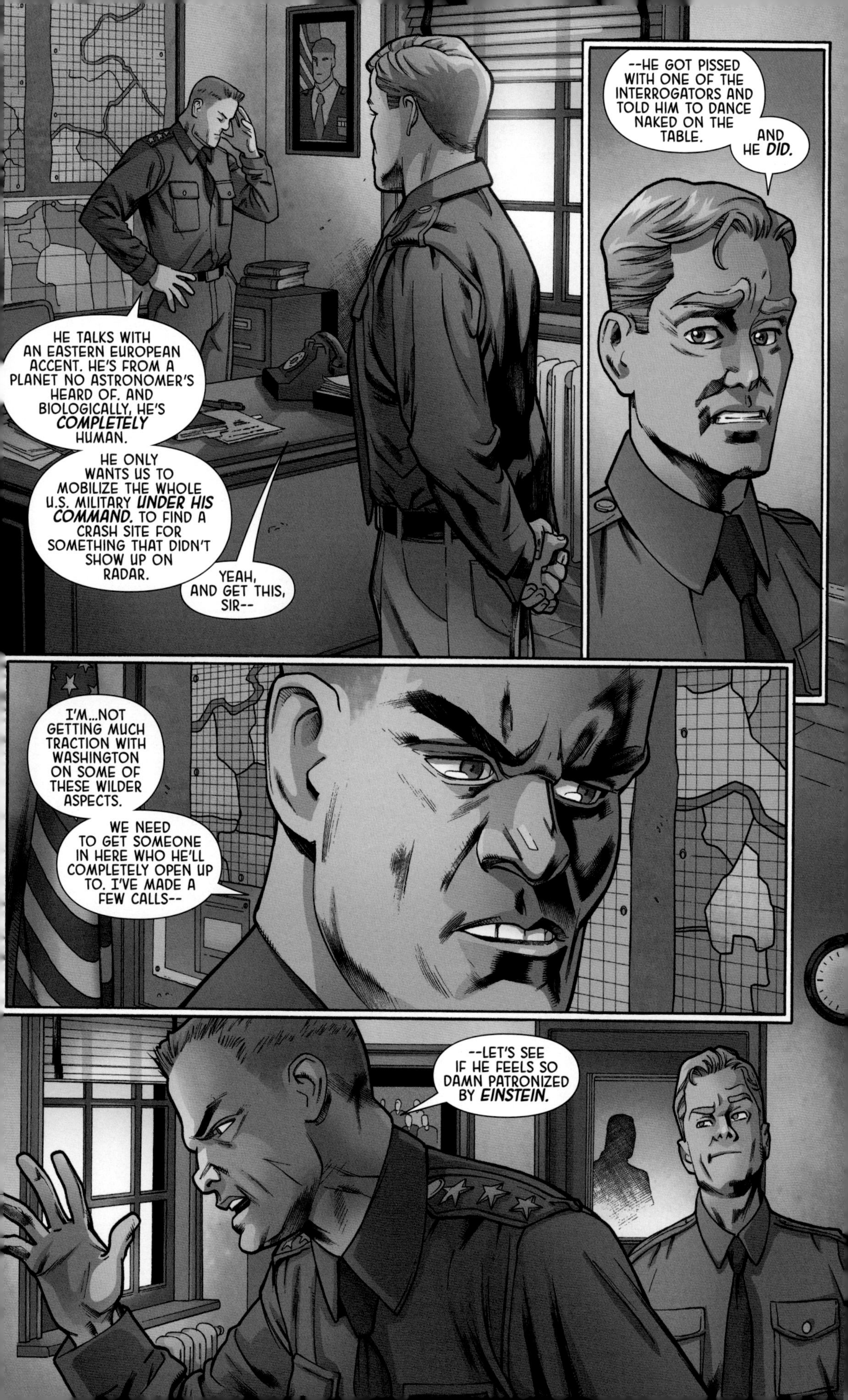
HE TALKS WITH AN EASTERN EUROPEAN ACCENT. HE'S FROM A PLANET NO ASTRONOMER'S HEARD OF. AND BIOLOGICALLY, HE'S *COMPLETELY* HUMAN.
HE ONLY WANTS US TO MOBILIZE THE WHOLE U.S. MILITARY *UNDER HIS COMMAND.* TO FIND A CRASH SITE FOR SOMETHING THAT DIDN'T SHOW UP ON RADAR.
YEAH, AND GET THIS, SIR--
--HE GOT PISSED WITH ONE OF THE INTERROGATORS AND TOLD HIM TO DANCE NAKED ON THE TABLE.
AND HE *DID.*
I'M...NOT GETTING MUCH TRACTION WITH WASHINGTON ON SOME OF THESE WILDER ASPECTS.
WE NEED TO GET SOMEONE IN HERE WHO HE'LL COMPLETELY OPEN UP TO. I'VE MADE A FEW CALLS--
--LET'S SEE IF HE FEELS SO DAMN PATRONIZED BY *EINSTEIN.*

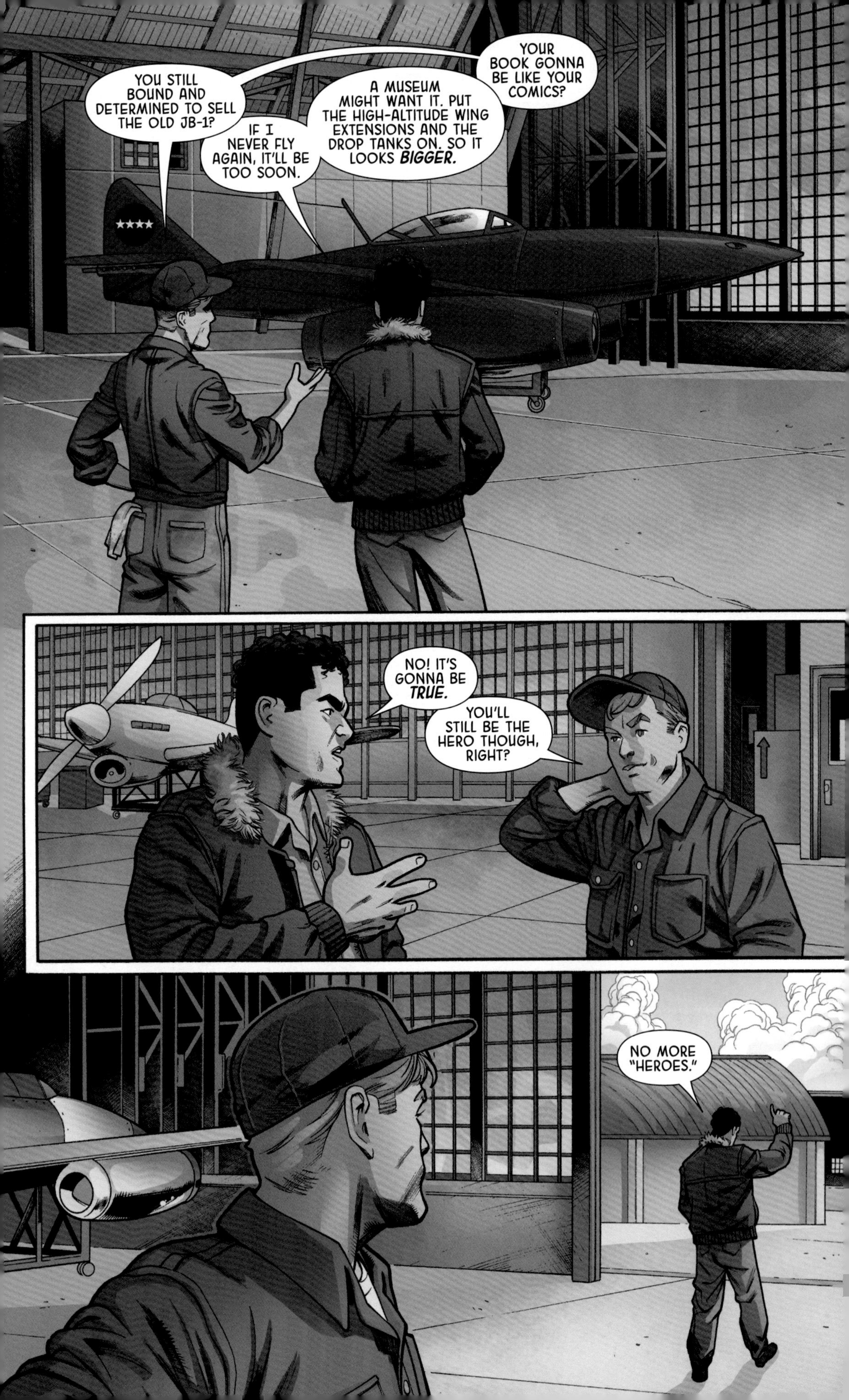
YOU STILL BOUND AND DETERMINED TO SELL THE OLD JB-1?
IF I NEVER FLY AGAIN, IT'LL BE TOO SOON.
A MUSEUM MIGHT WANT IT. PUT THE HIGH-ALTITUDE WING EXTENSIONS AND THE DROP TANKS ON. SO IT LOOKS BIGGER.
YOUR BOOK GONNA BE LIKE YOUR COMICS?
NO! IT'S GONNA BE TRUE.
YOU'LL STILL BE THE HERO THOUGH, RIGHT?
NO MORE "HEROES."

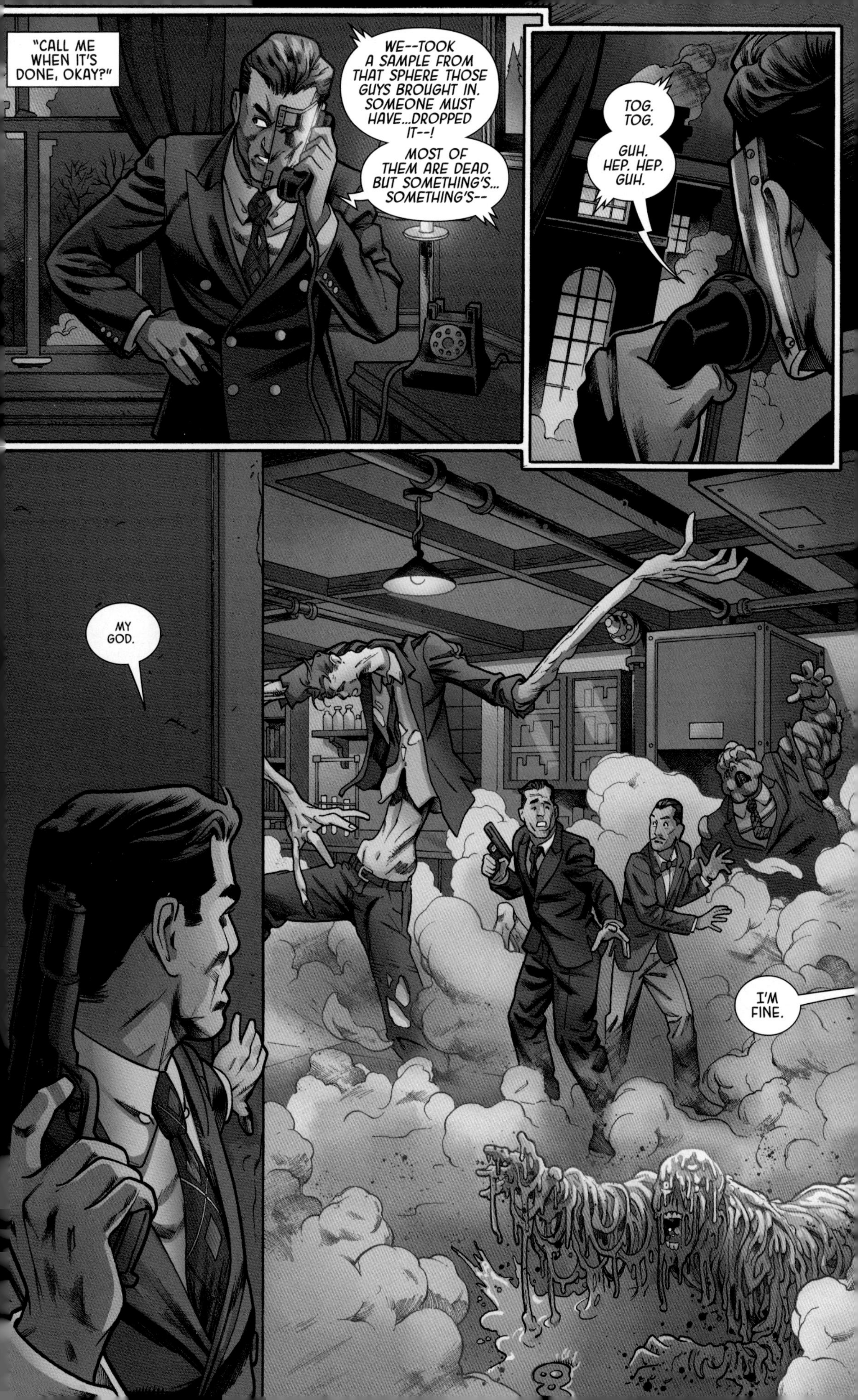
"CALL ME WHEN IT'S DONE, OKAY?"
WE--TOOK A SAMPLE FROM THAT SPHERE THOSE GUYS BROUGHT IN. SOMEONE MUST HAVE...DROPPED IT--!
MOST OF THEM ARE DEAD. BUT SOMETHING'S... SOMETHING'S--
TOG. TOG.
GUH. HEP. HEP. GUH.
MY GOD.
I'M FINE.

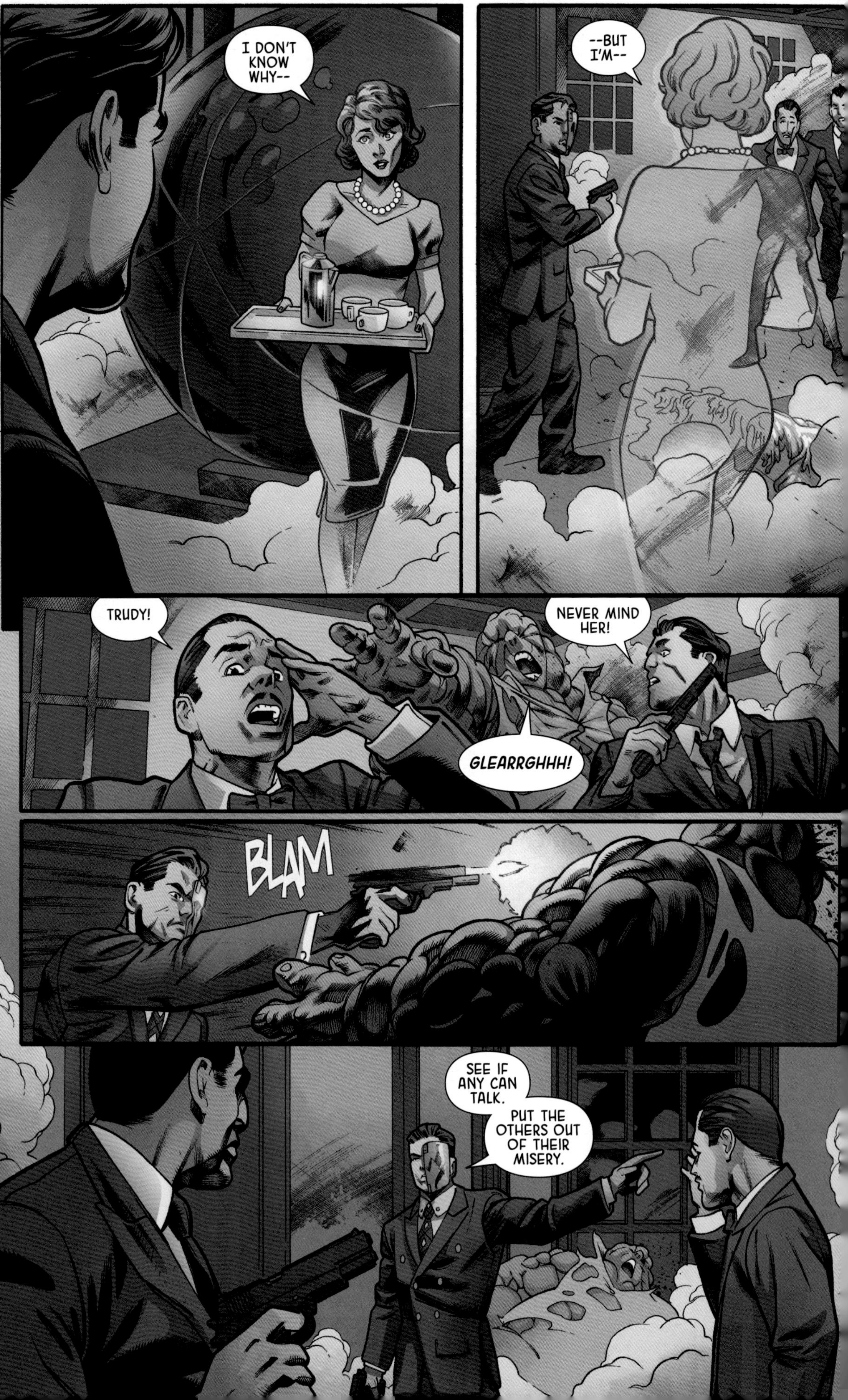
I DON'T KNOW WHY--
--BUT I'M--
TRUDY!
NEVER MIND HER!
GLEARRGHHH!
BLAM
SEE IF ANY CAN TALK.
PUT THE OTHERS OUT OF THEIR MISERY.

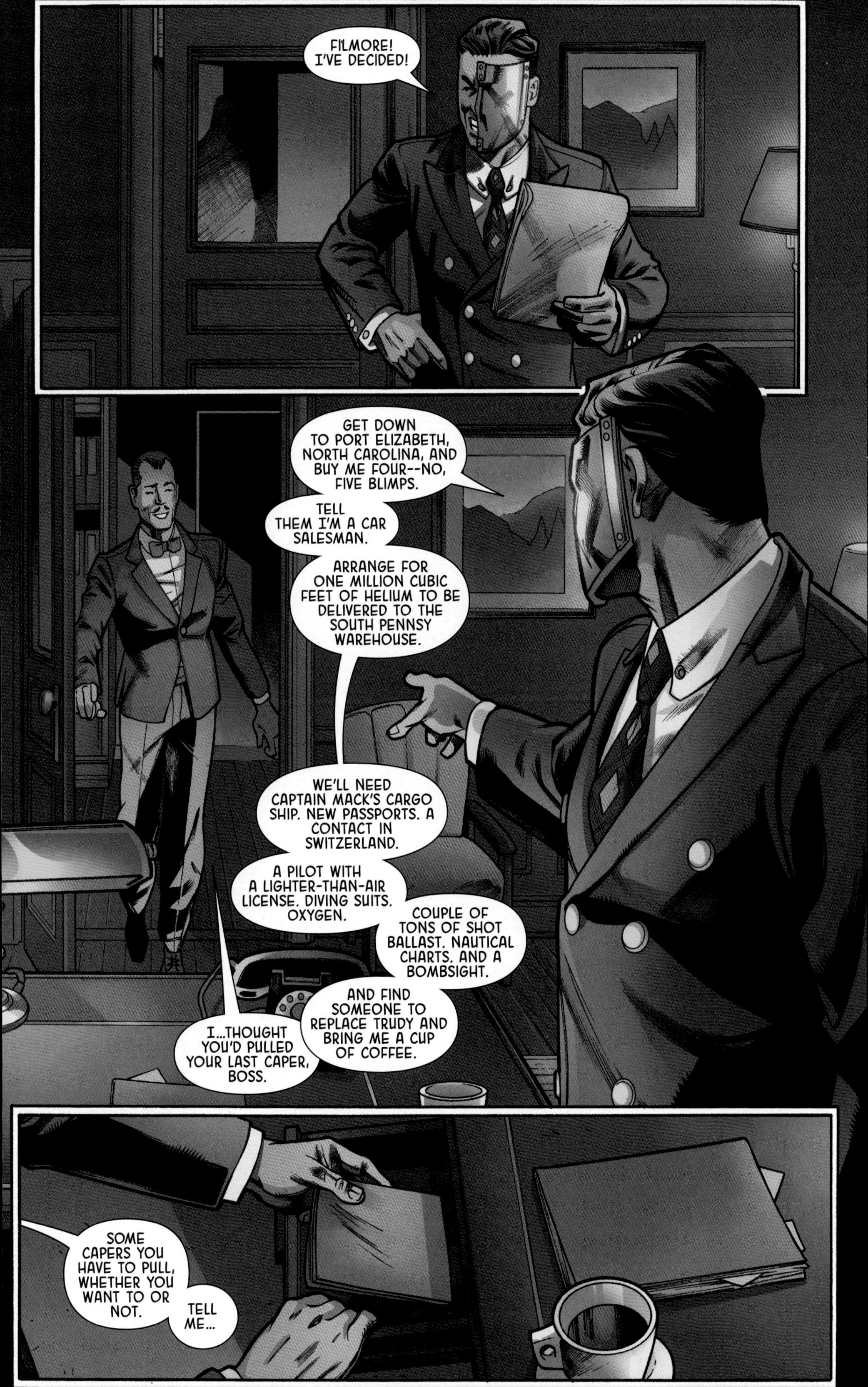
FILMORE! I'VE DECIDED!
GET DOWN TO PORT ELIZABETH, NORTH CAROLINA, AND BUY ME FOUR--NO, FIVE BLIMPS.
TELL THEM I'M A CAR SALESMAN.
ARRANGE FOR ONE MILLION CUBIC FEET OF HELIUM TO BE DELIVERED TO THE SOUTH PENNSY WAREHOUSE.
WE'LL NEED CAPTAIN MACK'S CARGO SHIP. NEW PASSPORTS. A CONTACT IN SWITZERLAND.
A PILOT WITH A LIGHTER-THAN-AIR LICENSE. DIVING SUITS. OXYGEN.
COUPLE OF TONS OF SHOT BALLAST. NAUTICAL CHARTS. AND A BOMBSIGHT.
AND FIND SOMEONE TO REPLACE TRUDY AND BRING ME A CUP OF COFFEE.
I...THOUGHT YOU'D PULLED YOUR LAST CAPER, BOSS.
SOME CAPERS YOU HAVE TO PULL, WHETHER YOU WANT TO OR NOT.
TELL ME...

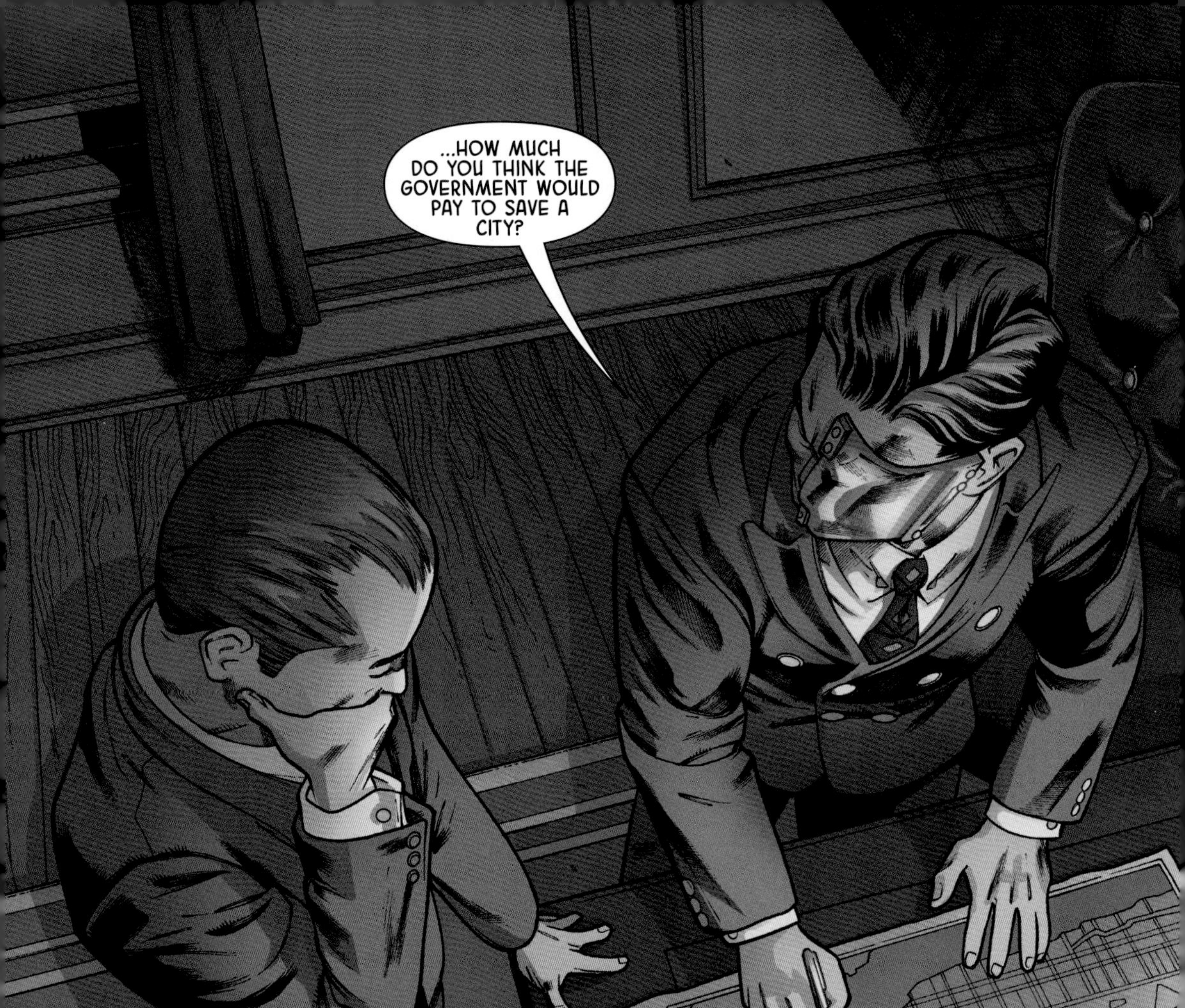
...HOW MUCH DO YOU THINK THE GOVERNMENT WOULD PAY TO SAVE A CITY?

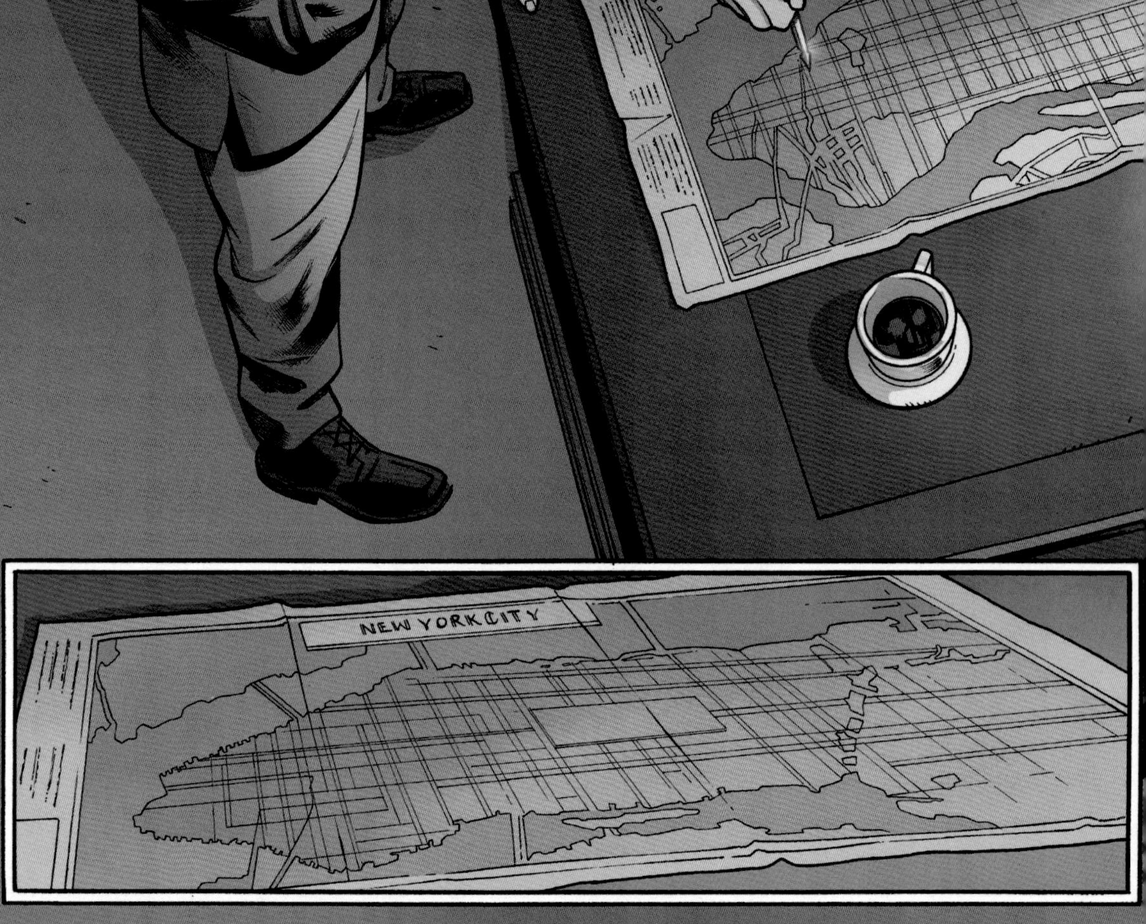
NEW YORK CITY

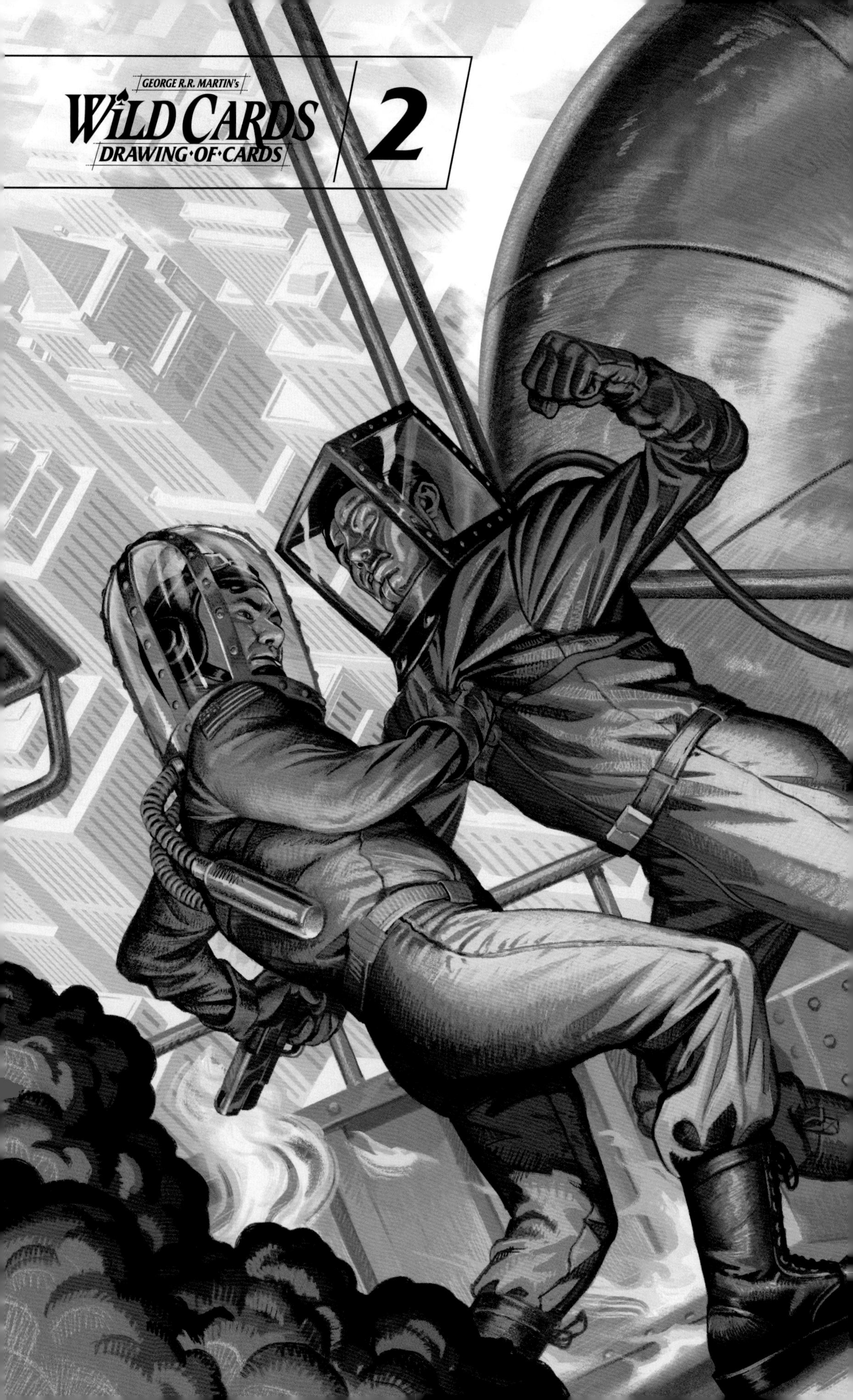
GEORGE R.R. MARTIN's
WILD CARDS
DRAWING·OF·CARDS
2

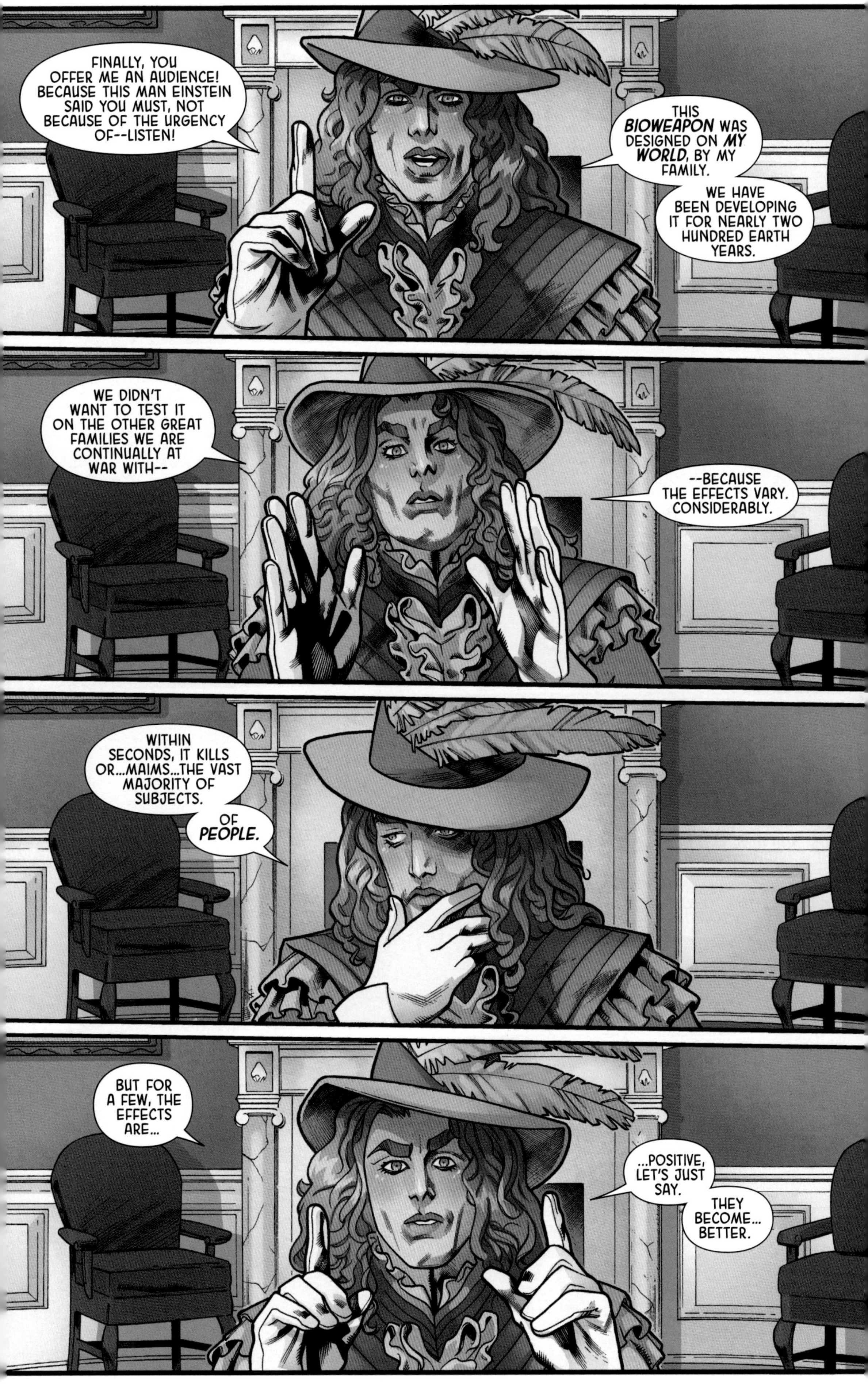
FINALLY, YOU OFFER ME AN AUDIENCE! BECAUSE THIS MAN EINSTEIN SAID YOU MUST, NOT BECAUSE OF THE URGENCY OF--LISTEN!
THIS BIOWEAPON WAS DESIGNED ON MY WORLD, BY MY FAMILY.
WE HAVE BEEN DEVELOPING IT FOR NEARLY TWO HUNDRED EARTH YEARS.
WE DIDN'T WANT TO TEST IT ON THE OTHER GREAT FAMILIES WE ARE CONTINUALLY AT WAR WITH--
--BECAUSE THE EFFECTS VARY. CONSIDERABLY.
WITHIN SECONDS, IT KILLS OR...MAIMS...THE VAST MAJORITY OF SUBJECTS.
OF PEOPLE.
BUT FOR A FEW, THE EFFECTS ARE...
...POSITIVE, LET'S JUST SAY.
THEY BECOME... BETTER.

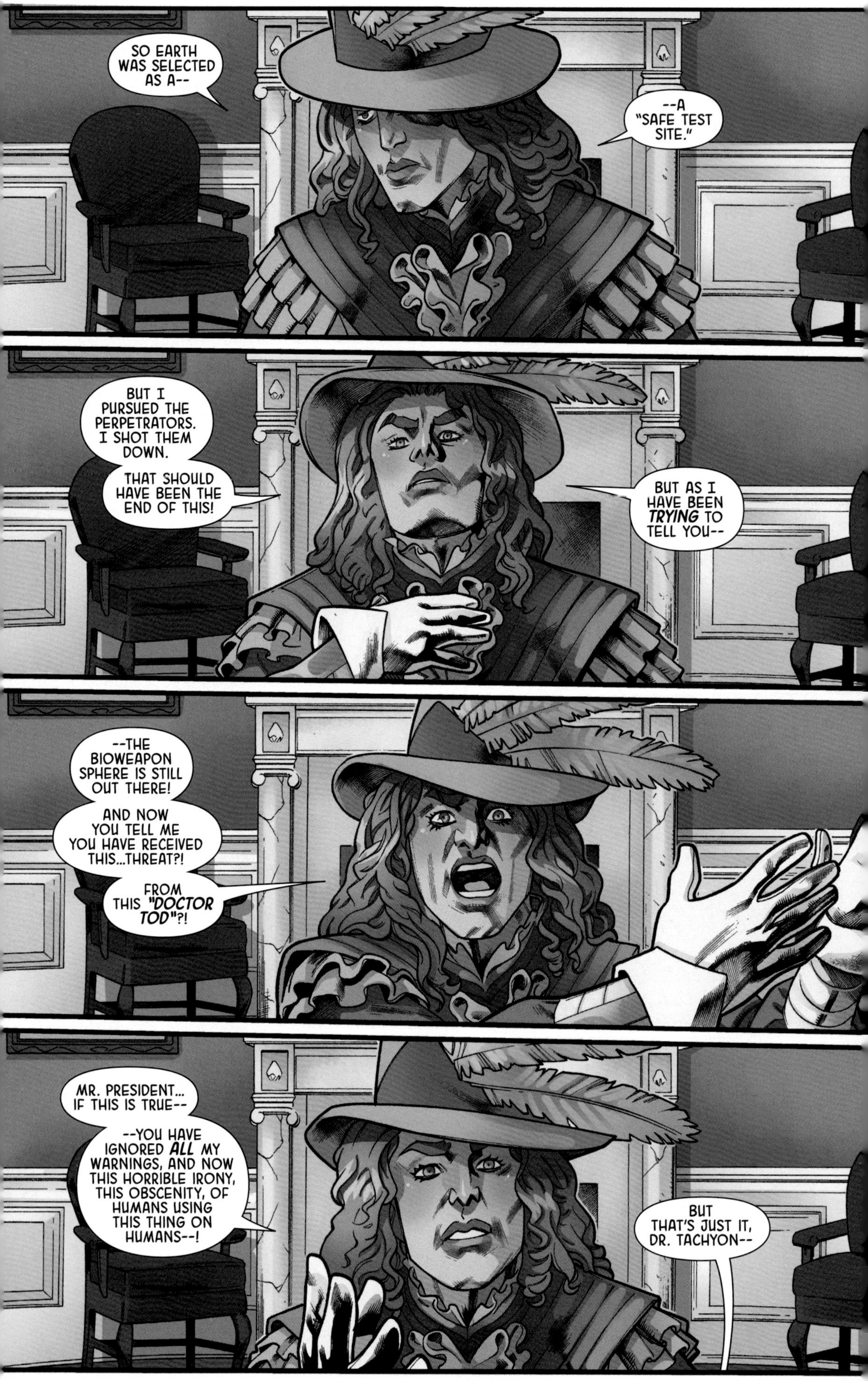
SO EARTH WAS SELECTED AS A--
--A "SAFE TEST SITE."
BUT I PURSUED THE PERPETRATORS. I SHOT THEM DOWN.
THAT SHOULD HAVE BEEN THE END OF THIS!
BUT AS I HAVE BEEN TRYING TO TELL YOU--
--THE BIOWEAPON SPHERE IS STILL OUT THERE!
AND NOW YOU TELL ME YOU HAVE RECEIVED THIS...THREAT?!
FROM THIS "DOCTOR TOD"?!
MR. PRESIDENT... IF THIS IS TRUE--
--YOU HAVE IGNORED ALL MY WARNINGS, AND NOW THIS HORRIBLE IRONY, THIS OBSCENITY, OF HUMANS USING THIS THING ON HUMANS--!
BUT THAT'S JUST IT, DR. TACHYON--

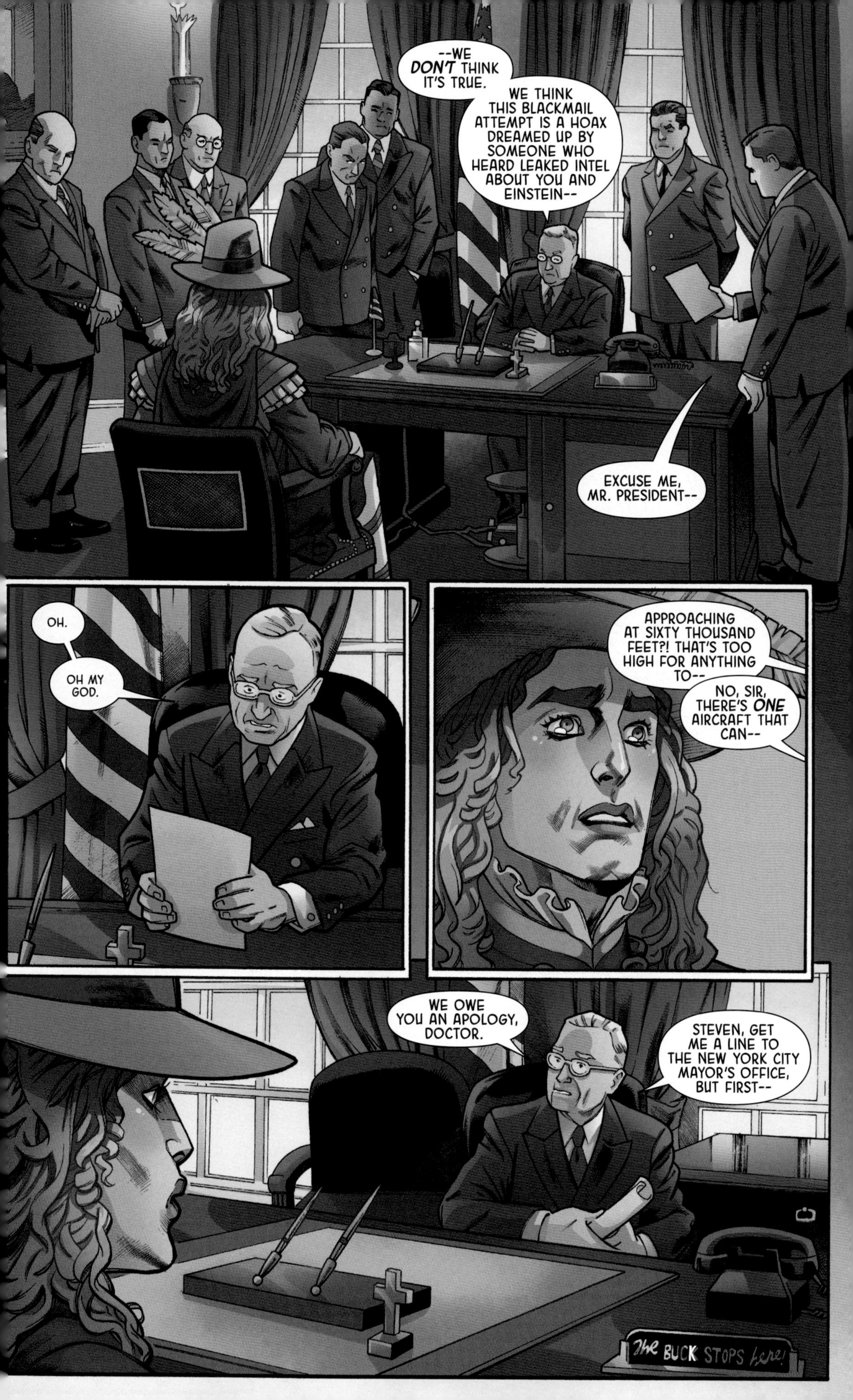
--WE DON'T THINK IT'S TRUE.
WE THINK THIS BLACKMAIL ATTEMPT IS A HOAX DREAMED UP BY SOMEONE WHO HEARD LEAKED INTEL ABOUT YOU AND EINSTEIN--
EXCUSE ME, MR. PRESIDENT--
OH.
OH MY GOD.
APPROACHING AT SIXTY THOUSAND FEET?! THAT'S TOO HIGH FOR ANYTHING TO--
NO, SIR, THERE'S ONE AIRCRAFT THAT CAN--
WE OWE YOU AN APOLOGY, DOCTOR.
STEVEN, GET ME A LINE TO THE NEW YORK CITY MAYOR'S OFFICE, BUT FIRST--
The BUCK STOPS here!

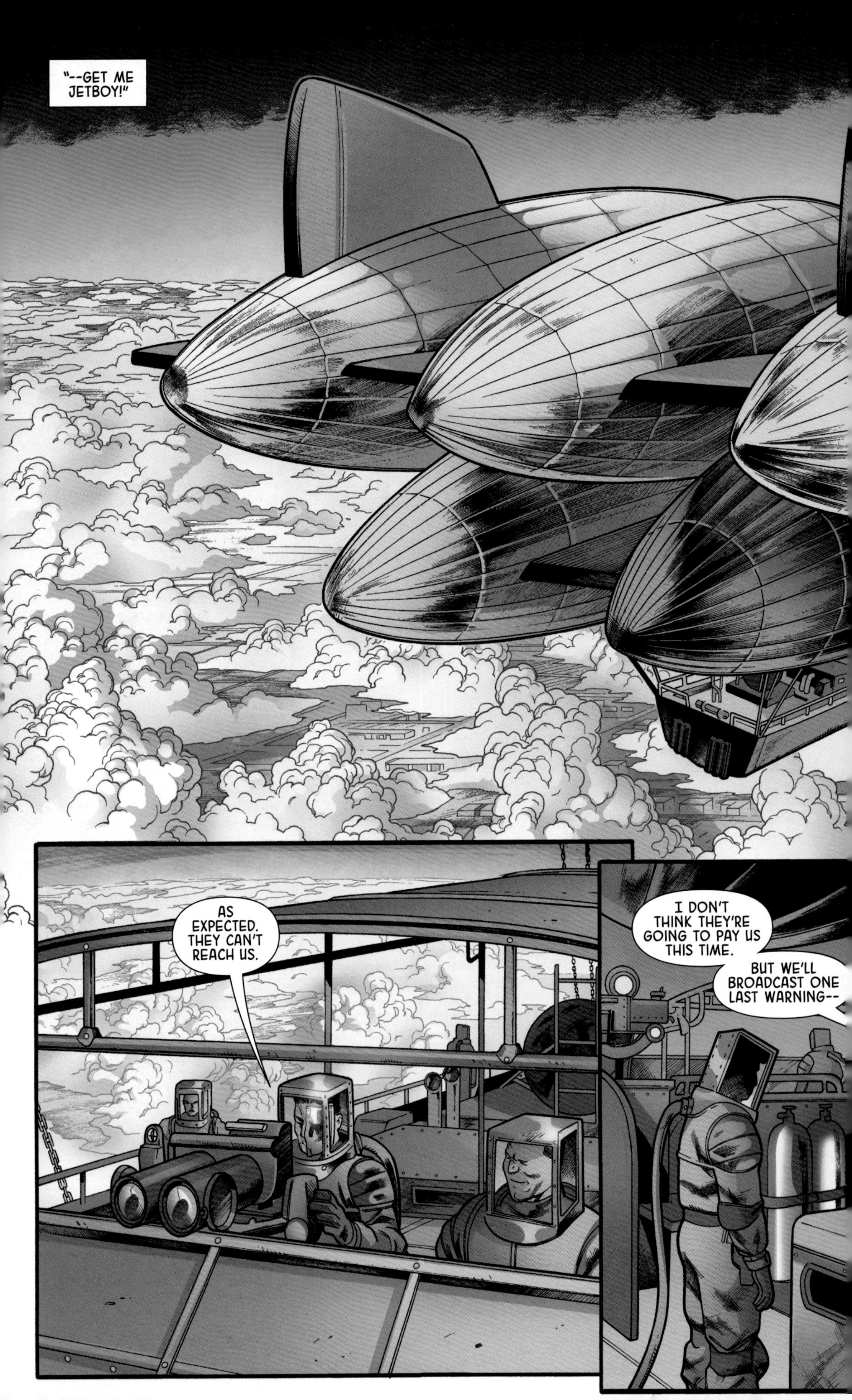
"--GET ME JETBOY!"
AS EXPECTED. THEY CAN'T REACH US.
I DON'T THINK THEY'RE GOING TO PAY US THIS TIME.
BUT WE'LL BROADCAST ONE LAST WARNING--

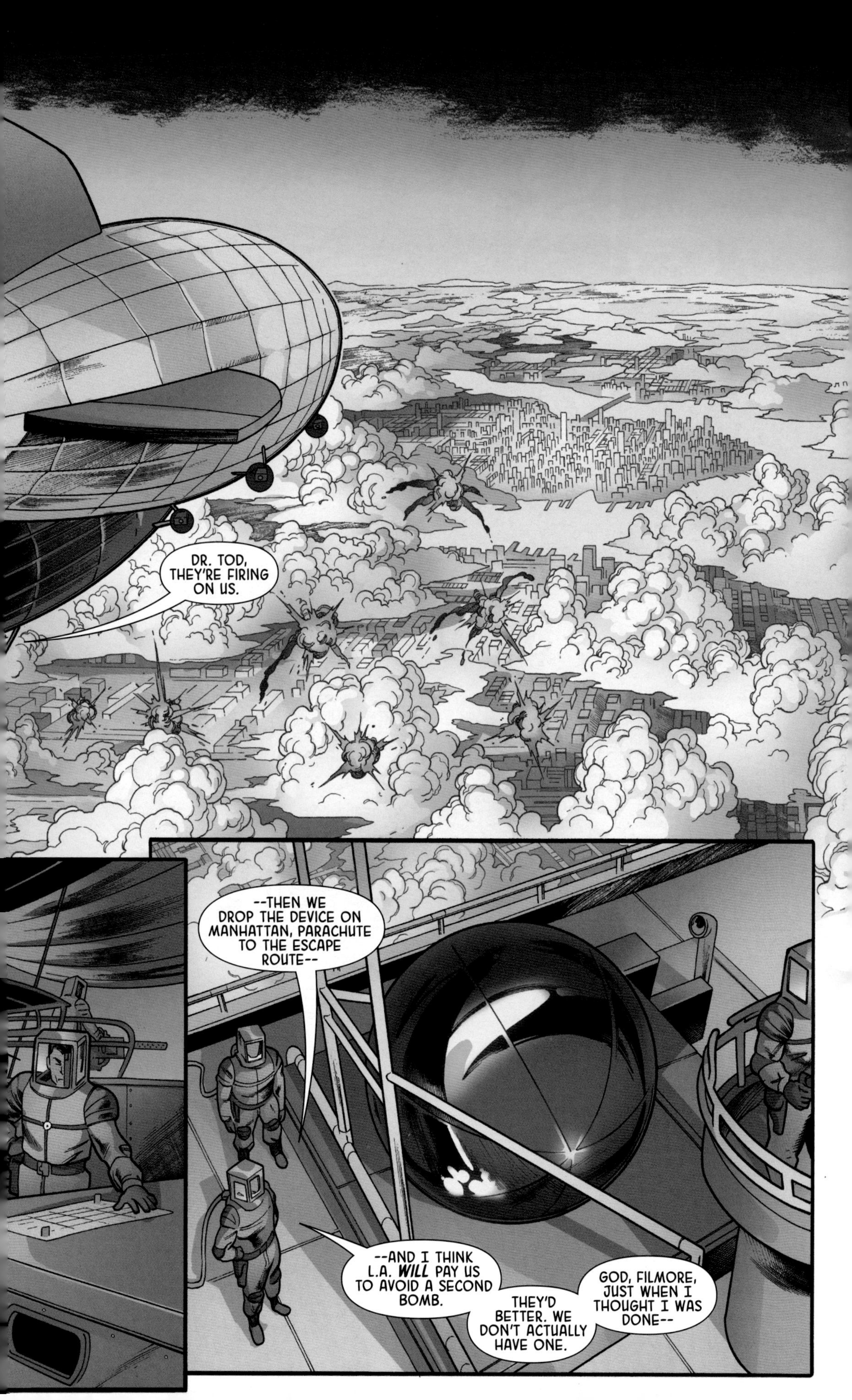
DR. TOD, THEY'RE FIRING ON US.
--THEN WE DROP THE DEVICE ON MANHATTAN, PARACHUTE TO THE ESCAPE ROUTE--
--AND I THINK L.A. WILL PAY US TO AVOID A SECOND BOMB.
THEY'D BETTER. WE DON'T ACTUALLY HAVE ONE.
GOD, FILMORE, JUST WHEN I THOUGHT I WAS DONE--

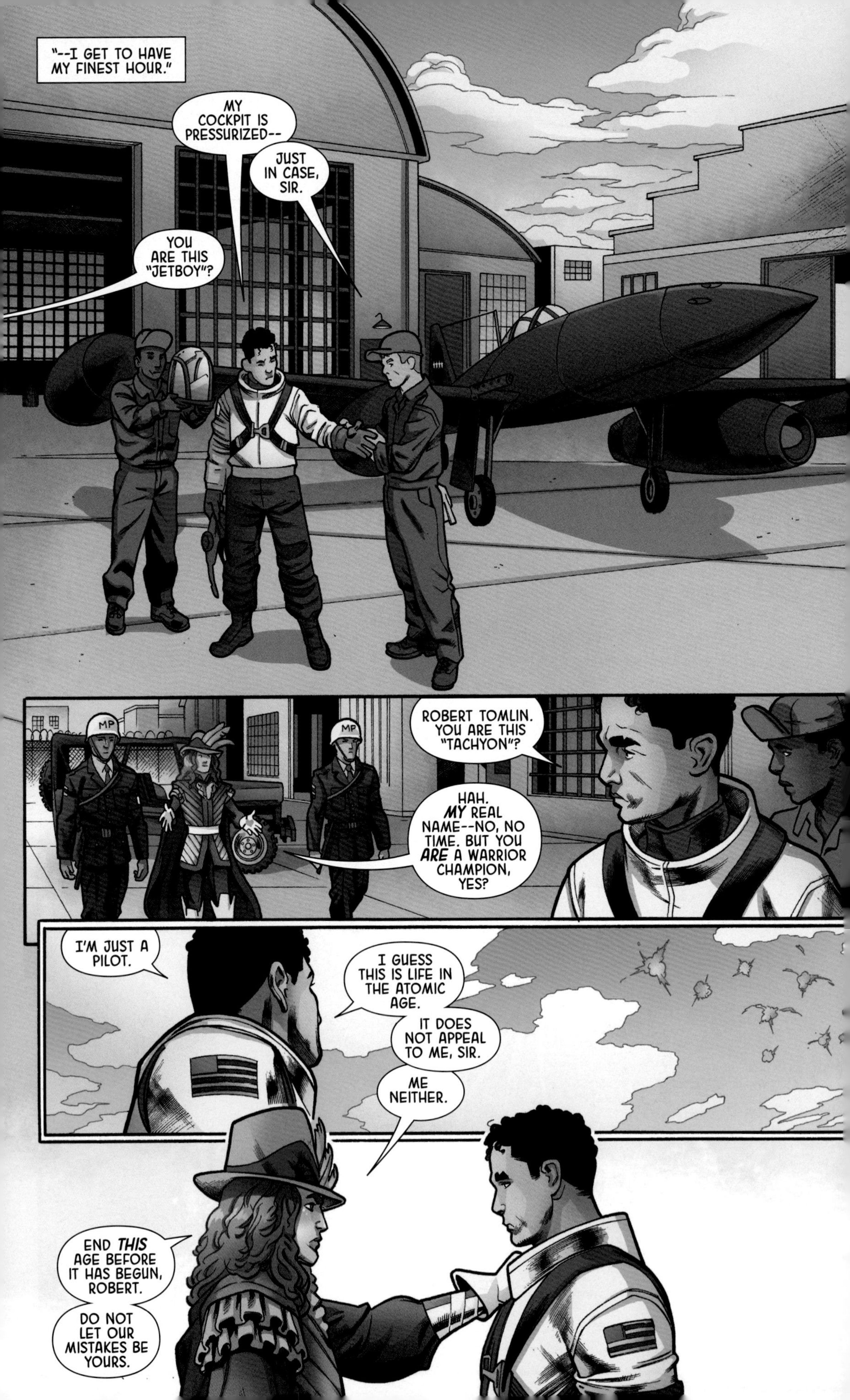
"--I GET TO HAVE MY FINEST HOUR."
MY COCKPIT IS PRESSURIZED--
JUST IN CASE, SIR.
YOU ARE THIS "JETBOY"?
ROBERT TOMLIN. YOU ARE THIS "TACHYON"?
HAH. MY REAL NAME--NO, NO TIME. BUT YOU ARE A WARRIOR CHAMPION, YES?
MP
MP
I'M JUST A PILOT.
I GUESS THIS IS LIFE IN THE ATOMIC AGE.
IT DOES NOT APPEAL TO ME, SIR.
ME NEITHER.
END THIS AGE BEFORE IT HAS BEGUN, ROBERT.
DO NOT LET OUR MISTAKES BE YOURS.

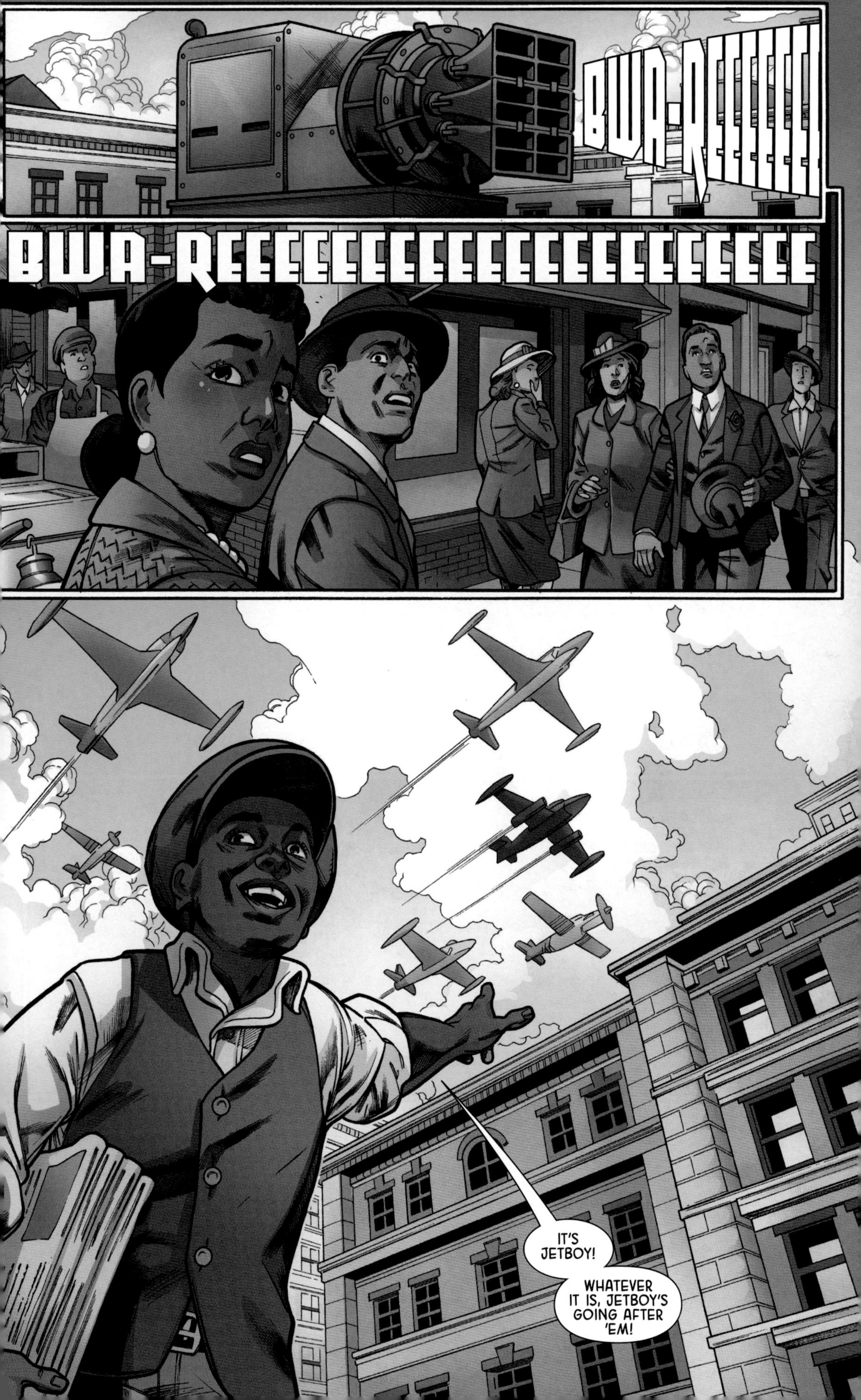
BWA-REEEEEE!
BWA-REEEEEEEEEEEEEEEEEEEEEE
IT'S JETBOY!
WHATEVER IT IS, JETBOY'S GOING AFTER 'EM!

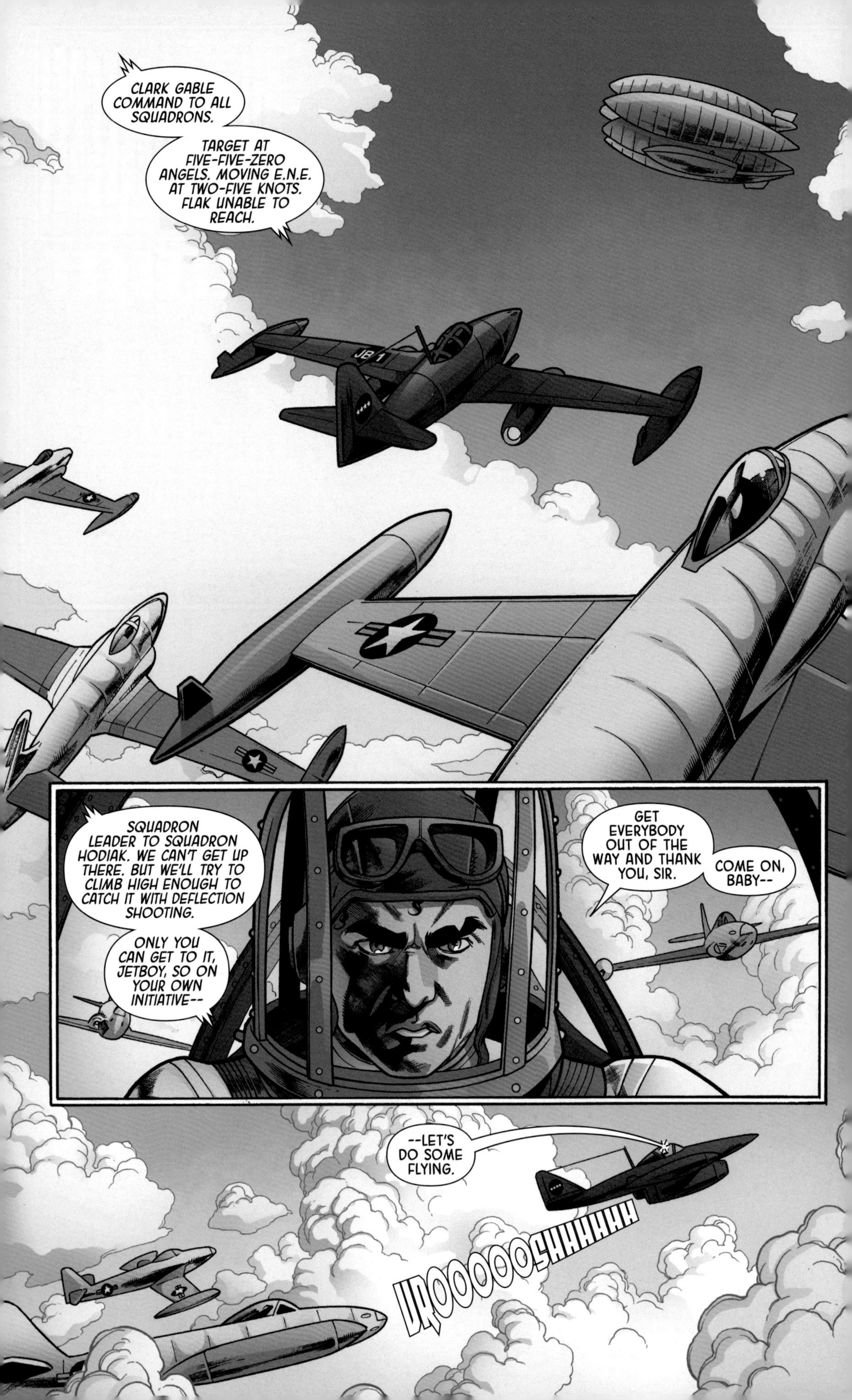
CLARK GABLE COMMAND TO ALL SQUADRONS.
TARGET AT FIVE-FIVE-ZERO ANGELS. MOVING E.N.E. AT TWO-FIVE KNOTS. FLAK UNABLE TO REACH.
JB 1
SQUADRON LEADER TO SQUADRON HODIAK. WE CAN'T GET UP THERE. BUT WE'LL TRY TO CLIMB HIGH ENOUGH TO CATCH IT WITH DEFLECTION SHOOTING.
ONLY YOU CAN GET TO IT, JETBOY, SO ON YOUR OWN INITIATIVE--
GET EVERYBODY OUT OF THE WAY AND THANK YOU, SIR.
COME ON, BABY--
--LET'S DO SOME FLYING.
VROOOOOOSHHHHHH

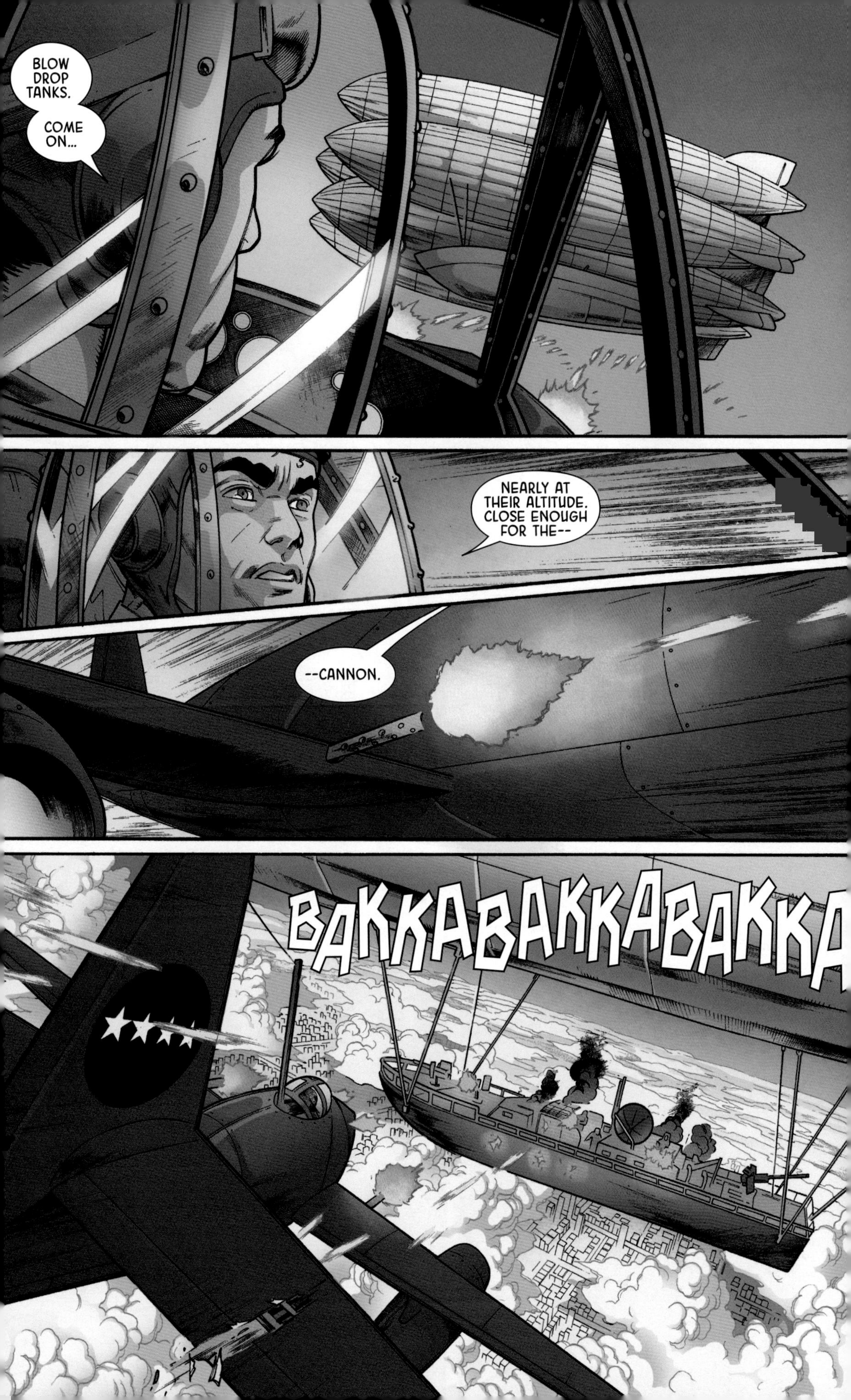
BLOW DROP TANKS.
COME ON...
NEARLY AT THEIR ALTITUDE. CLOSE ENOUGH FOR THE--
--CANNON.
BAKKABAKKABAKKA

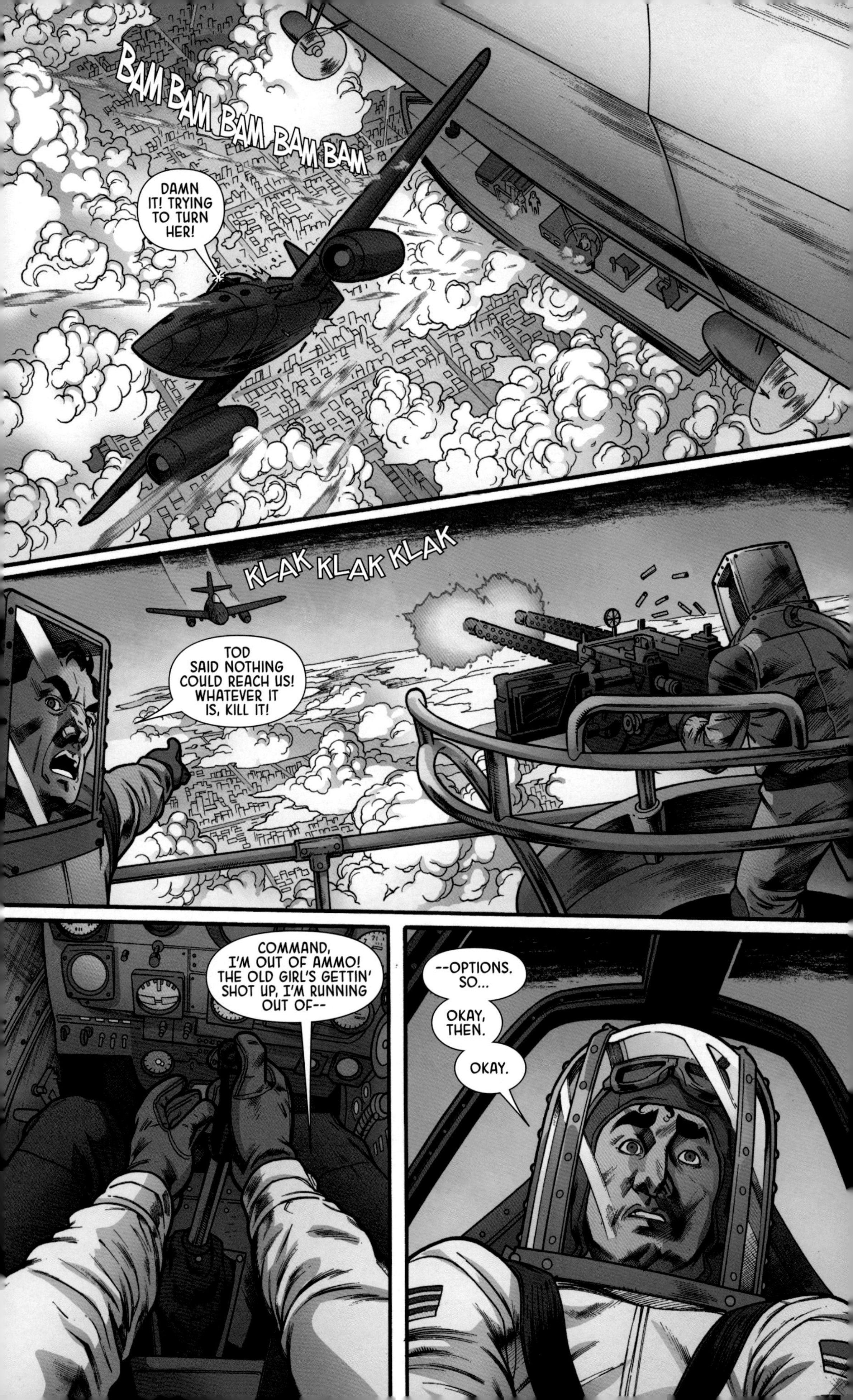
BAM BAM BAM BAM BAM
DAMN IT! TRYING TO TURN HER!
KLAK KLAK KLAK
TOD SAID NOTHING COULD REACH US! WHATEVER IT IS, KILL IT!
COMMAND, I'M OUT OF AMMO! THE OLD GIRL'S GETTIN' SHOT UP, I'M RUNNING OUT OF--
--OPTIONS. SO...
OKAY, THEN.
OKAY.

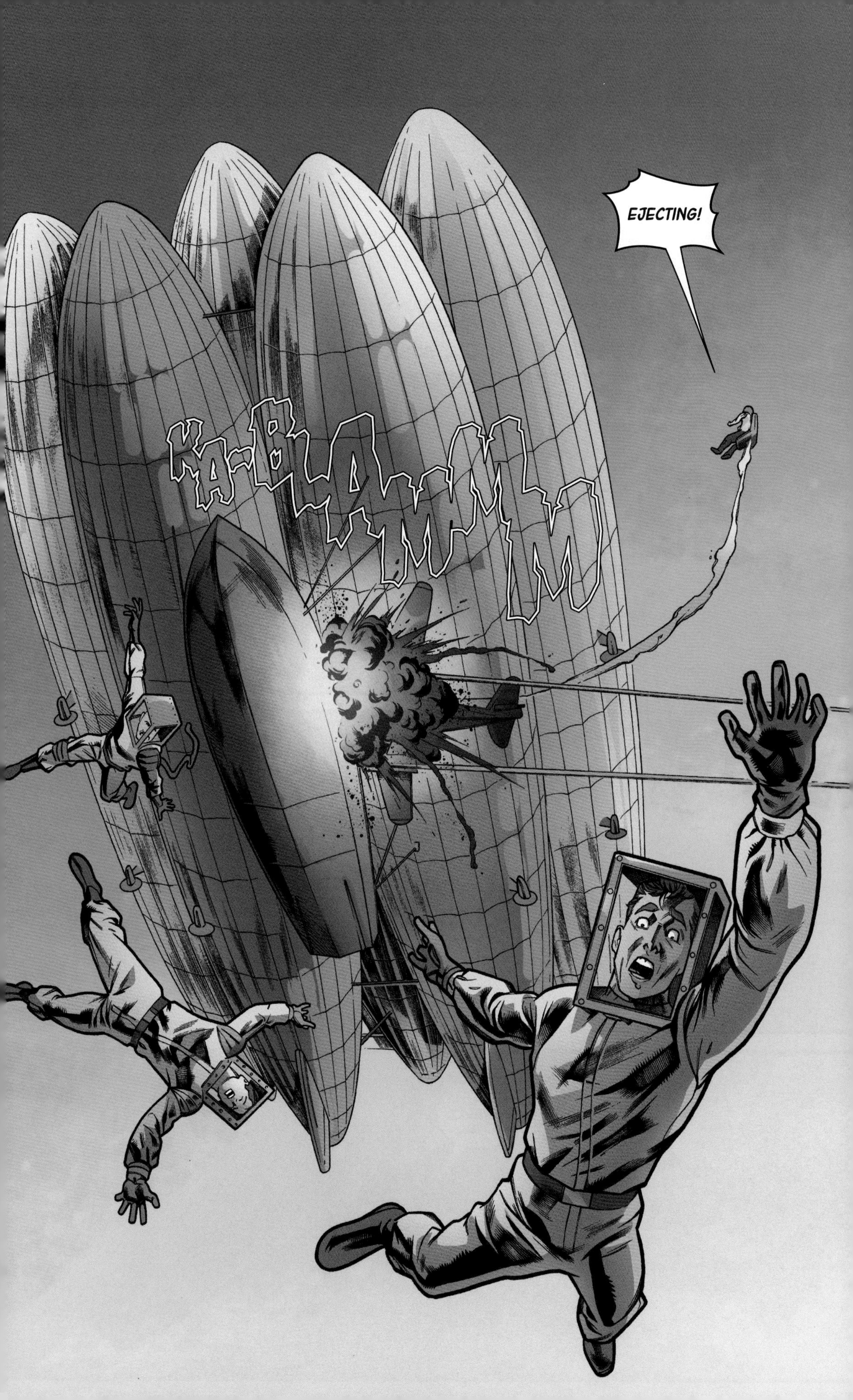
EJECTING!
KA-BLAMMMM

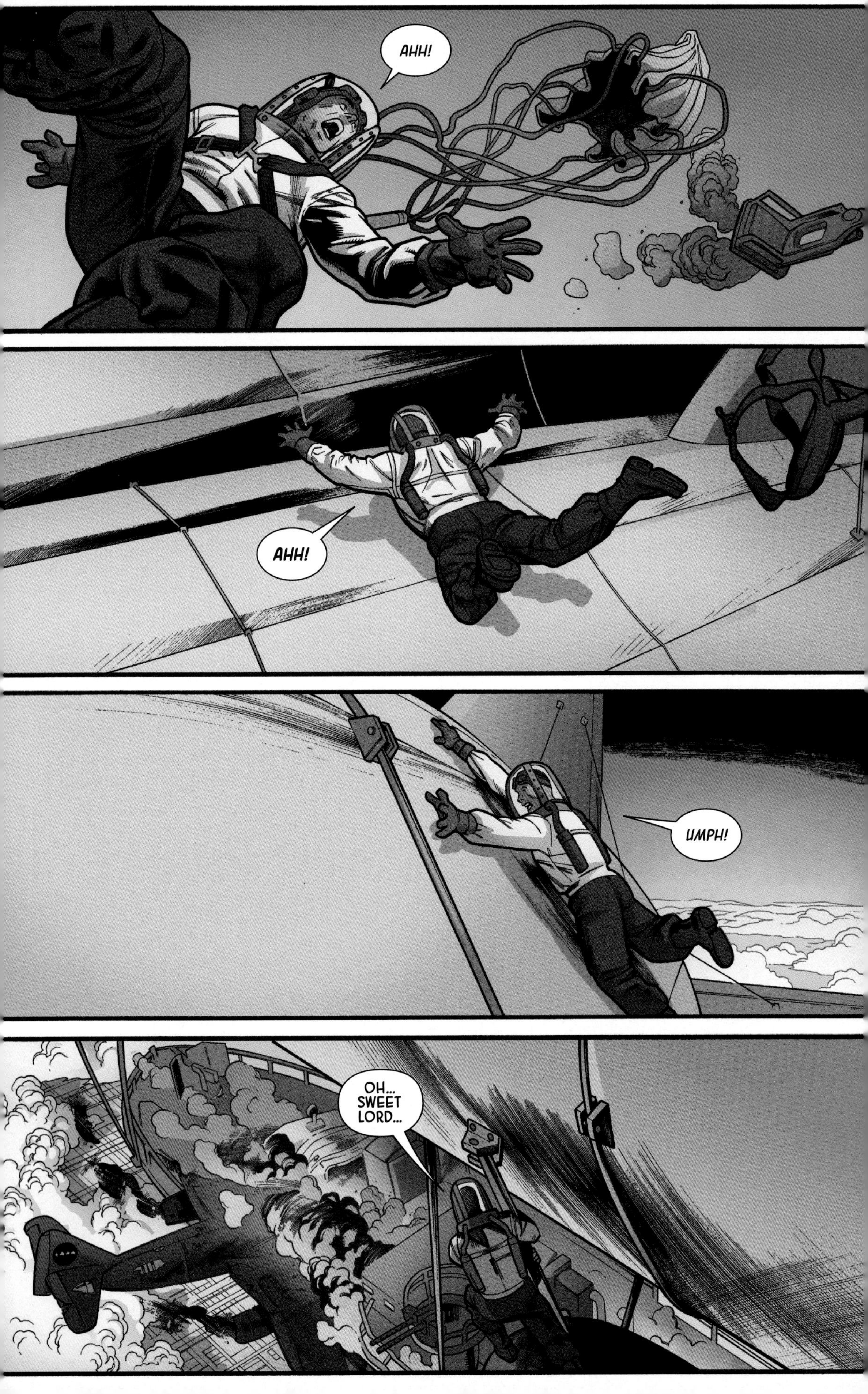
AHH!
AHH!
UMPH!
OH... SWEET LORD...

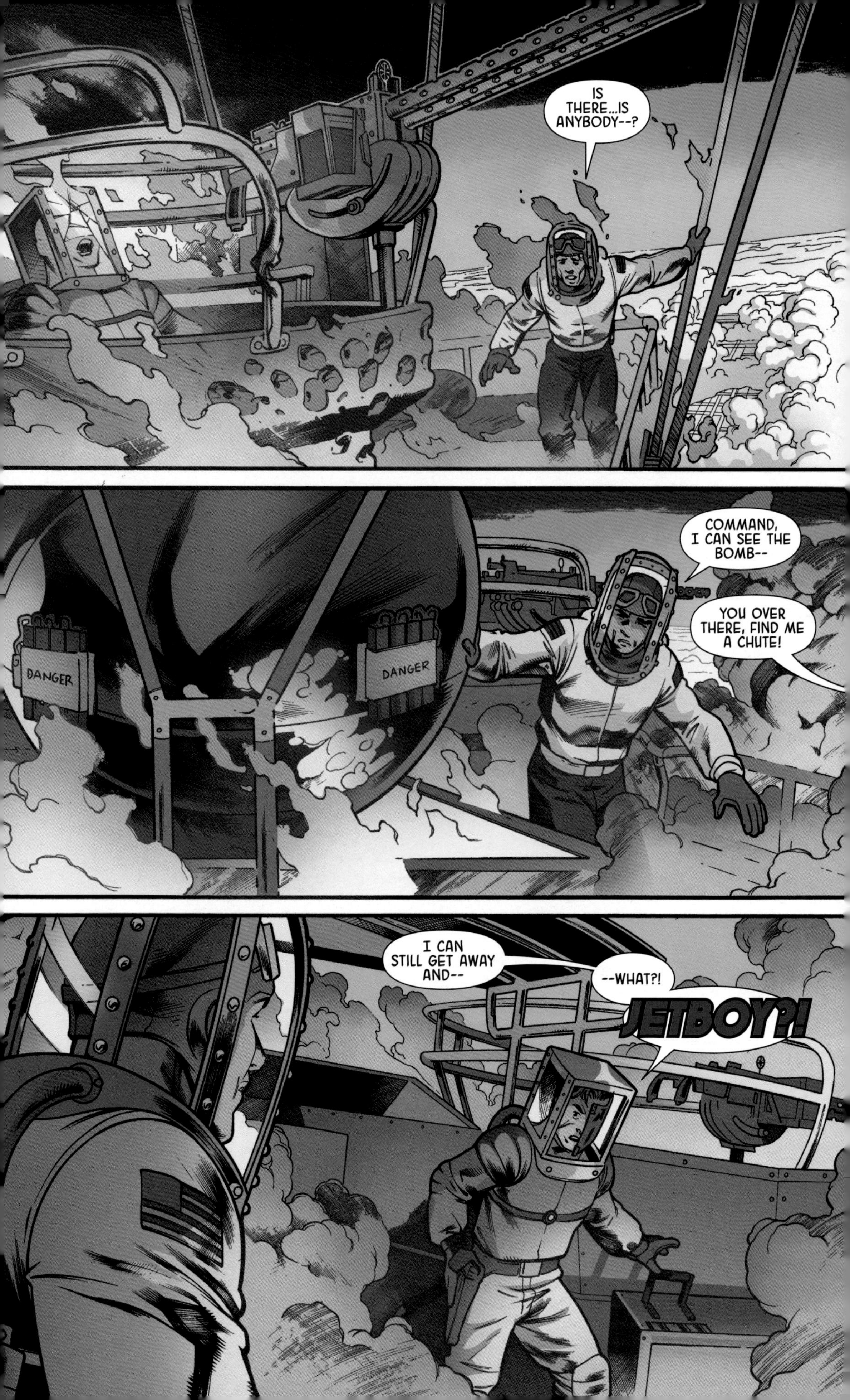
IS THERE...IS ANYBODY--?
COMMAND, I CAN SEE THE BOMB--
YOU OVER THERE, FIND ME A CHUTE!
DANGER
DANGER
I CAN STILL GET AWAY AND--
--WHAT?!
JETBOY?!

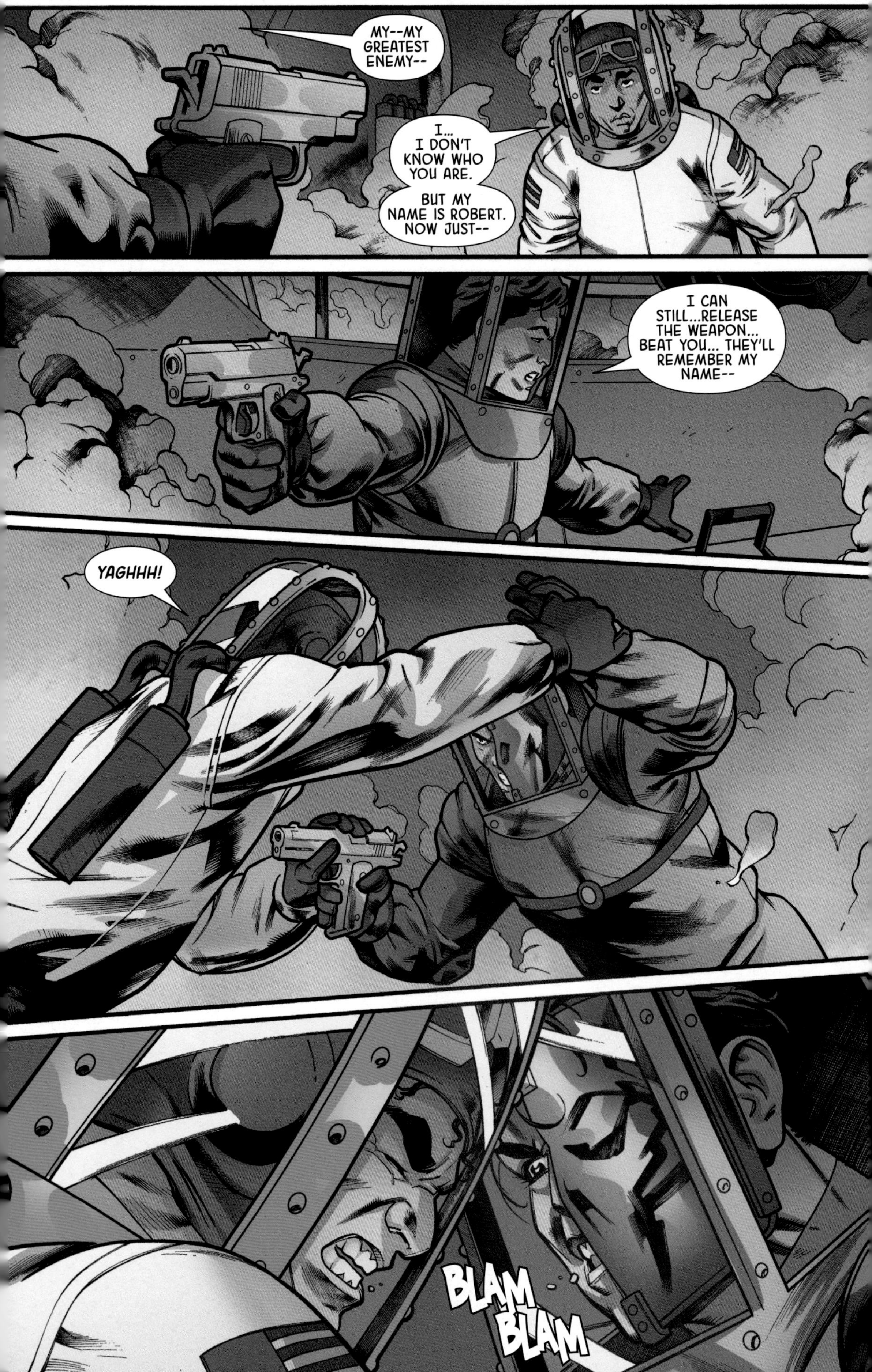

MY--MY GREATEST ENEMY--
I... I DON'T KNOW WHO YOU ARE.
BUT MY NAME IS ROBERT. NOW JUST--
I CAN STILL...RELEASE THE WEAPON... BEAT YOU... THEY'LL REMEMBER MY NAME--
YAGHHH!
BLAM BLAM

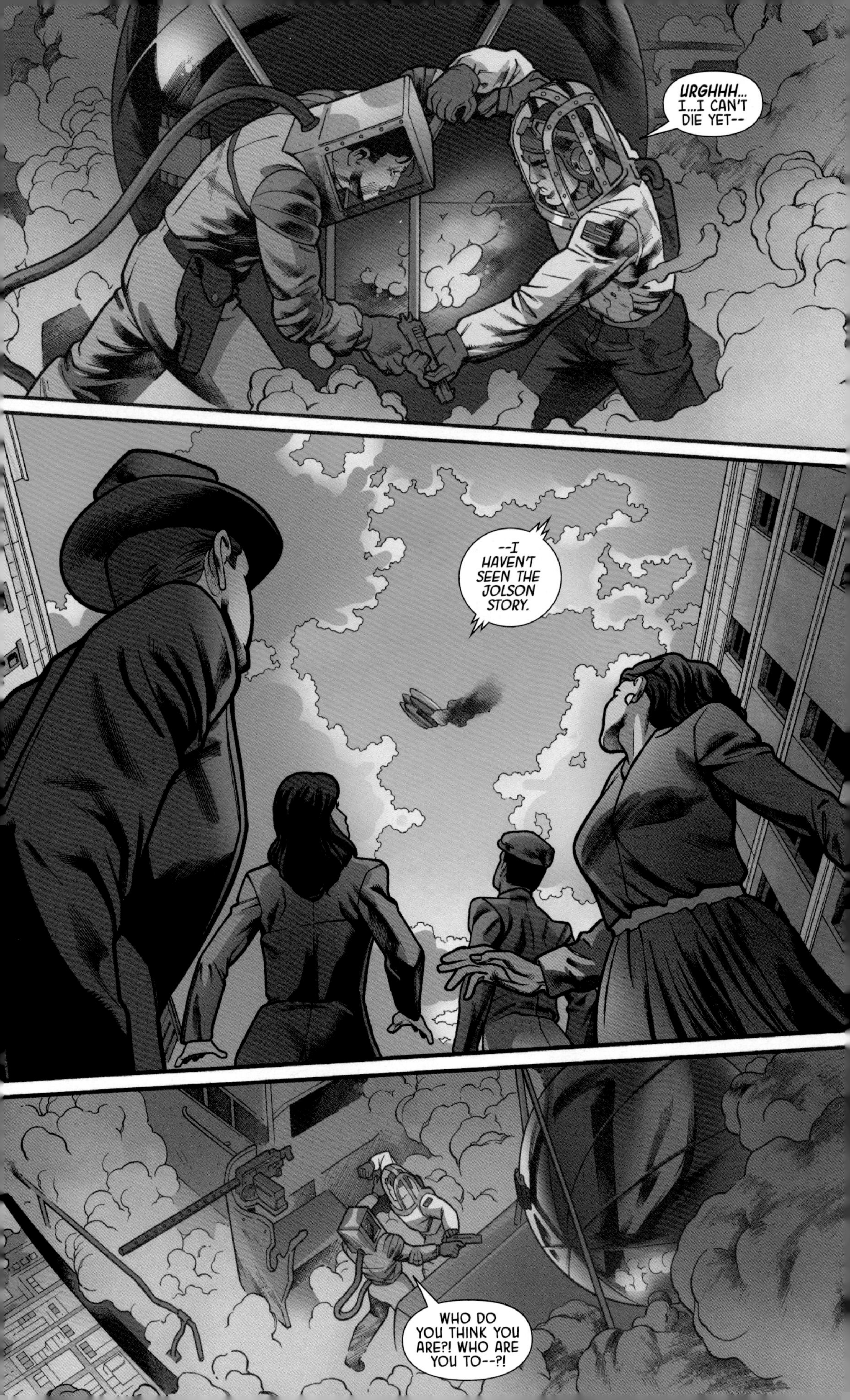
URGHHH... I...I CAN'T DIE YET--
--I HAVEN'T SEEN THE JOLSON STORY.
WHO DO YOU THINK YOU ARE?! WHO ARE YOU TO--?!

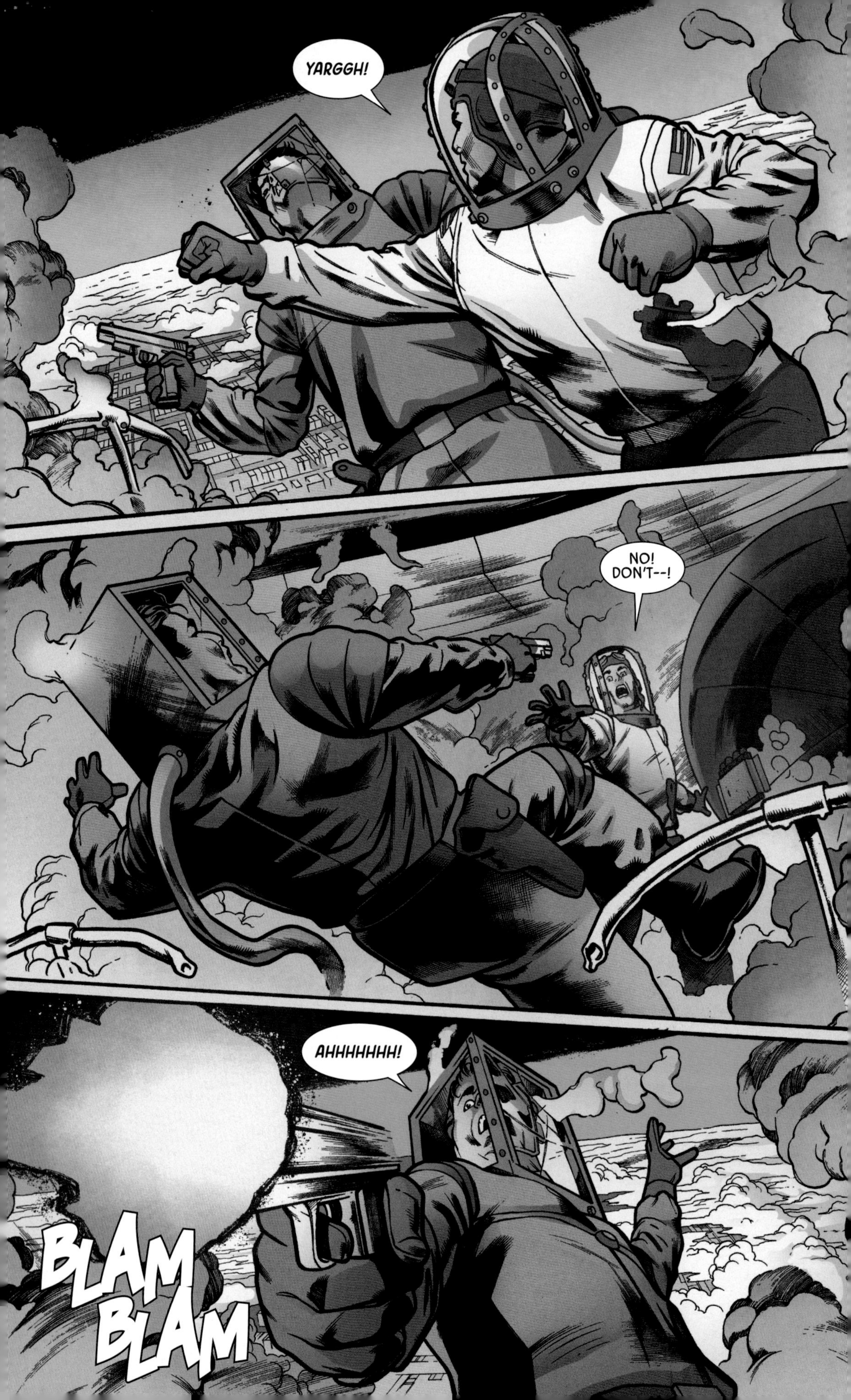
YARGGH!
NO! DON'T--!
AHHHHHHH!
BLAM
BLAM

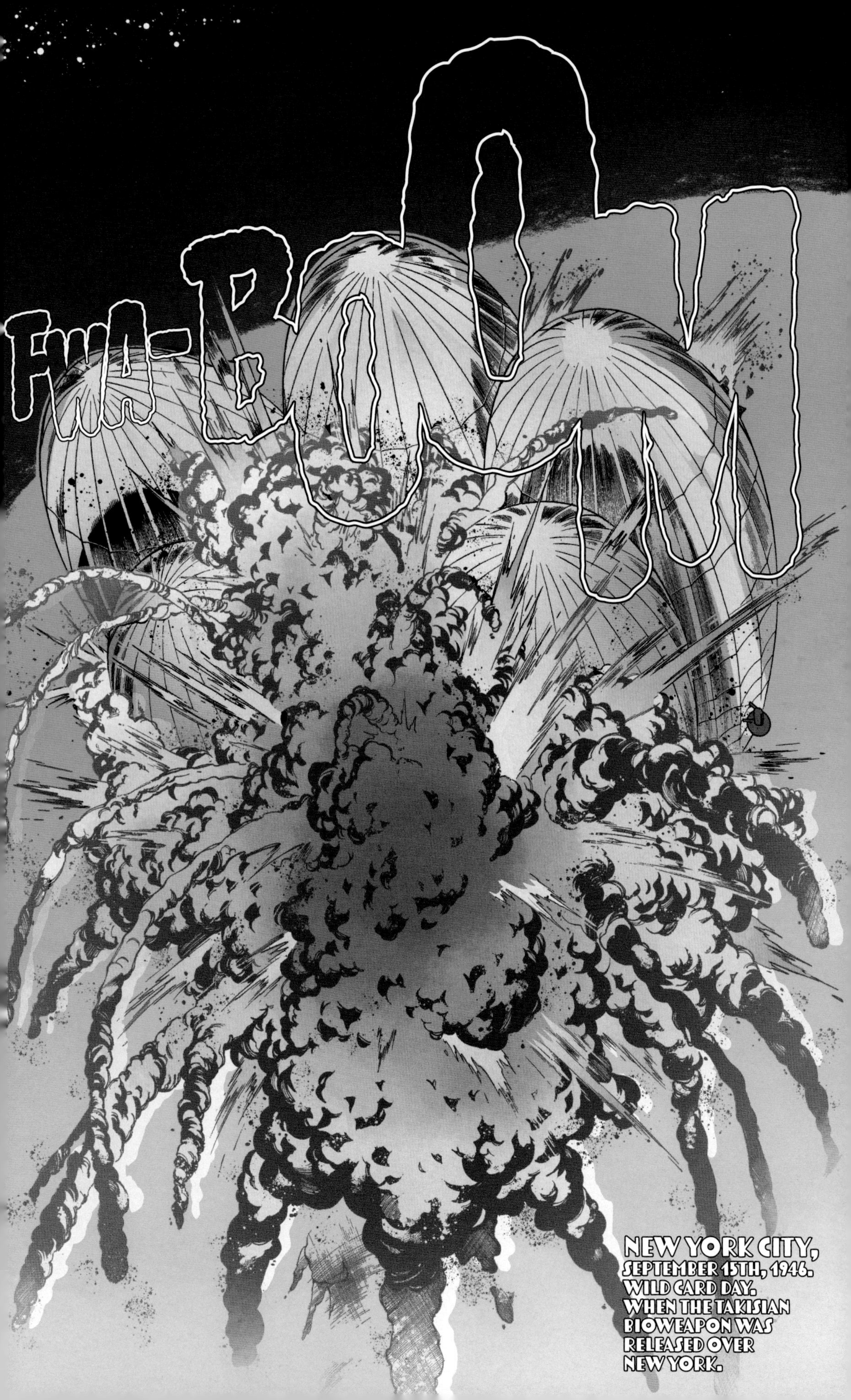
FWA-BOOM
NEW YORK CITY,
SEPTEMBER 15TH, 1946.
WILD CARD DAY.
WHEN THE TAKISIAN
BIOWEAPON WAS
RELEASED OVER
NEW YORK.

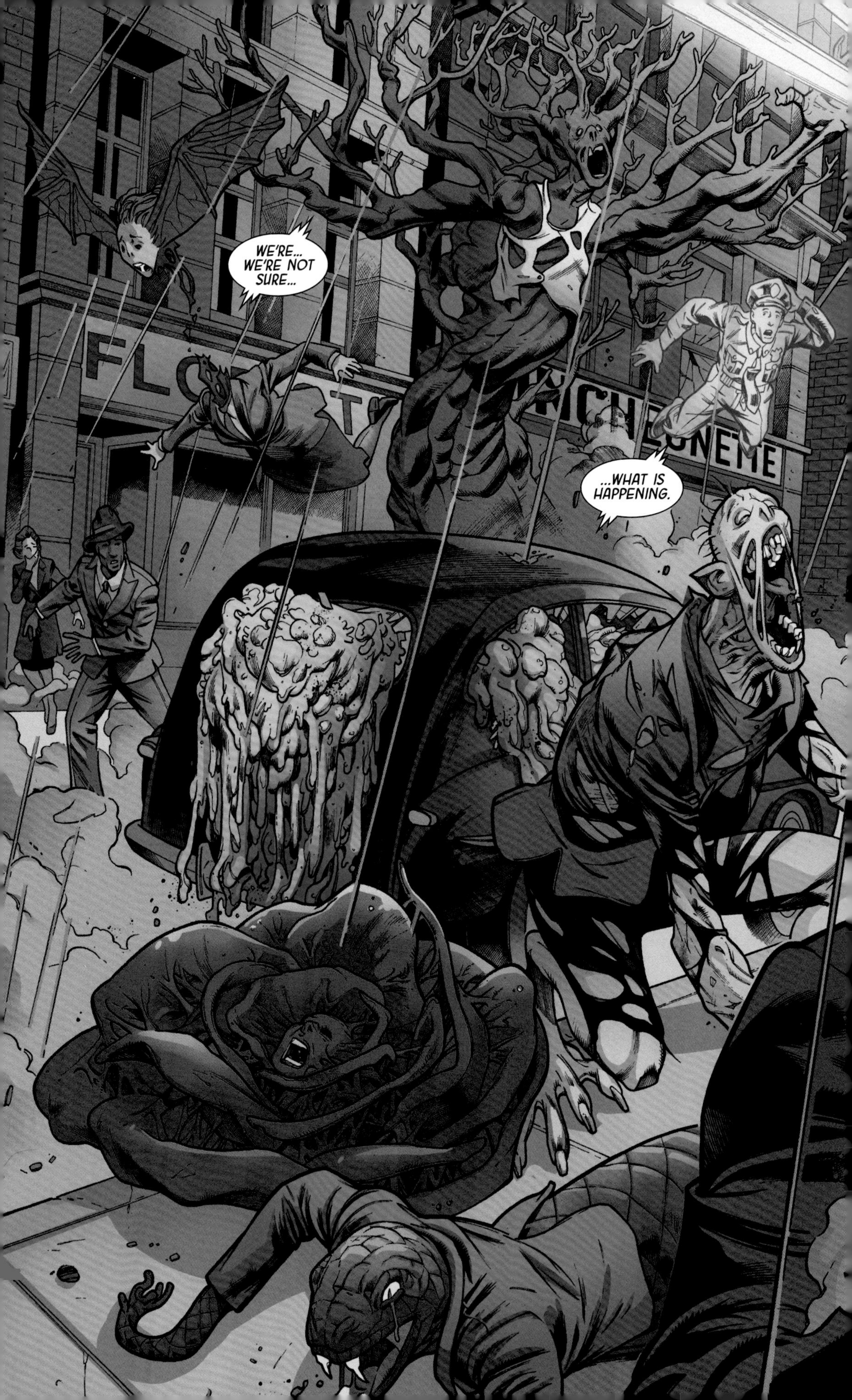
WE'RE... WE'RE NOT SURE...
...WHAT IS HAPPENING.

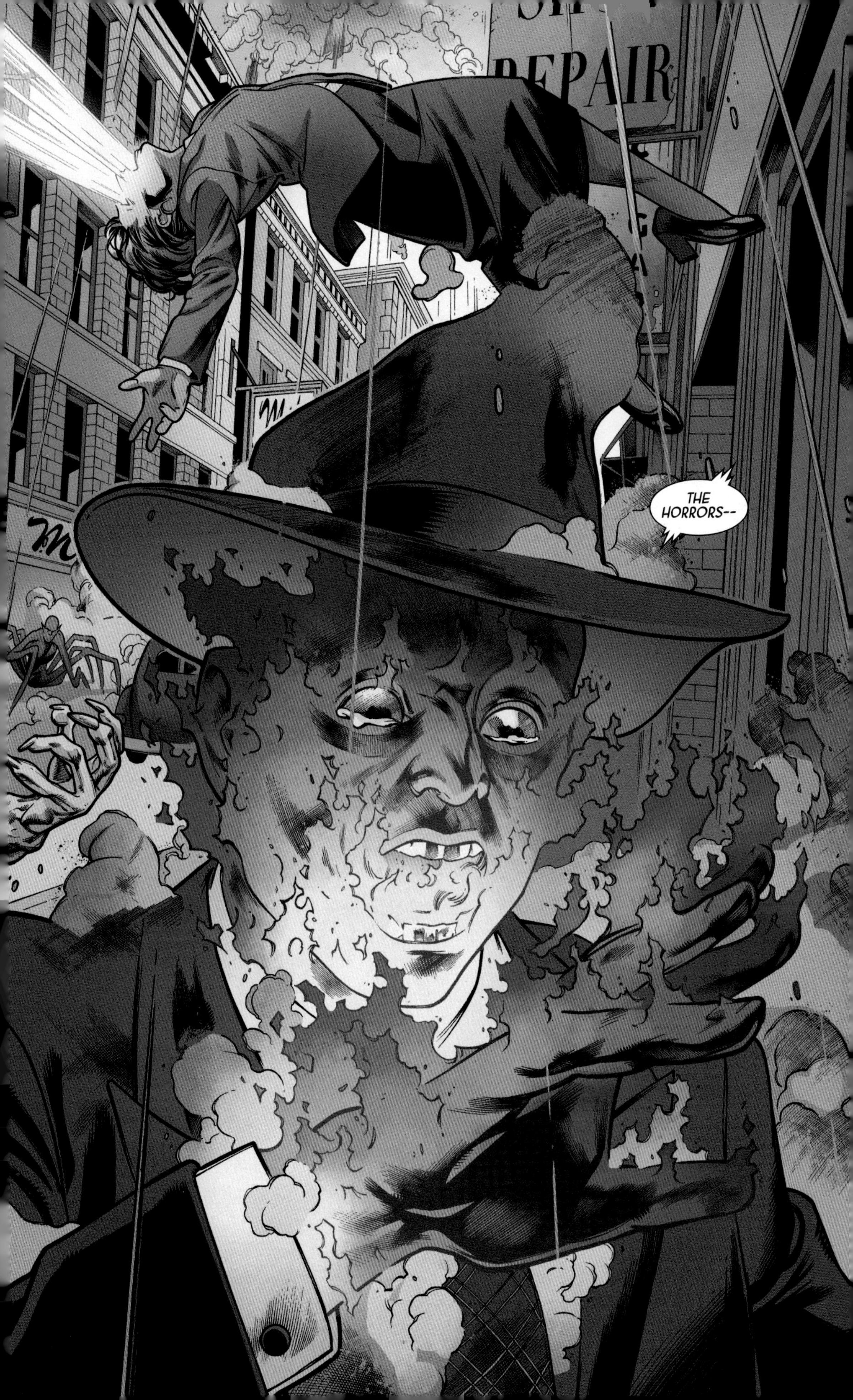
REPAIR
THE HORRORS--

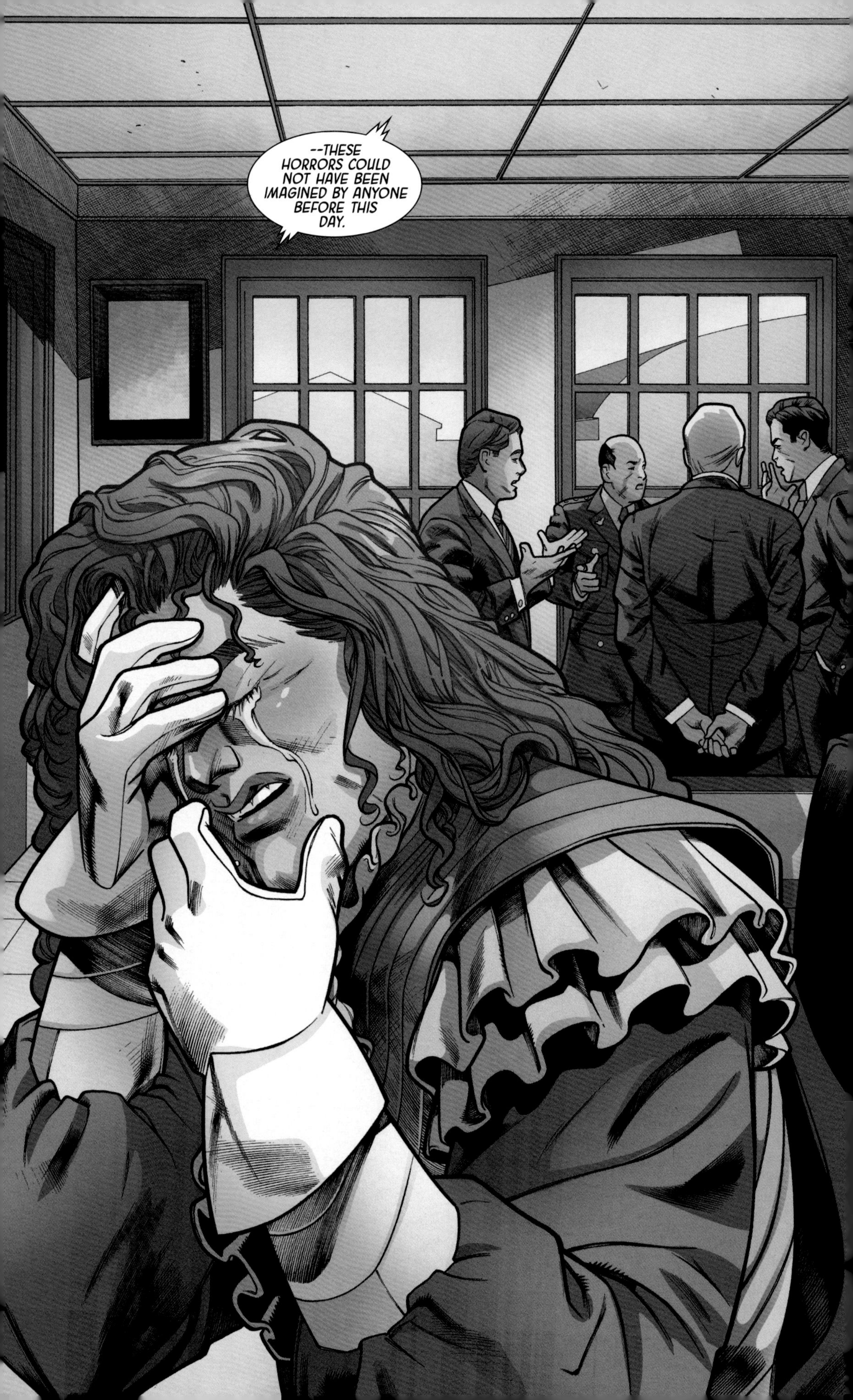
--THESE HORRORS COULD NOT HAVE BEEN IMAGINED BY ANYONE BEFORE THIS DAY.

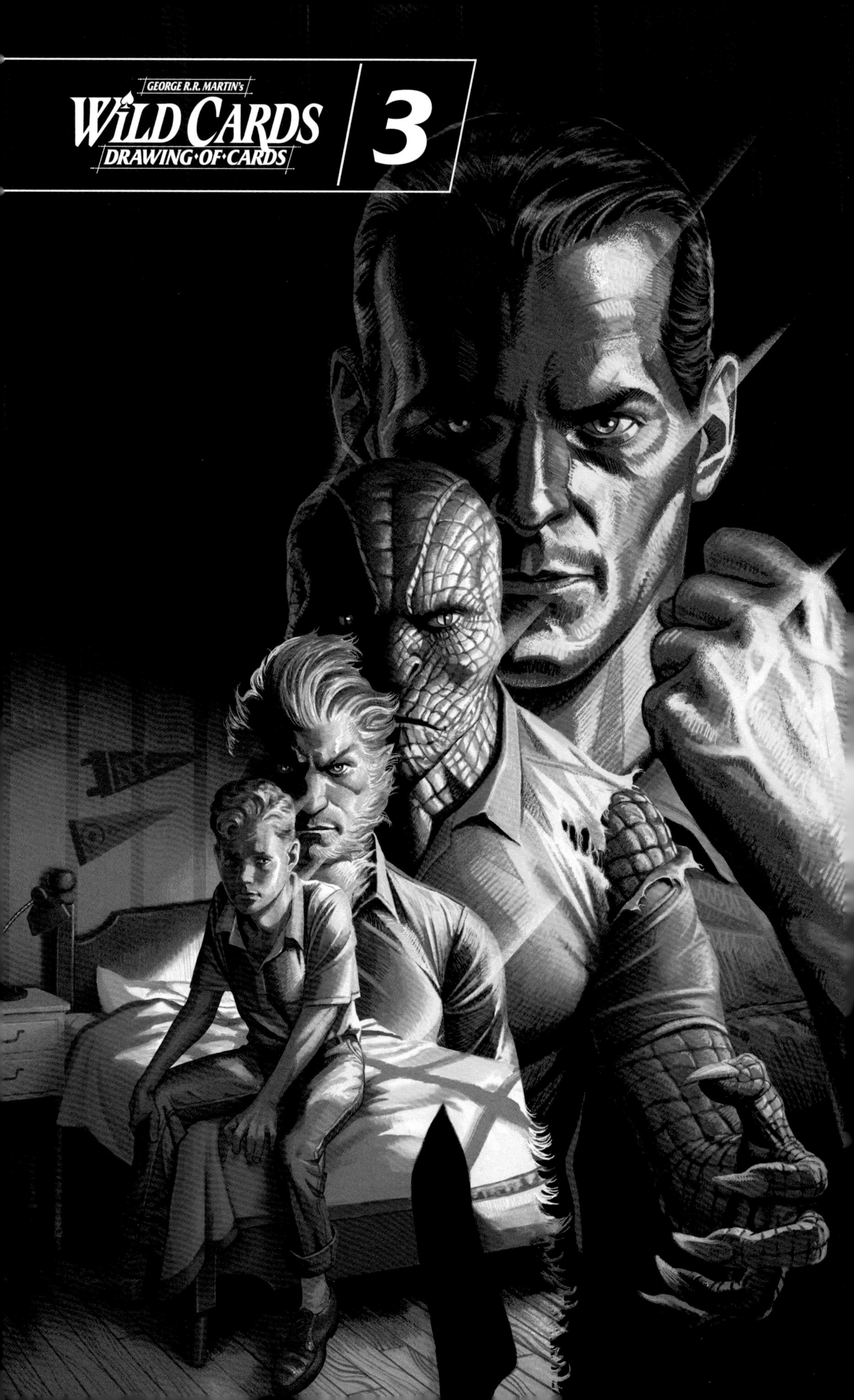
GEORGE R.R. MARTIN's
WILD CARDS
DRAWING·OF·CARDS
3

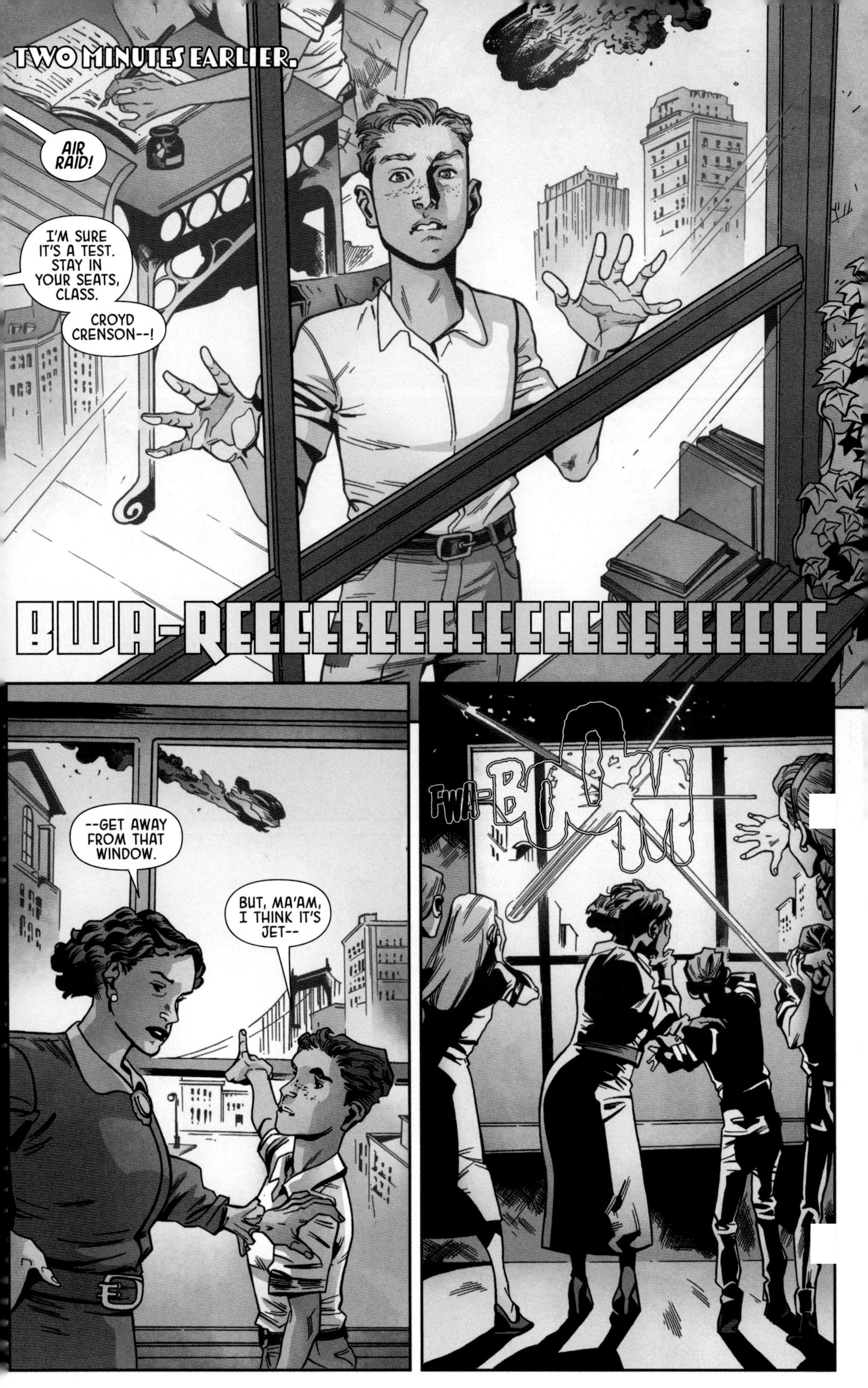
TWO MINUTES EARLIER.
AIR RAID!
I'M SURE IT'S A TEST. STAY IN YOUR SEATS, CLASS.
CROYD CRENSON--!
BWA-REEEEEEEEEEEEEEEEEEEEE
--GET AWAY FROM THAT WINDOW.
BUT, MA'AM, I THINK IT'S JET--
FWA-BOOM

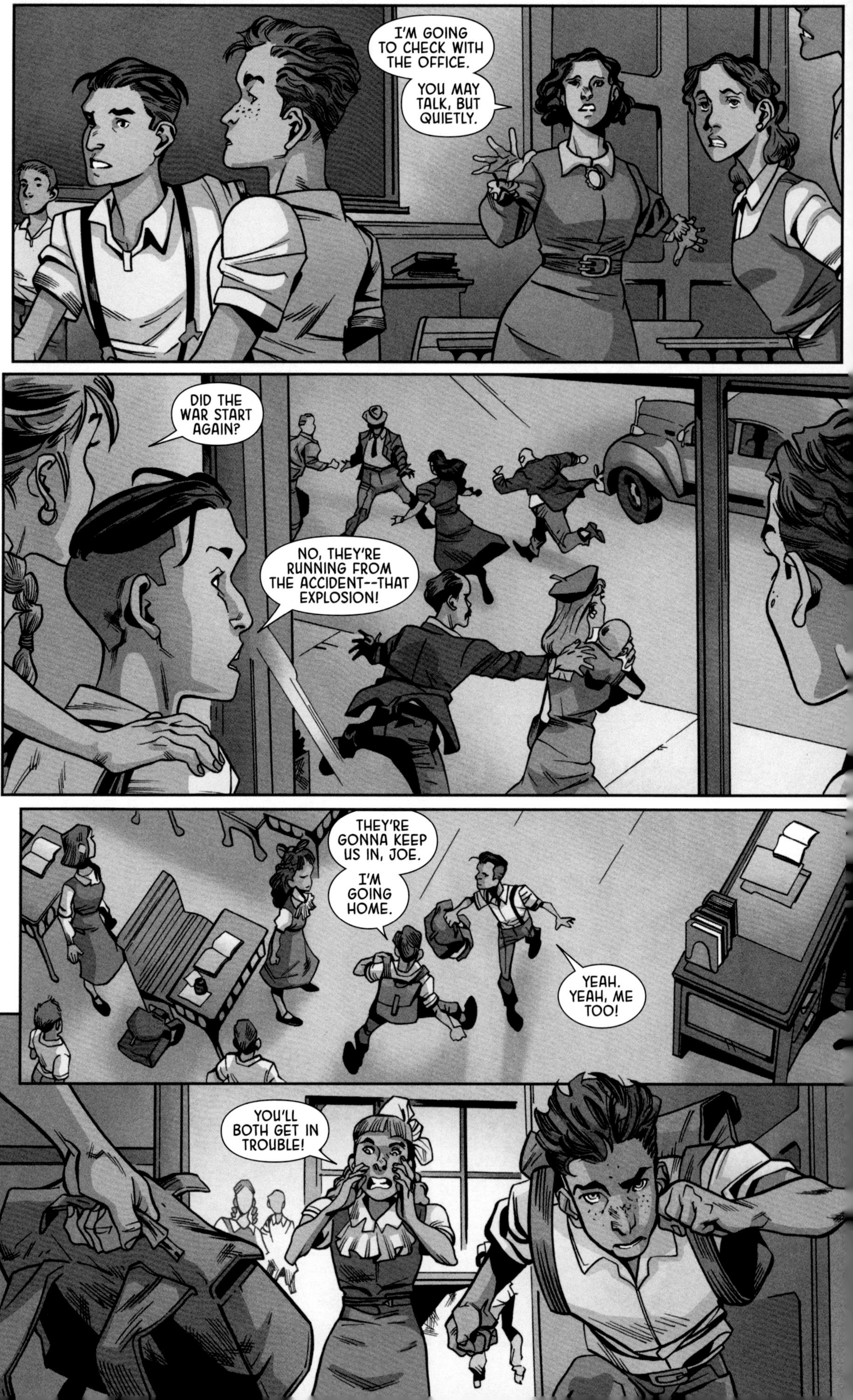
I'M GOING TO CHECK WITH THE OFFICE.
YOU MAY TALK, BUT QUIETLY.
DID THE WAR START AGAIN?
NO, THEY'RE RUNNING FROM THE ACCIDENT--THAT EXPLOSION!
THEY'RE GONNA KEEP US IN, JOE.
I'M GOING HOME.
YEAH. YEAH, ME TOO!
YOU'LL BOTH GET IN TROUBLE!

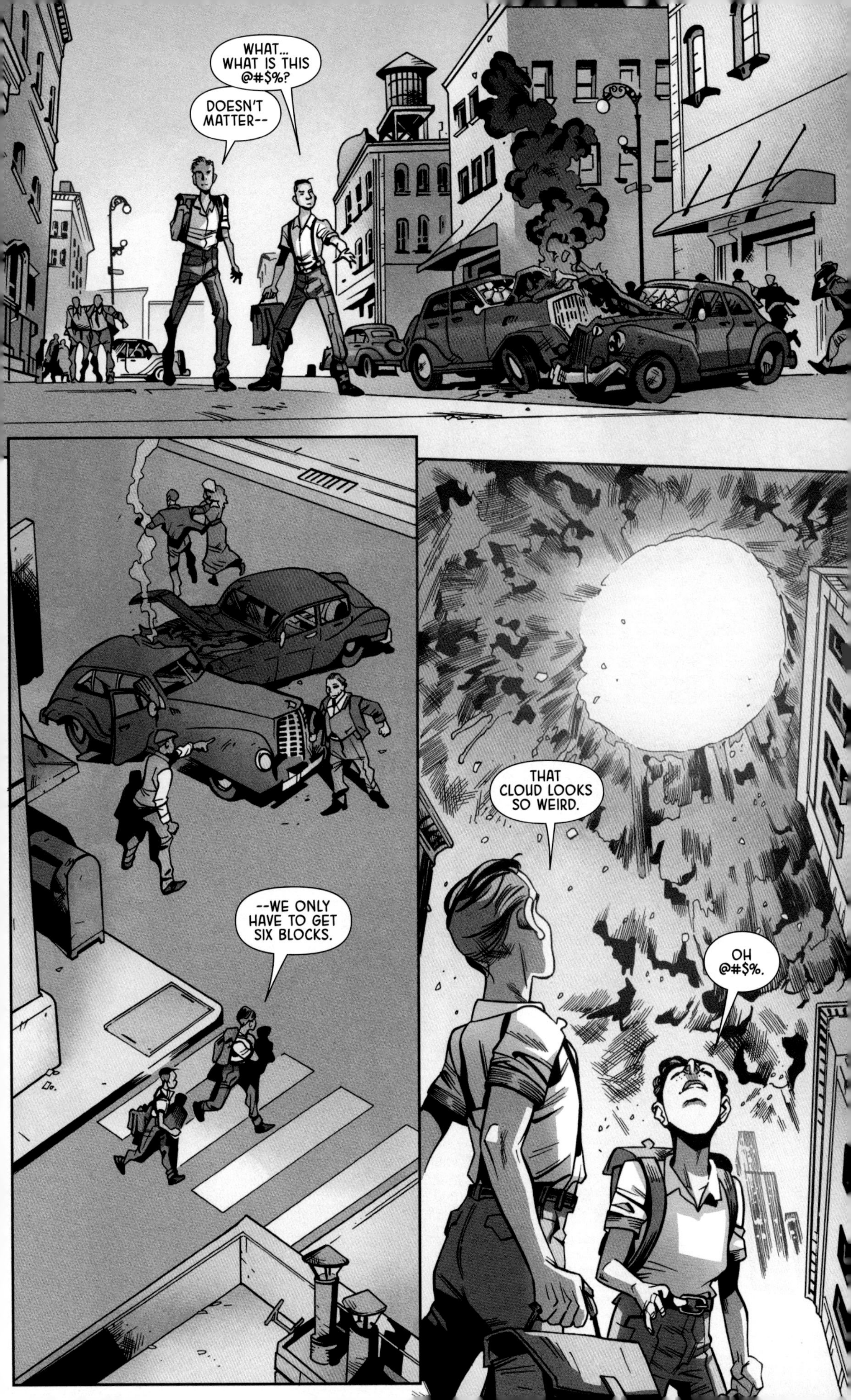
WHAT... WHAT IS THIS @#$%?
DOESN'T MATTER--
--WE ONLY HAVE TO GET SIX BLOCKS.
THAT CLOUD LOOKS SO WEIRD.
OH @#$%.

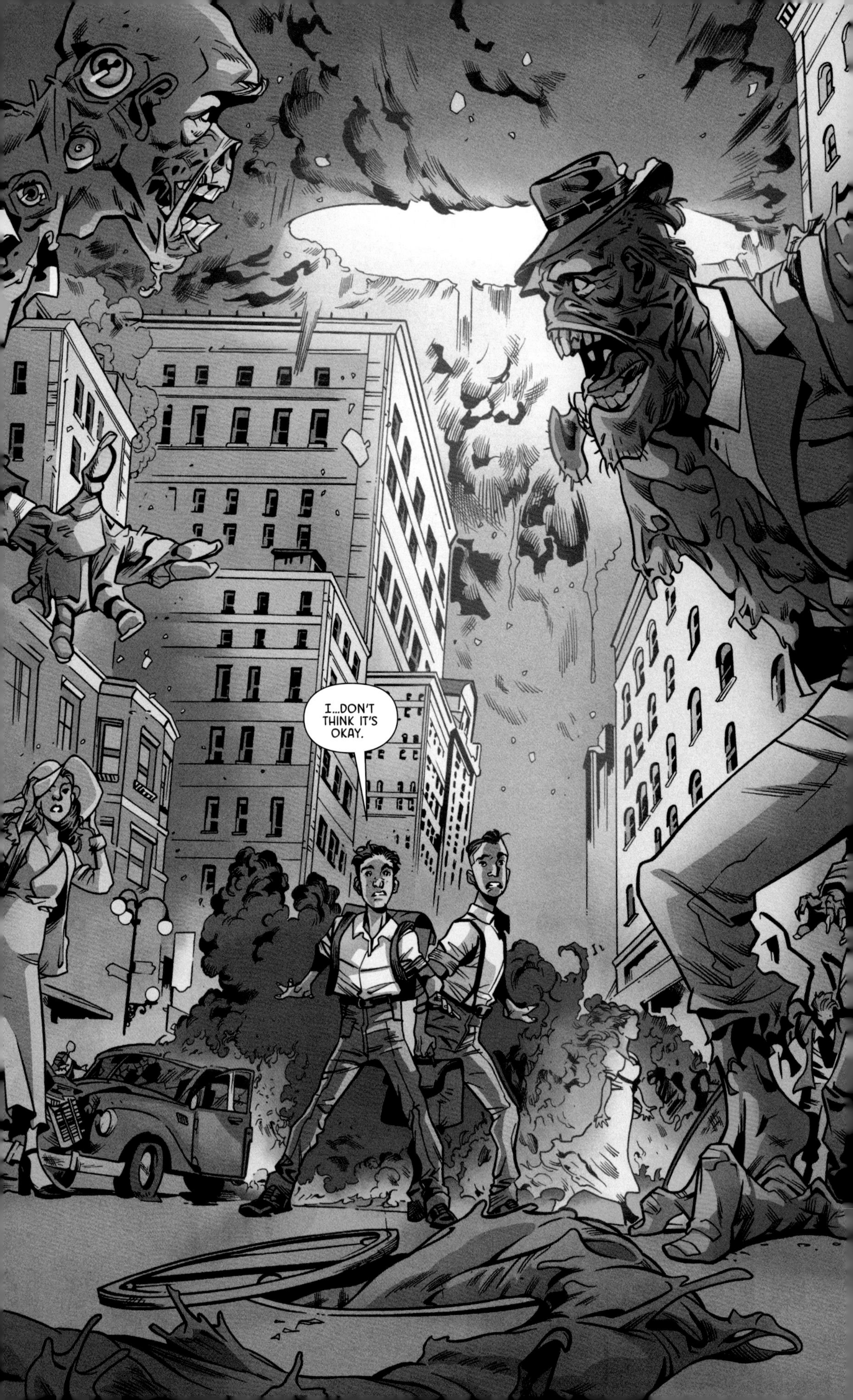
I...DON'T THINK IT'S OKAY.

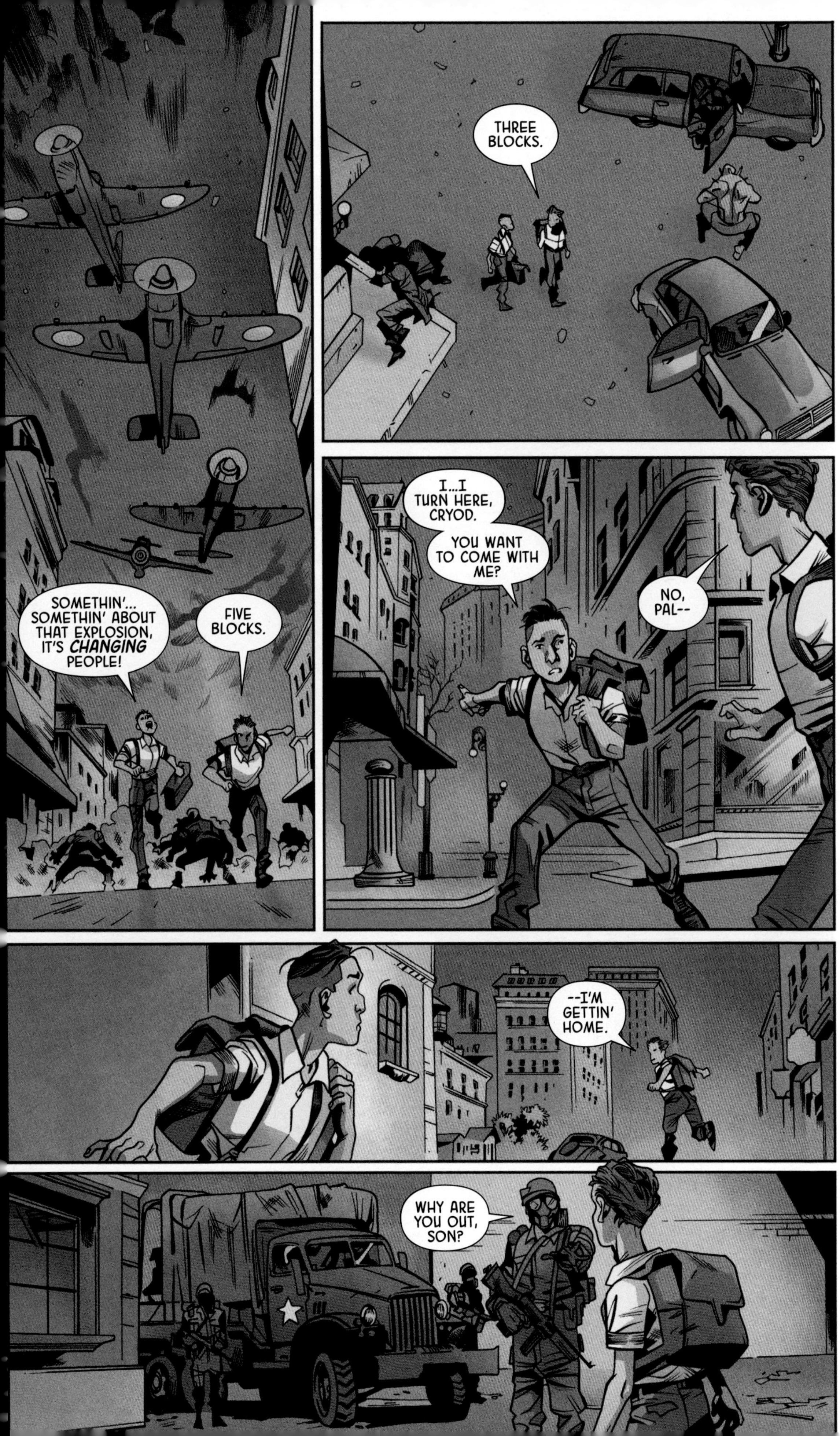
SOMETHIN'... SOMETHIN' ABOUT THAT EXPLOSION, IT'S *CHANGING* PEOPLE!
FIVE BLOCKS.
THREE BLOCKS.
I...I TURN HERE, CRYOD.
YOU WANT TO COME WITH ME?
NO, PAL--
--I'M GETTIN' HOME.
WHY ARE YOU OUT, SON?

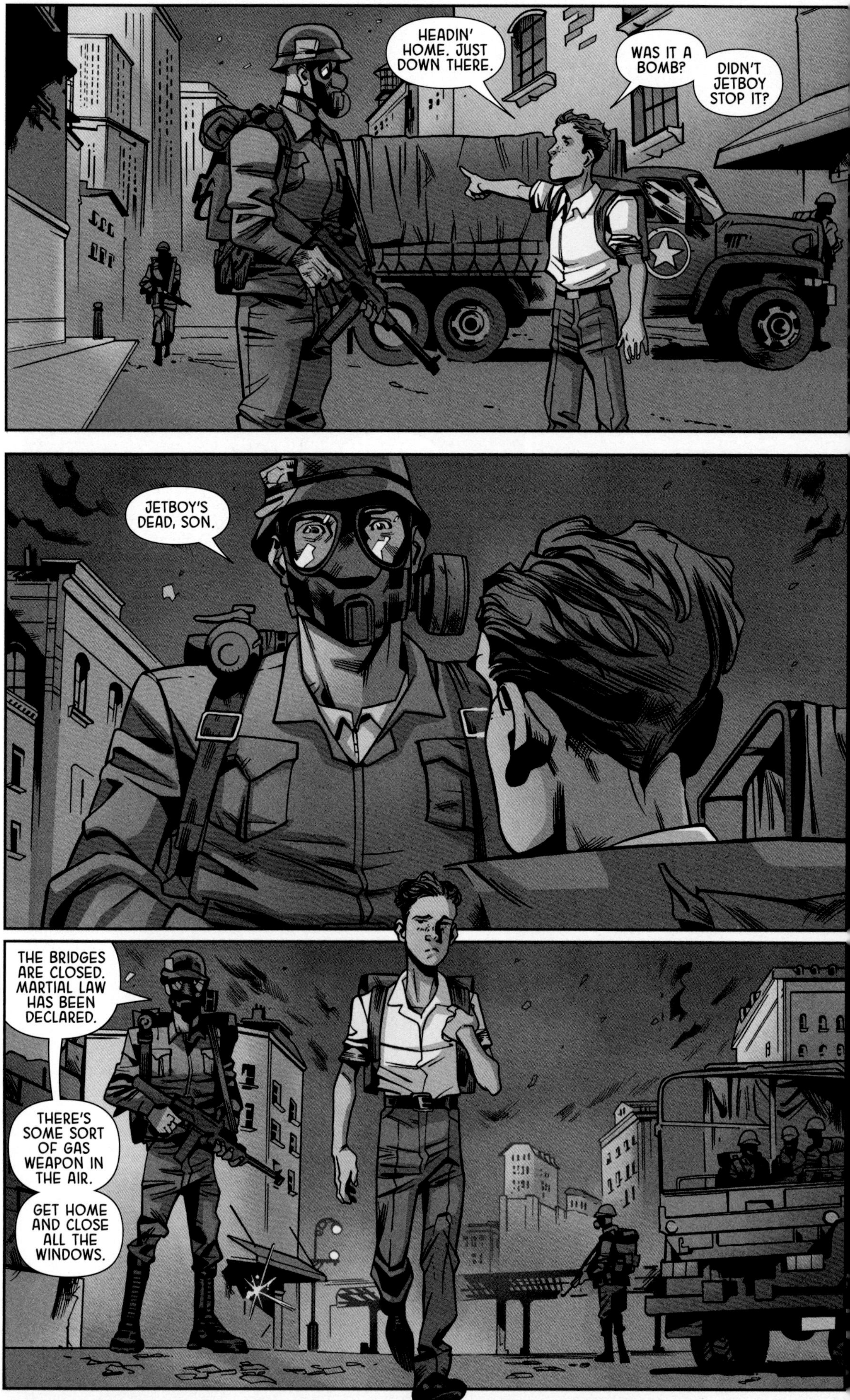
HEADIN' HOME. JUST DOWN THERE.
WAS IT A BOMB?
DIDN'T JETBOY STOP IT?
JETBOY'S DEAD, SON.
THE BRIDGES ARE CLOSED. MARTIAL LAW HAS BEEN DECLARED.
THERE'S SOME SORT OF GAS WEAPON IN THE AIR.
GET HOME AND CLOSE ALL THE WINDOWS.

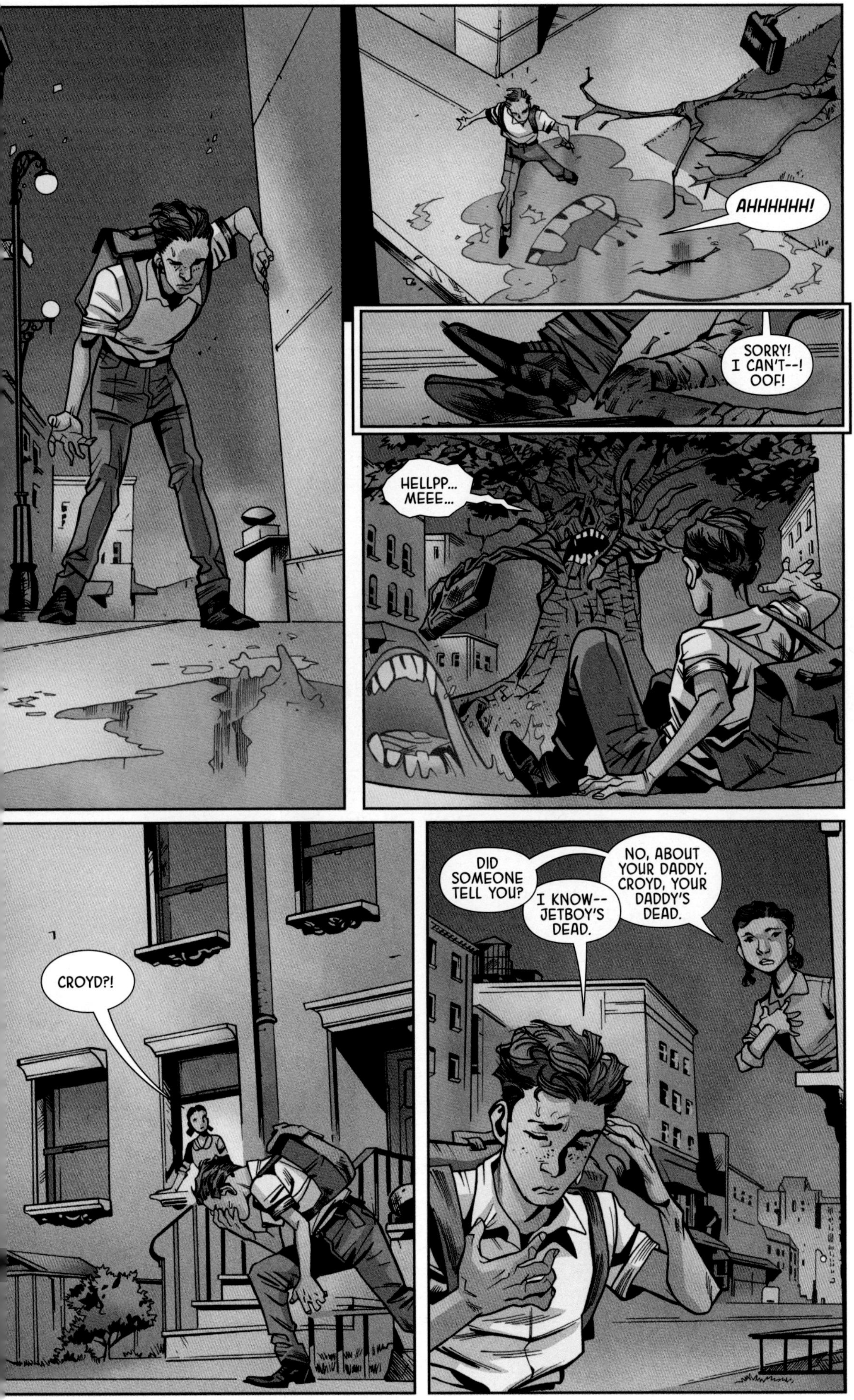
AHHHHHH!
SORRY! I CAN'T--! OOF!
HELLPP... MEEE...
CROYD?!
DID SOMEONE TELL YOU?
I KNOW-- JETBOY'S DEAD.
NO, ABOUT YOUR DADDY. CROYD, YOUR DADDY'S DEAD.

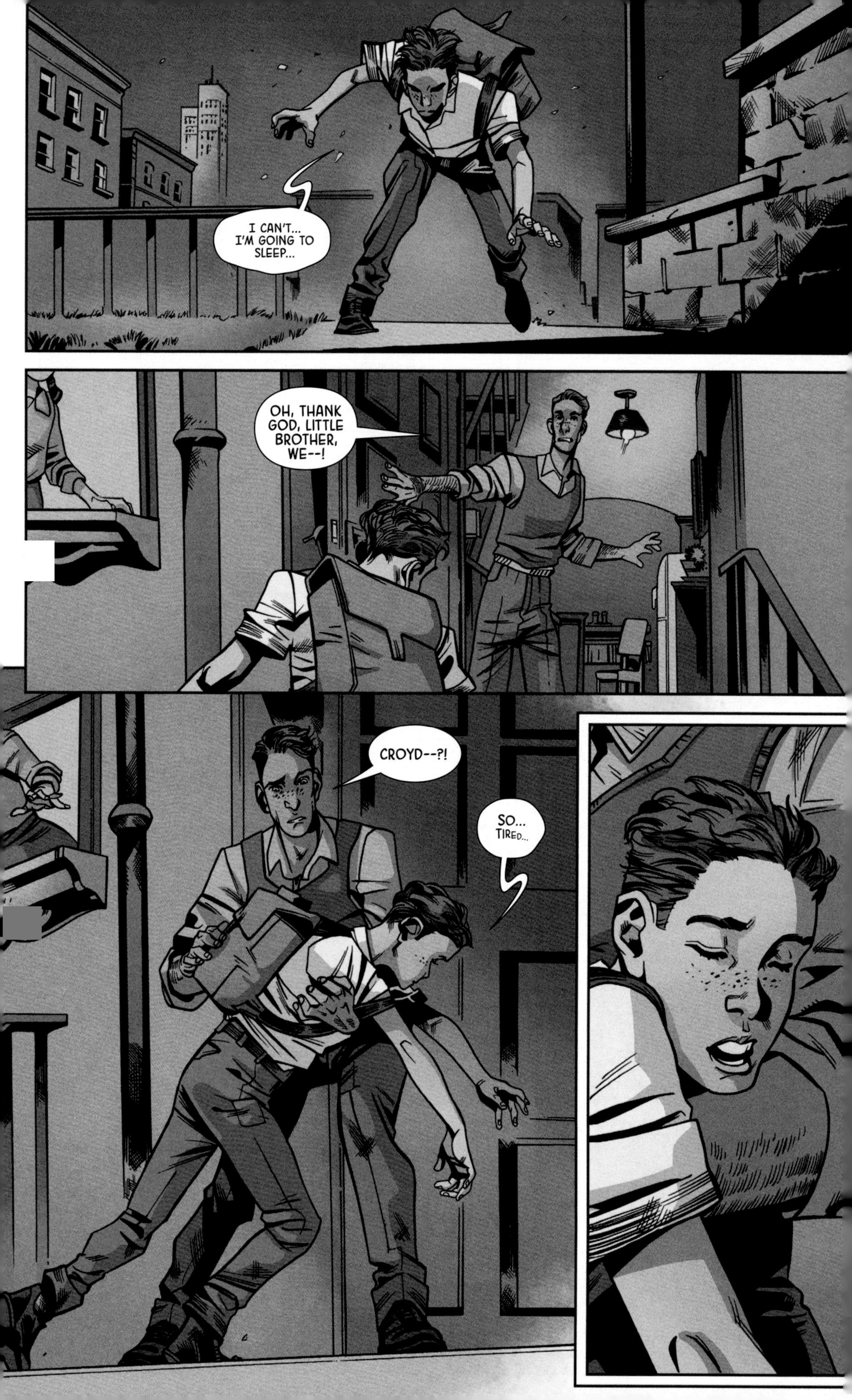
I CAN'T... I'M GOING TO SLEEP...
OH, THANK GOD, LITTLE BROTHER, WE--!
CROYD--?!
SO... TIRED...

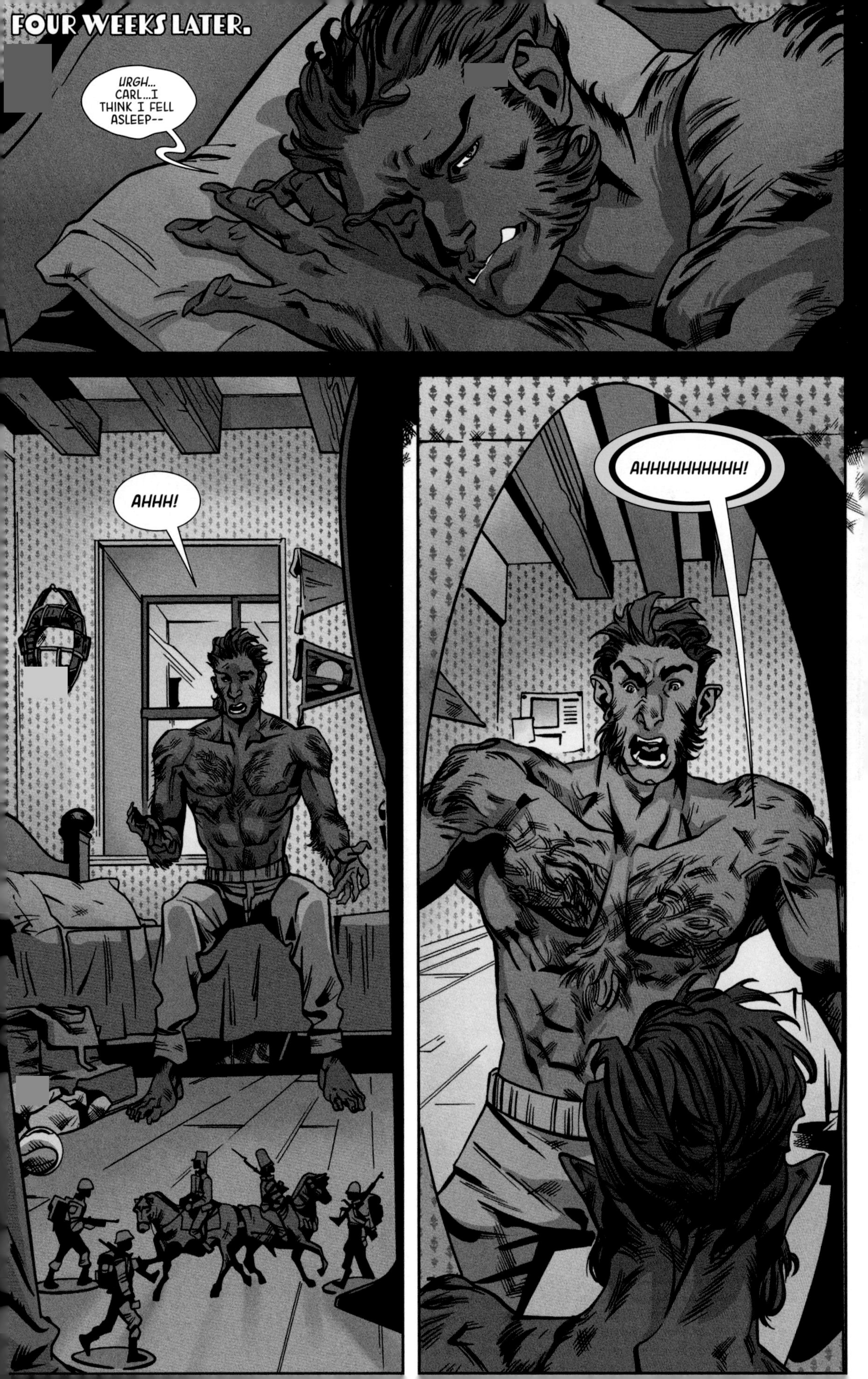
FOUR WEEKS LATER.
URGH... CARL...I THINK I FELL ASLEEP--
AHHH!
AHHHHHHHHHH!

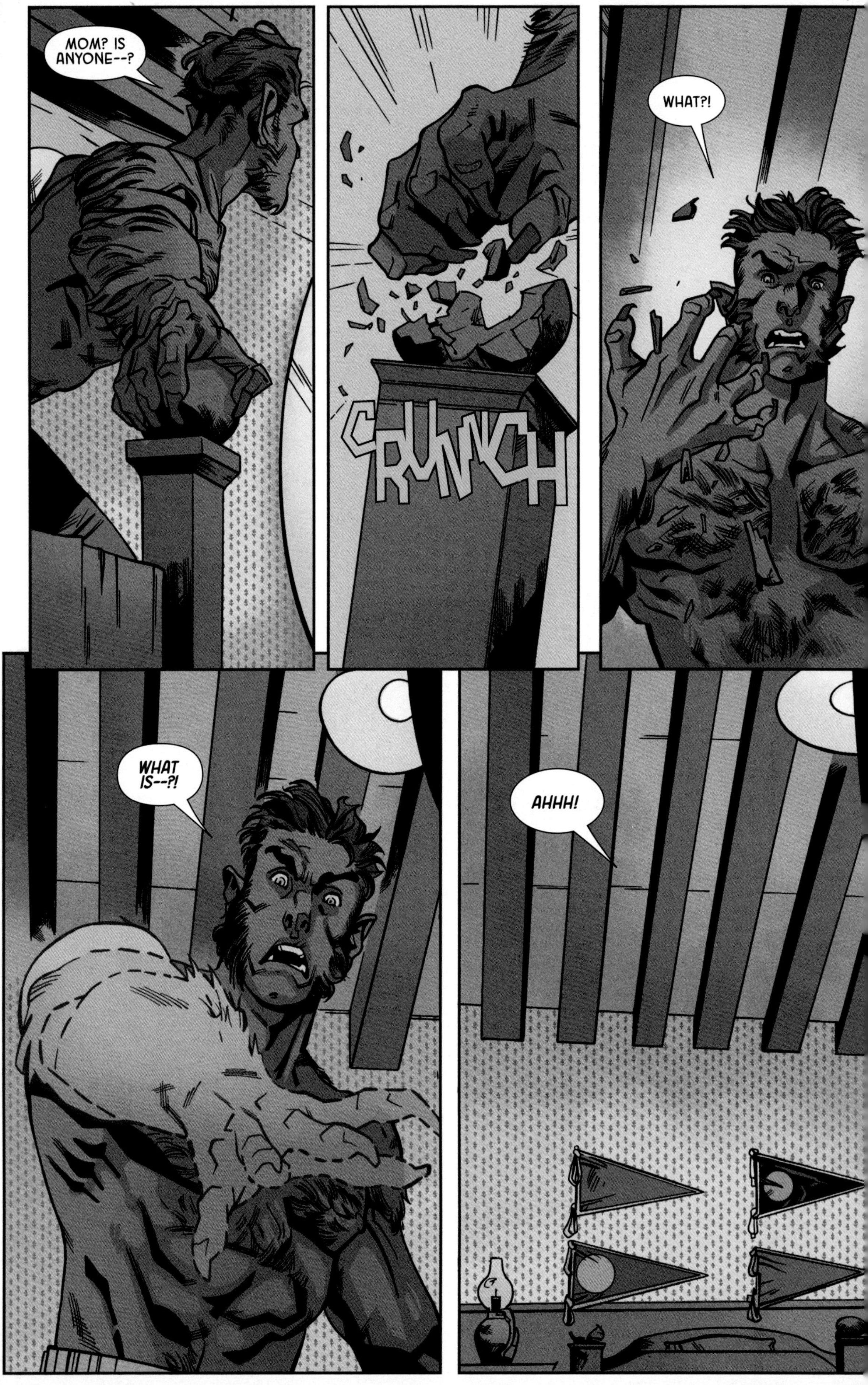
MOM? IS ANYONE--?
CRUNCH
WHAT?!
WHAT IS--?!
AHHH!

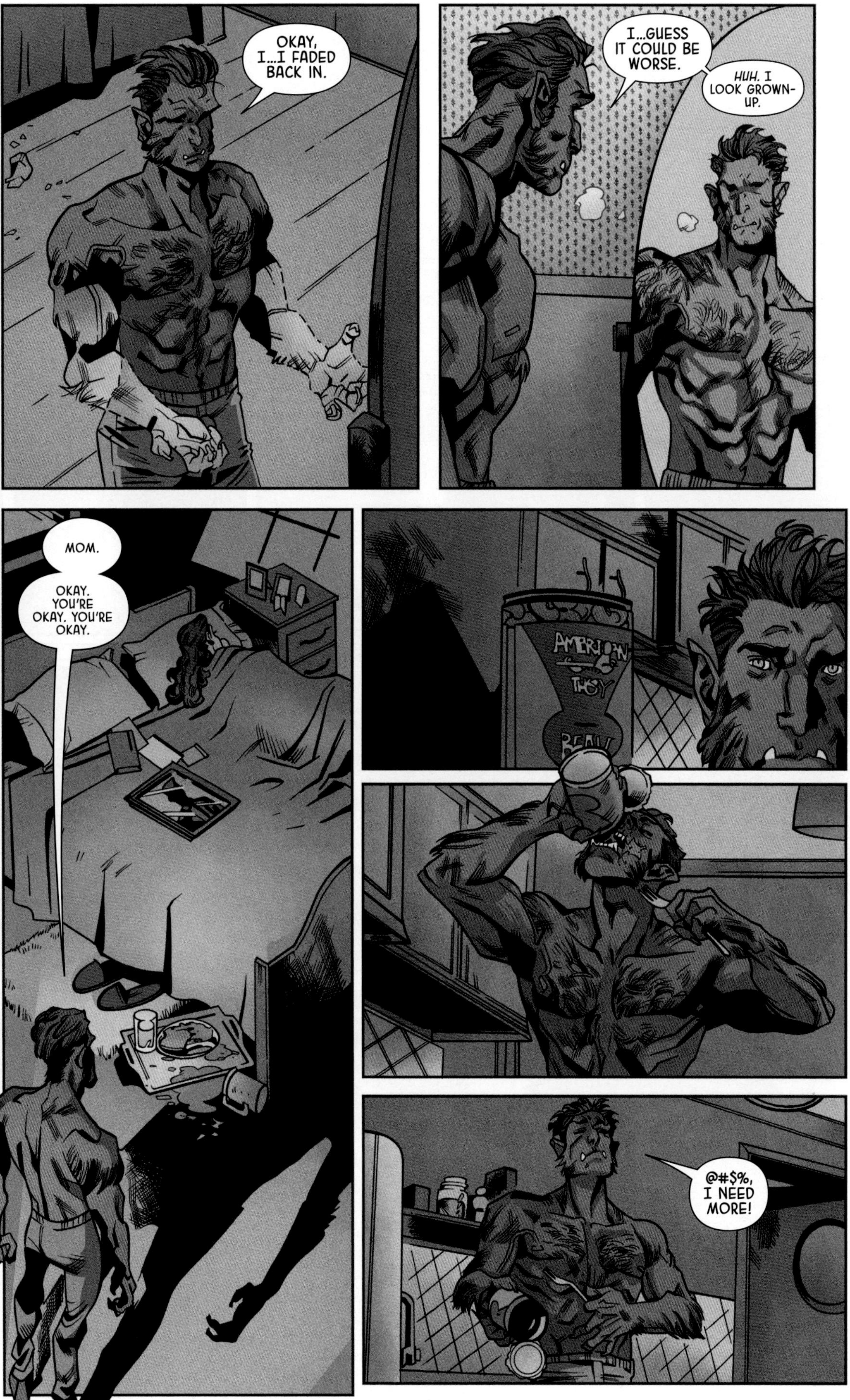
OKAY, I...I FADED BACK IN.
I...GUESS IT COULD BE WORSE.
HUH. I LOOK GROWN-UP.
MOM.
OKAY. YOU'RE OKAY. YOU'RE OKAY.
AMERICAN THGY
@#$%, I NEED MORE!

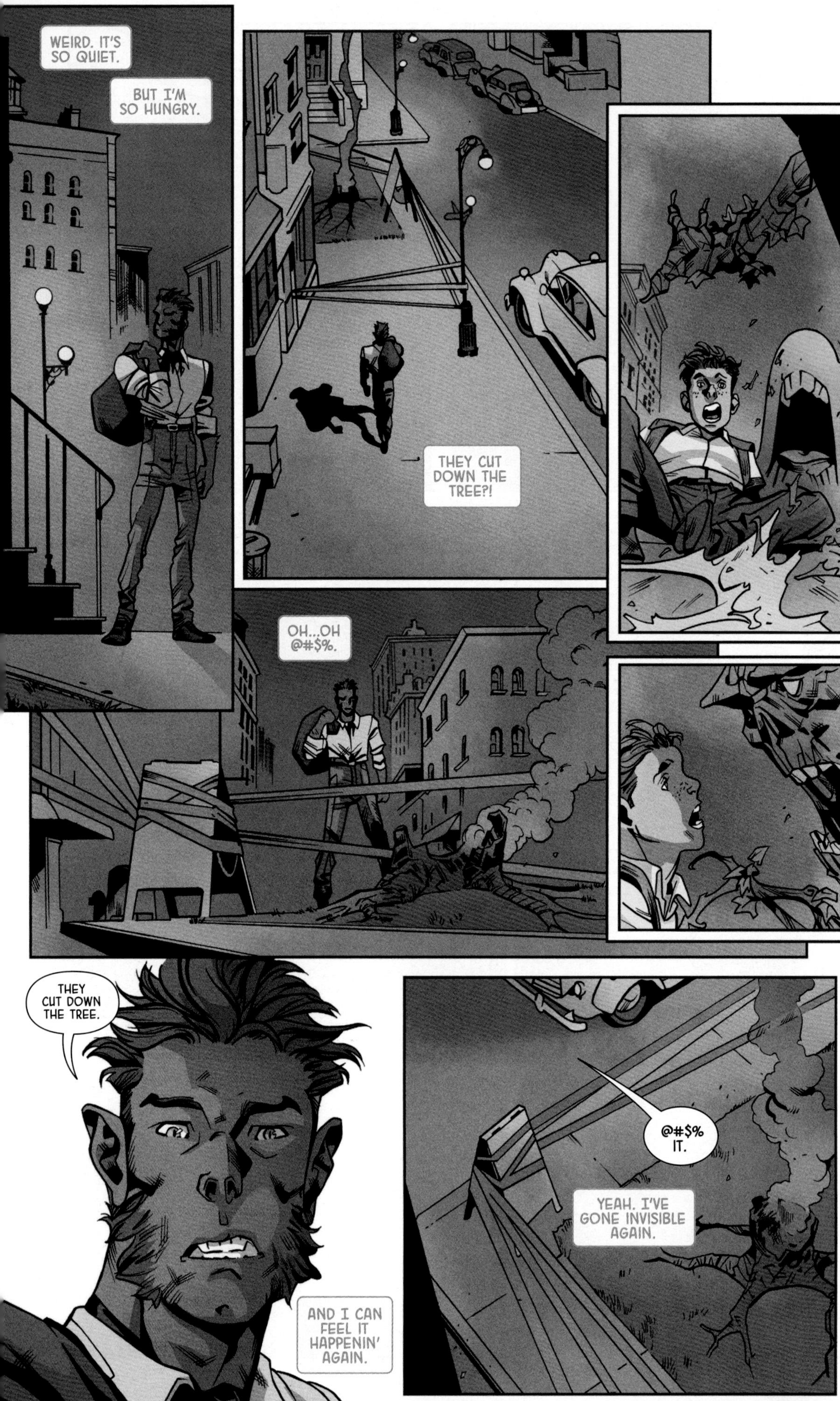
WEIRD. IT'S SO QUIET.
BUT I'M SO HUNGRY.
THEY CUT DOWN THE TREE?!
OH...OH @#$%.
THEY CUT DOWN THE TREE.
AND I CAN FEEL IT HAPPENIN' AGAIN.
@#$% IT.
YEAH. I'VE GONE INVISIBLE AGAIN.

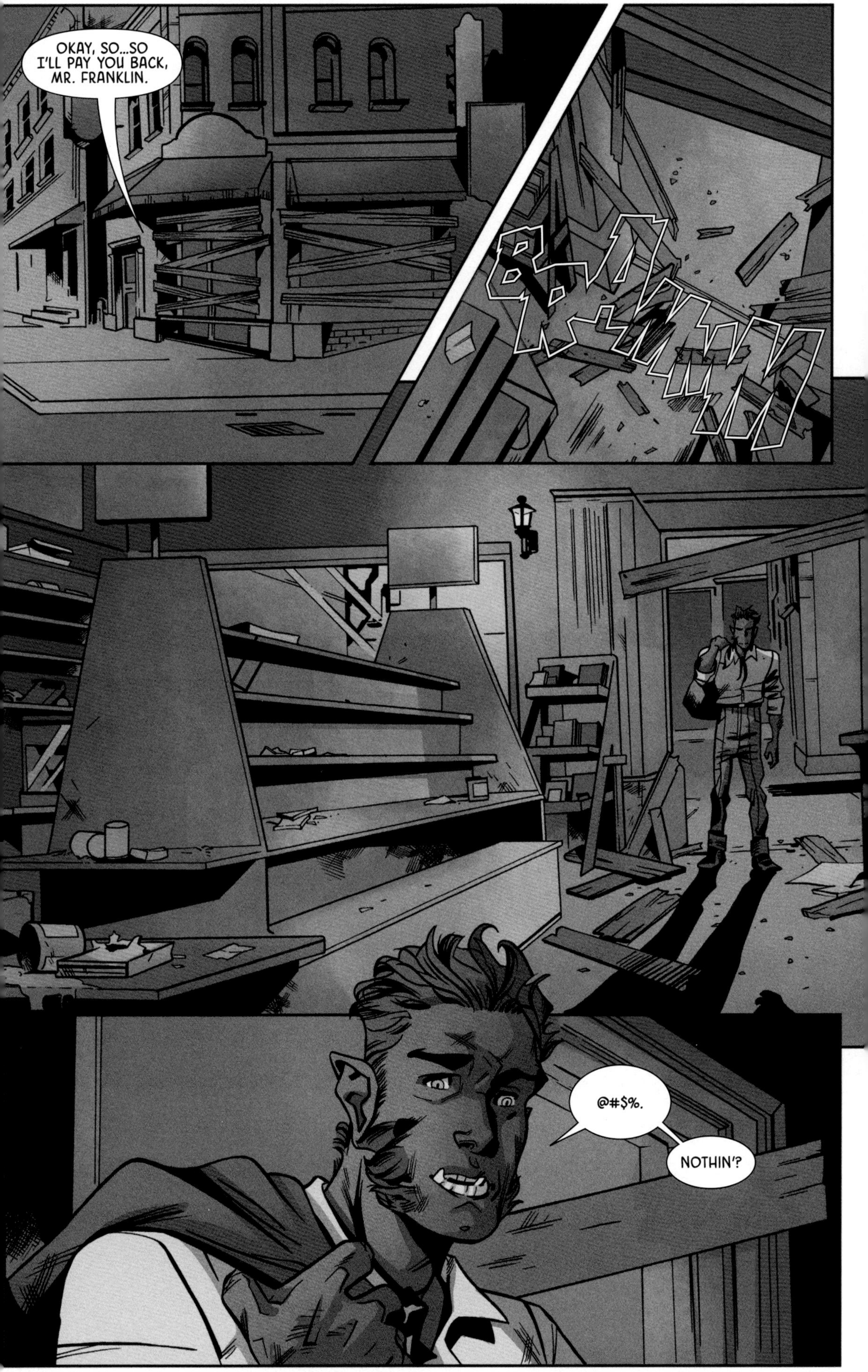
OKAY, SO...SO I'LL PAY YOU BACK, MR. FRANKLIN.
@#$%.
NOTHIN'?

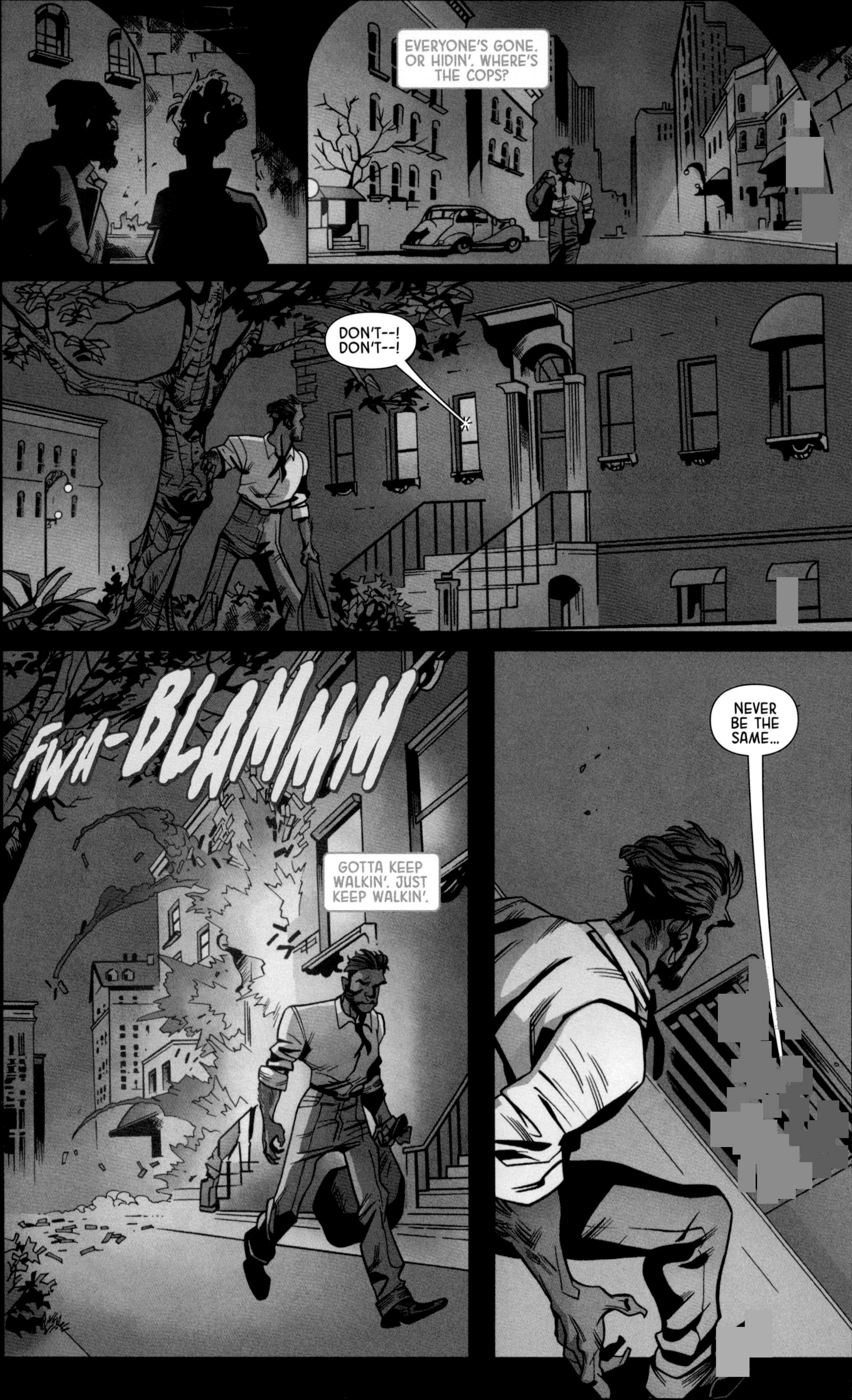

EVERYONE'S GONE. OR HIDIN'. WHERE'S THE COPS?
DON'T--! DON'T--!
FWA-BLAMMM
GOTTA KEEP WALKIN'. JUST KEEP WALKIN'.
NEVER BE THE SAME...

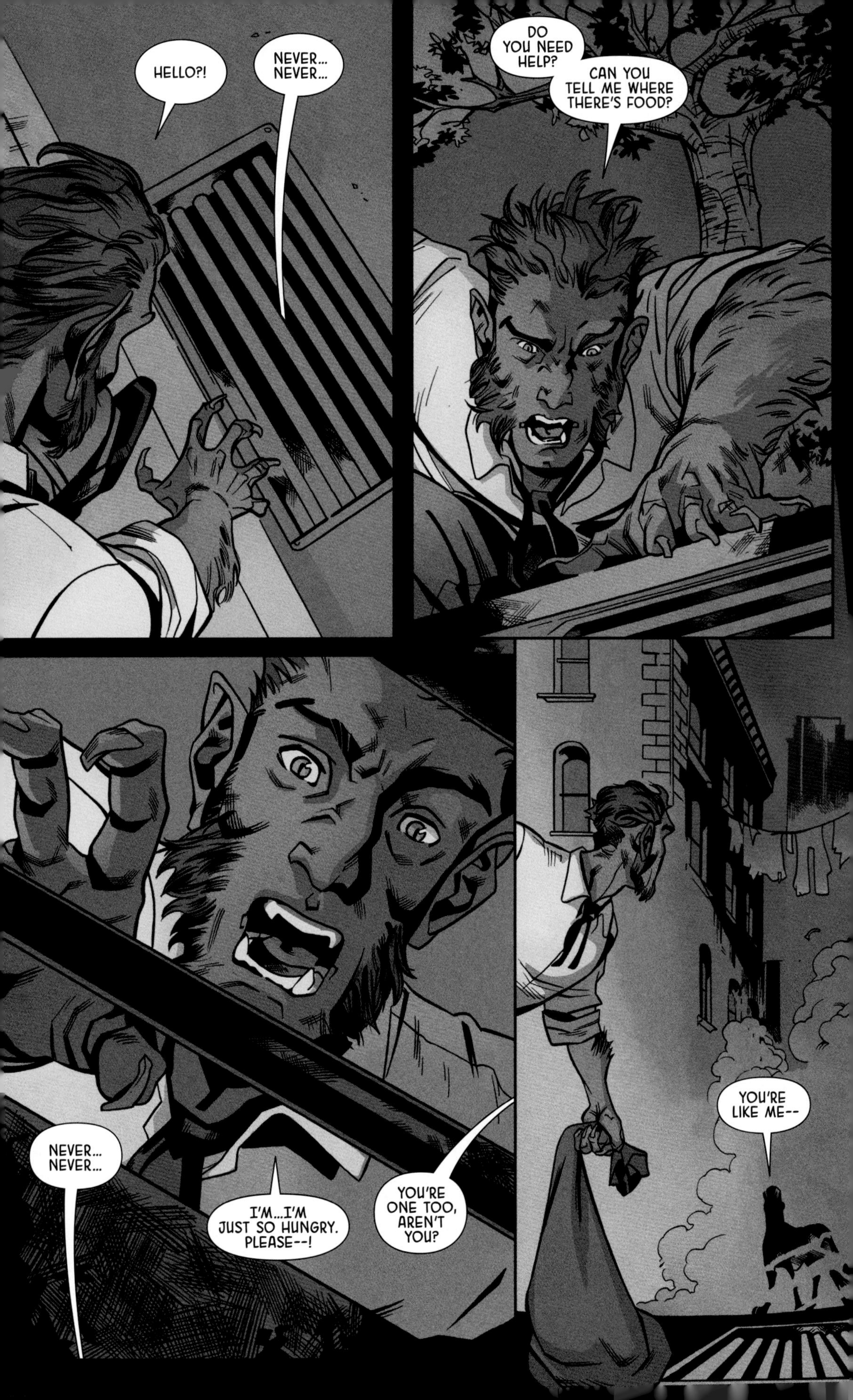
HELLO?!
NEVER... NEVER...
DO YOU NEED HELP?
CAN YOU TELL ME WHERE THERE'S FOOD?
NEVER... NEVER...
I'M...I'M JUST SO HUNGRY. PLEASE--!
YOU'RE ONE TOO, AREN'T YOU?
YOU'RE LIKE ME--

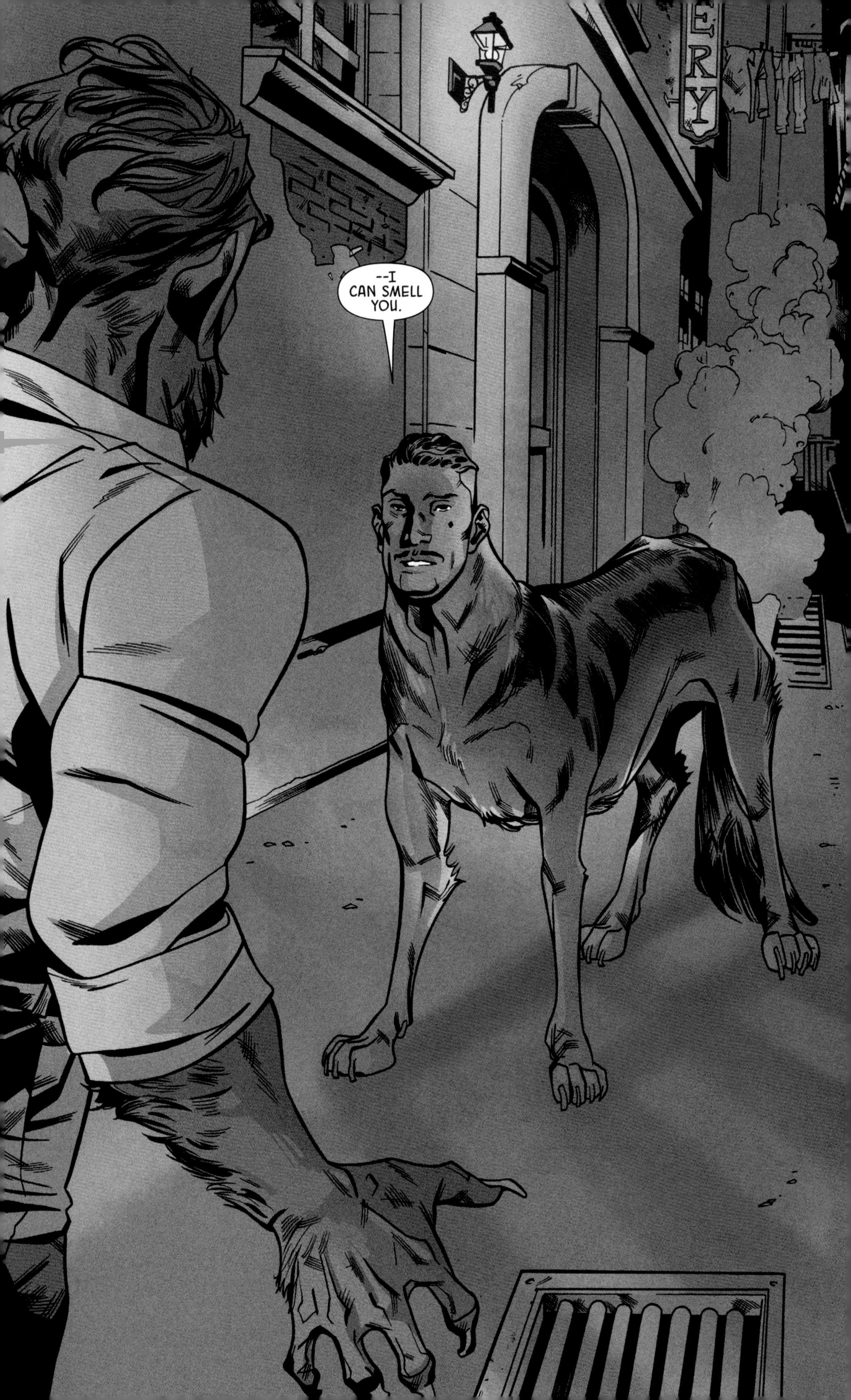
--I CAN SMELL YOU.

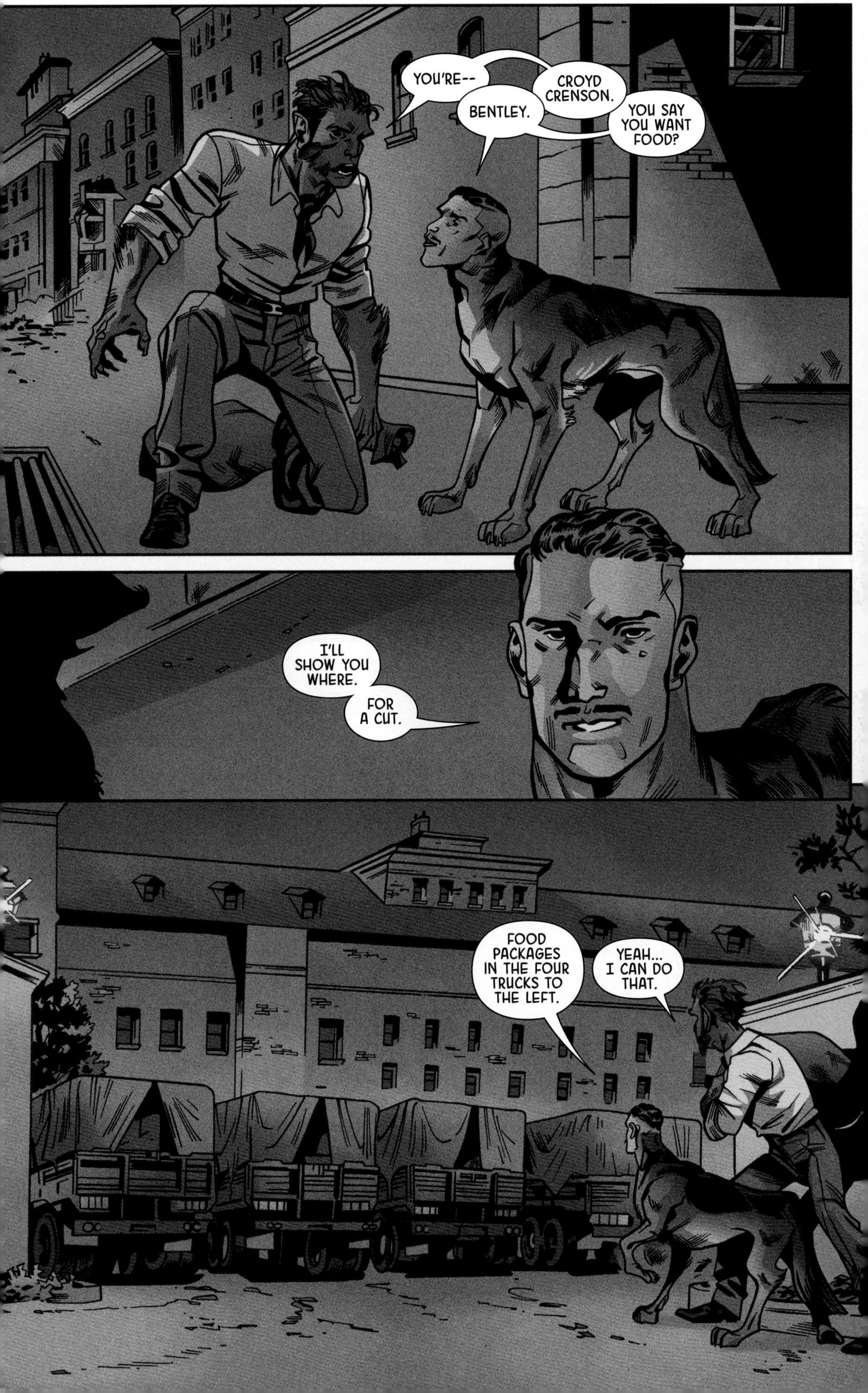
YOU'RE--
CROYD CRENSON.
BENTLEY.
YOU SAY YOU WANT FOOD?
I'LL SHOW YOU WHERE.
FOR A CUT.
FOOD PACKAGES IN THE FOUR TRUCKS TO THE LEFT.
YEAH... I CAN DO THAT.

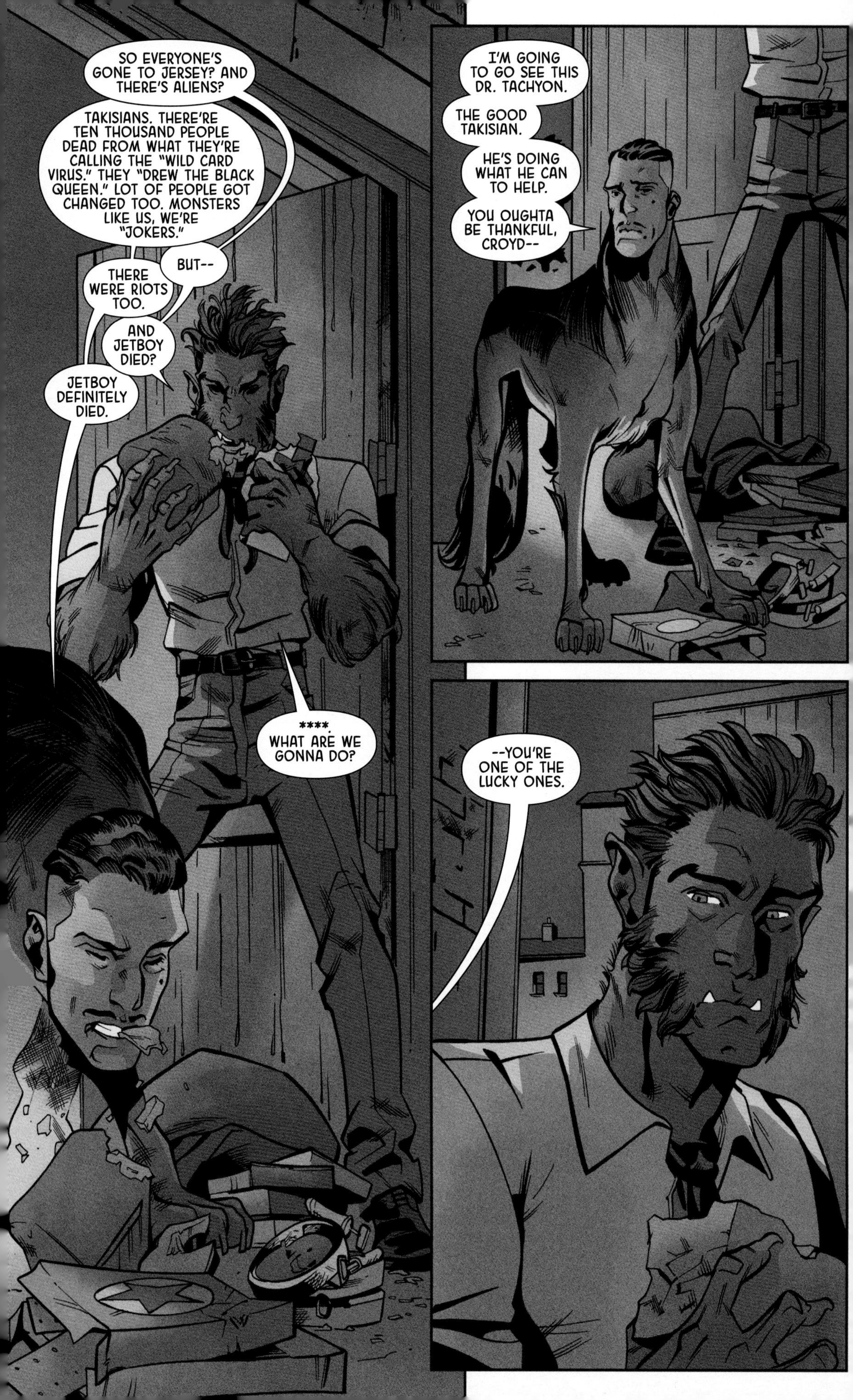
SO EVERYONE'S GONE TO JERSEY? AND THERE'S ALIENS?
TAKISIANS. THERE'RE TEN THOUSAND PEOPLE DEAD FROM WHAT THEY'RE CALLING THE "WILD CARD VIRUS." THEY "DREW THE BLACK QUEEN." LOT OF PEOPLE GOT CHANGED TOO. MONSTERS LIKE US, WE'RE "JOKERS."
BUT--
THERE WERE RIOTS TOO.
AND JETBOY DIED?
JETBOY DEFINITELY DIED.
****. WHAT ARE WE GONNA DO?
I'M GOING TO GO SEE THIS DR. TACHYON.
THE GOOD TAKISIAN.
HE'S DOING WHAT HE CAN TO HELP.
YOU OUGHTA BE THANKFUL, CROYD--
--YOU'RE ONE OF THE LUCKY ONES.

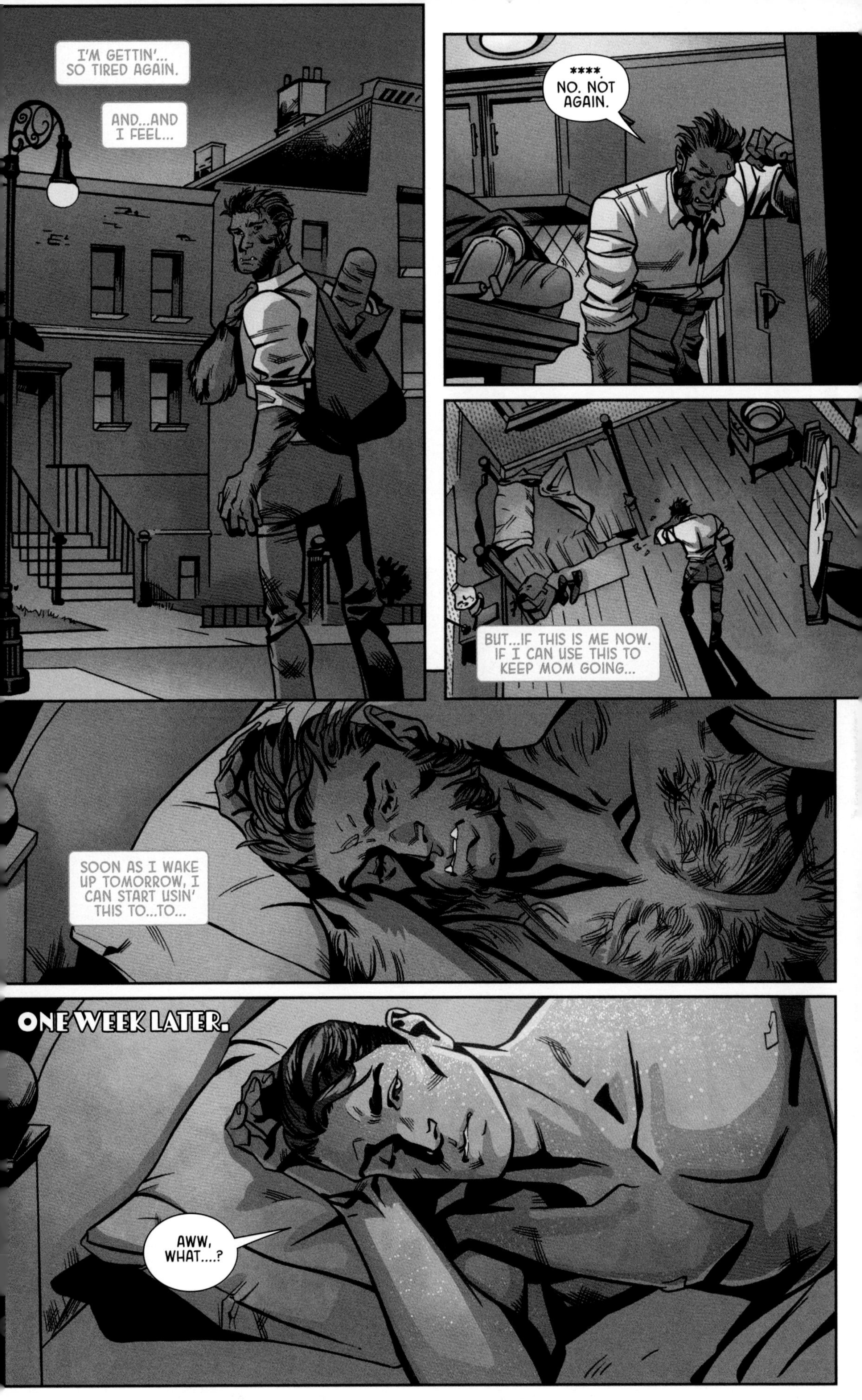
I'M GETTIN'... SO TIRED AGAIN.
AND...AND I FEEL...
****. NO. NOT AGAIN.
BUT...IF THIS IS ME NOW. IF I CAN USE THIS TO KEEP MOM GOING...
SOON AS I WAKE UP TOMORROW, I CAN START USIN' THIS TO...TO...
ONE WEEK LATER.
AWW, WHAT....?

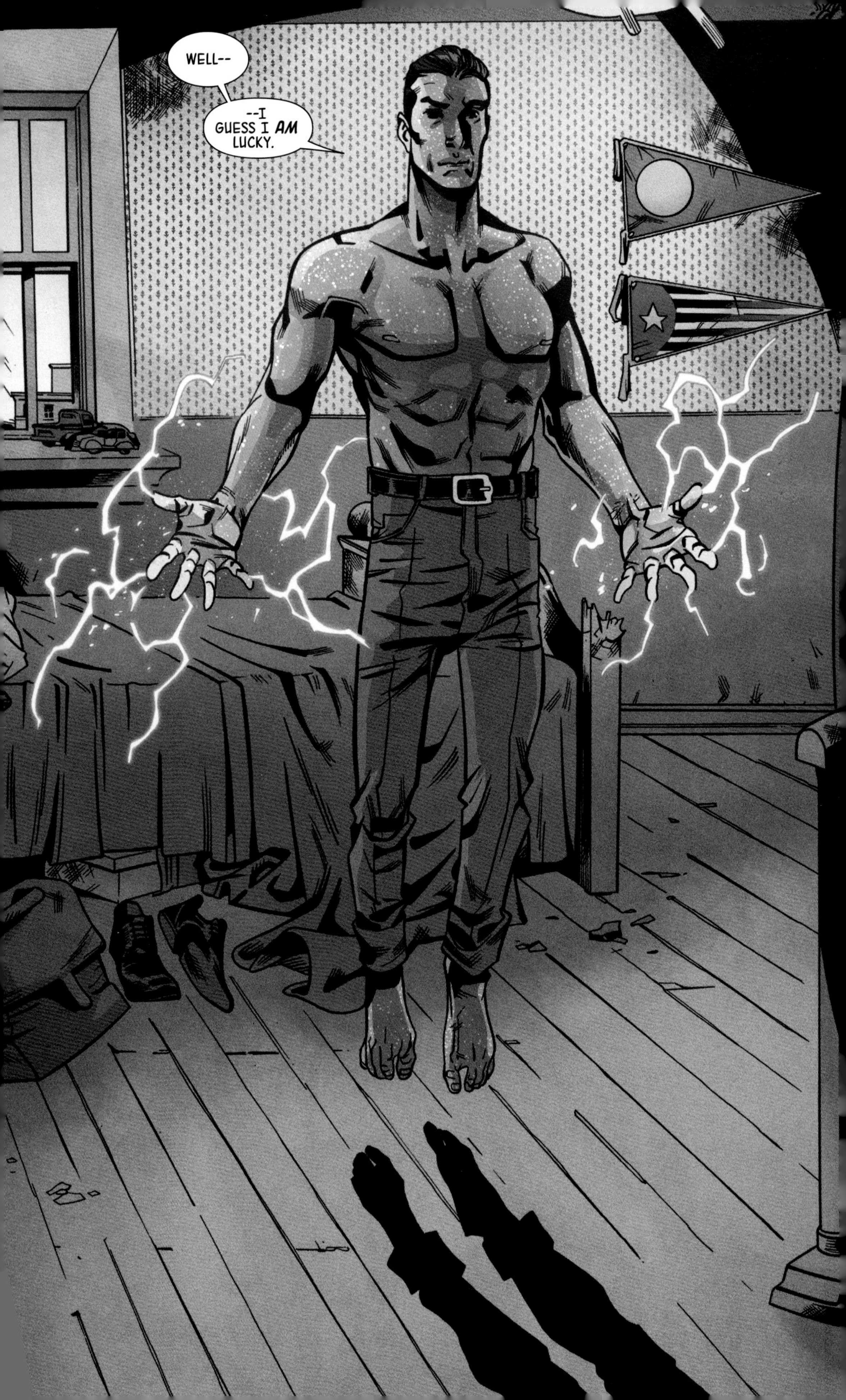
WELL--
--I GUESS I **AM** LUCKY.

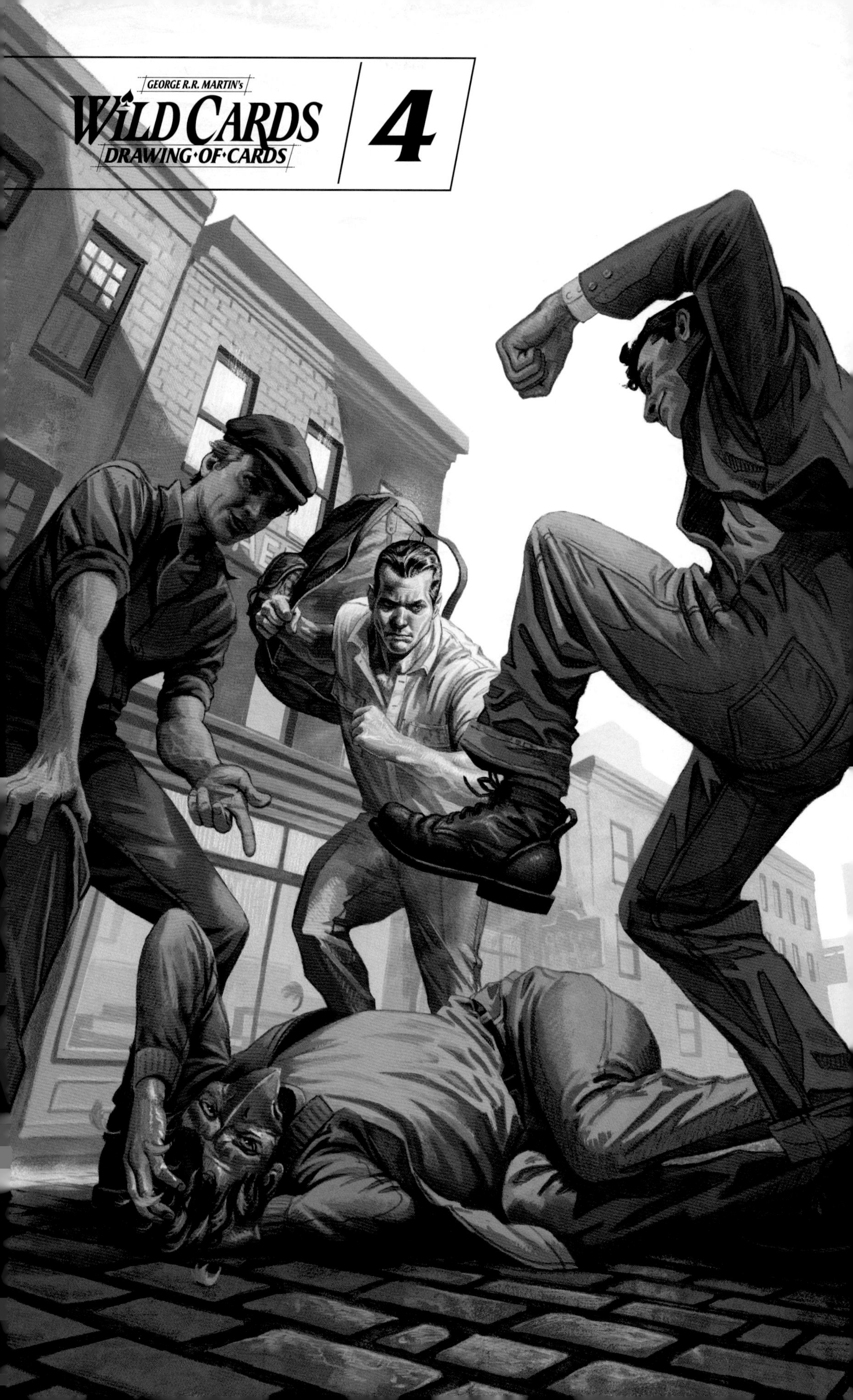
GEORGE R.R. MARTIN's
WILD CARDS
DRAWING·OF·CARDS
4

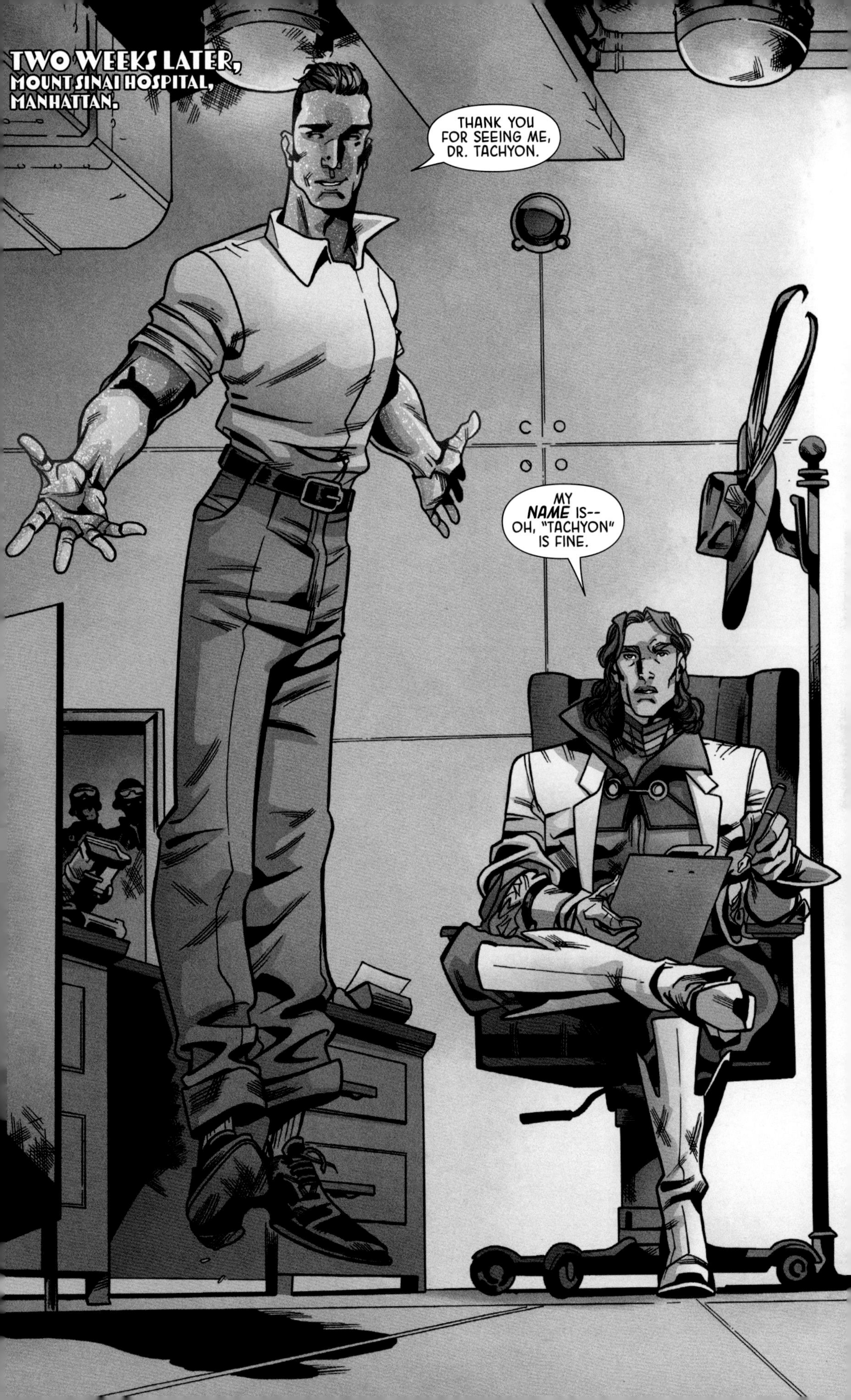
TWO WEEKS LATER, MOUNT SINAI HOSPITAL, MANHATTAN.
THANK YOU FOR SEEING ME, DR. TACHYON.
MY NAME IS-- OH, "TACHYON" IS FINE.

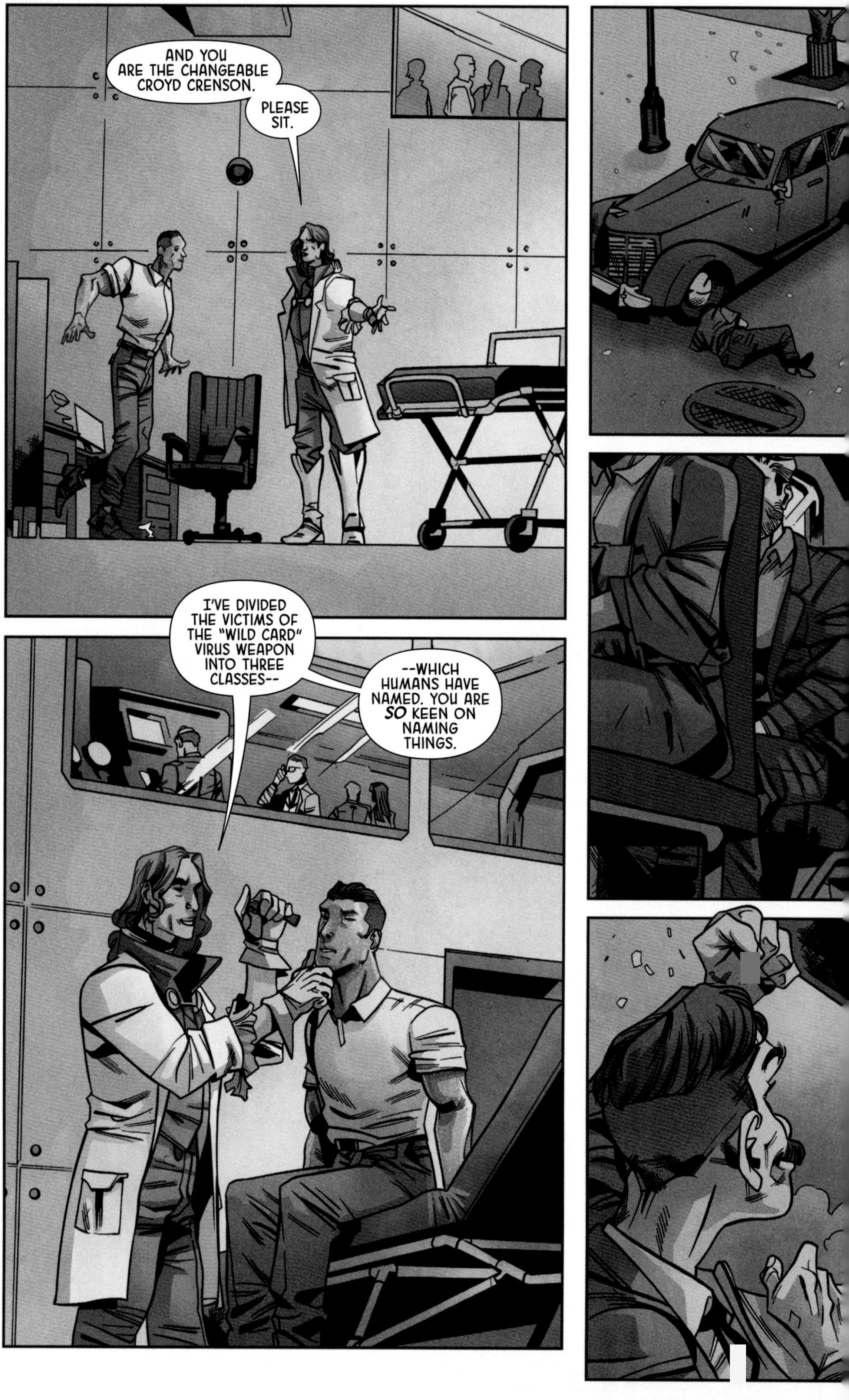
AND YOU ARE THE CHANGEABLE CROYD CRENSON.
PLEASE SIT.
I'VE DIVIDED THE VICTIMS OF THE "WILD CARD" VIRUS WEAPON INTO THREE CLASSES--
--WHICH HUMANS HAVE NAMED. YOU ARE SO KEEN ON NAMING THINGS.

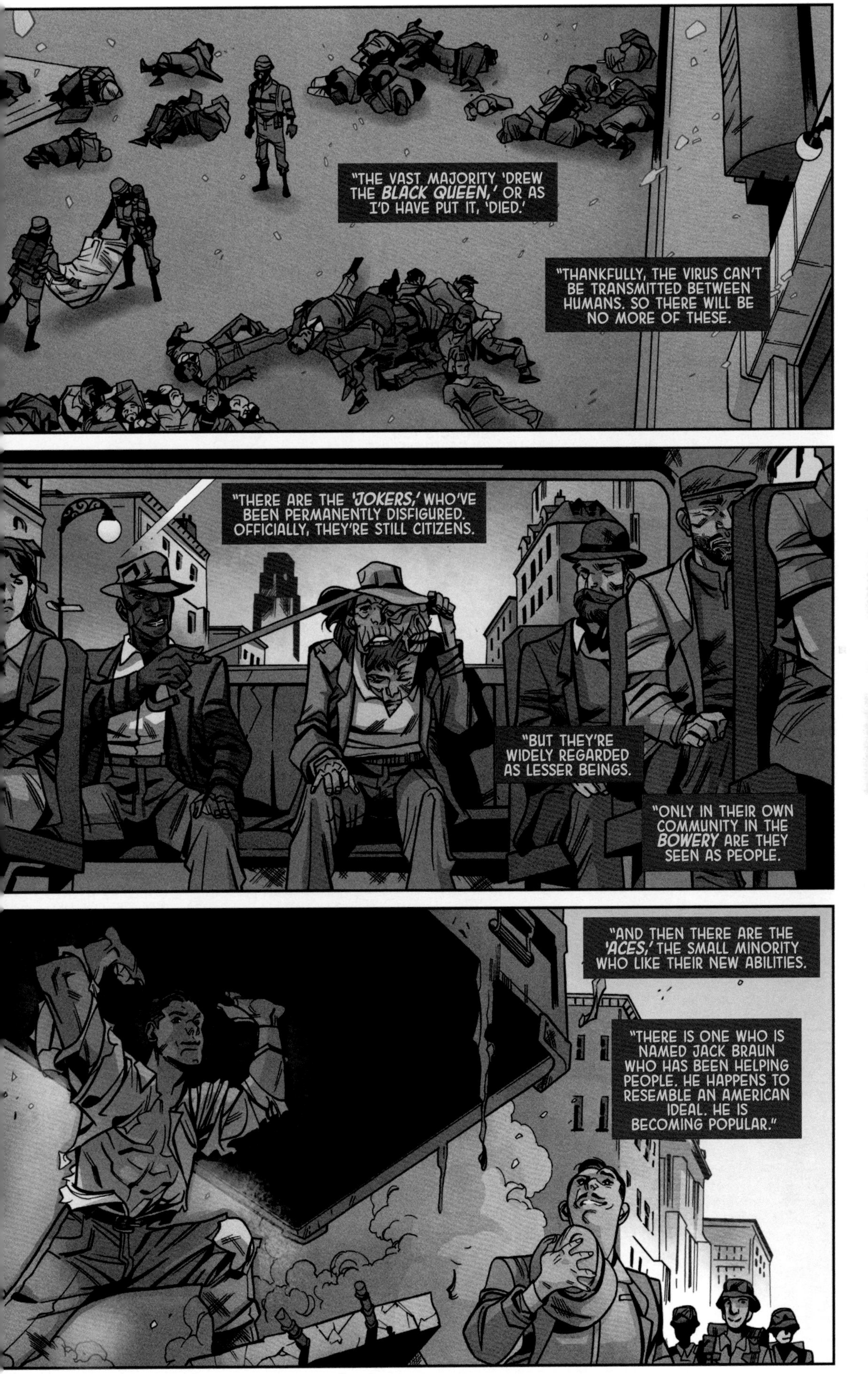
"THE VAST MAJORITY 'DREW THE BLACK QUEEN,' OR AS I'D HAVE PUT IT, 'DIED.'
"THANKFULLY, THE VIRUS CAN'T BE TRANSMITTED BETWEEN HUMANS. SO THERE WILL BE NO MORE OF THESE.
"THERE ARE THE 'JOKERS,' WHO'VE BEEN PERMANENTLY DISFIGURED. OFFICIALLY, THEY'RE STILL CITIZENS.
"BUT THEY'RE WIDELY REGARDED AS LESSER BEINGS.
"ONLY IN THEIR OWN COMMUNITY IN THE BOWERY ARE THEY SEEN AS PEOPLE.
"AND THEN THERE ARE THE 'ACES,' THE SMALL MINORITY WHO LIKE THEIR NEW ABILITIES.
"THERE IS ONE WHO IS NAMED JACK BRAUN WHO HAS BEEN HELPING PEOPLE. HE HAPPENS TO RESEMBLE AN AMERICAN IDEAL. HE IS BECOMING POPULAR."

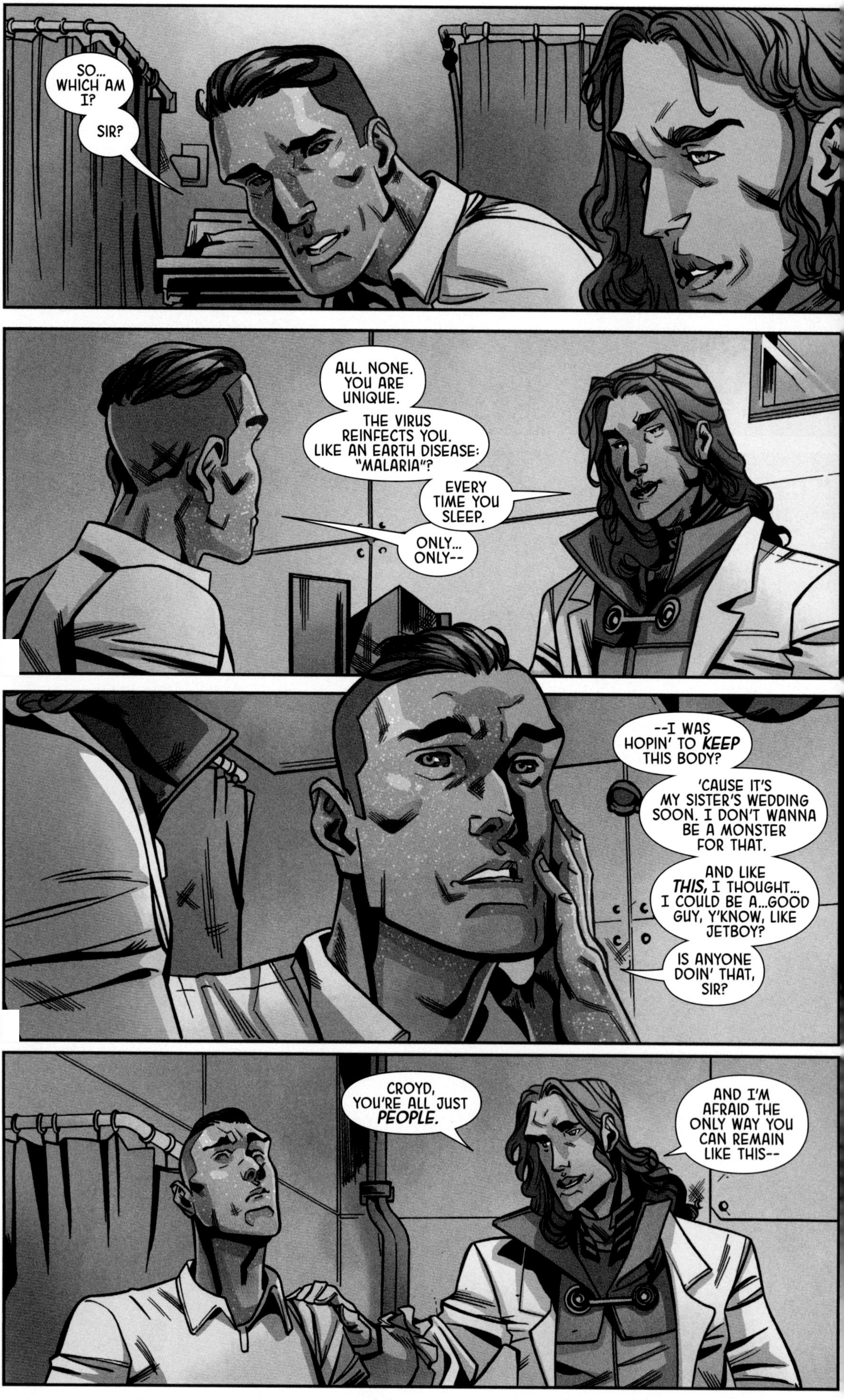
SO... WHICH AM I?
SIR?
ALL. NONE. YOU ARE UNIQUE.
THE VIRUS REINFECTS YOU. LIKE AN EARTH DISEASE: "MALARIA"?
EVERY TIME YOU SLEEP.
ONLY... ONLY--
--I WAS HOPIN' TO KEEP THIS BODY?
'CAUSE IT'S MY SISTER'S WEDDING SOON. I DON'T WANNA BE A MONSTER FOR THAT.
AND LIKE THIS, I THOUGHT... I COULD BE A...GOOD GUY, Y'KNOW, LIKE JETBOY?
IS ANYONE DOIN' THAT, SIR?
CROYD, YOU'RE ALL JUST PEOPLE.
AND I'M AFRAID THE ONLY WAY YOU CAN REMAIN LIKE THIS--

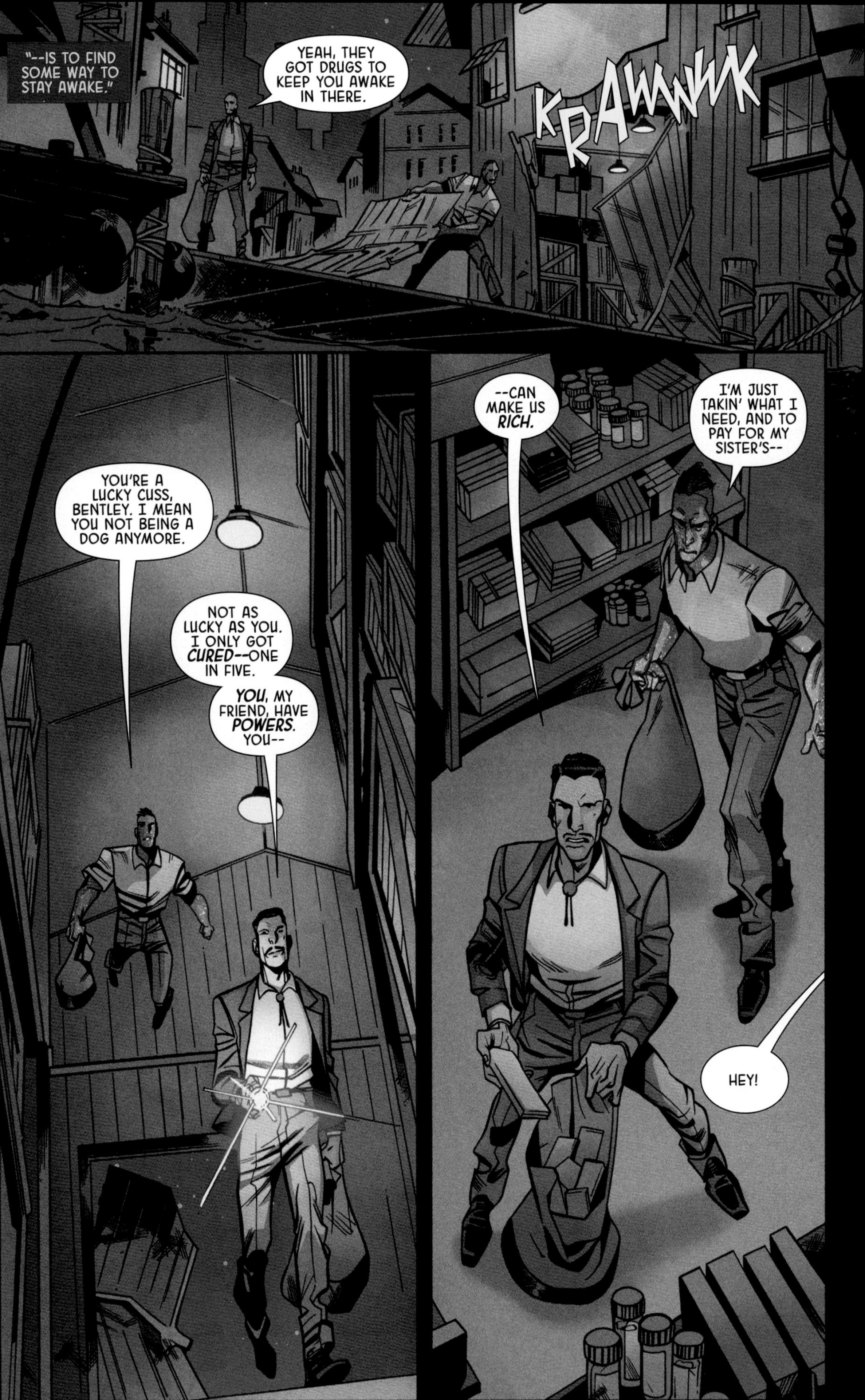
"--IS TO FIND SOME WAY TO STAY AWAKE."
YEAH, THEY GOT DRUGS TO KEEP YOU AWAKE IN THERE.
KRAWWK
YOU'RE A LUCKY CUSS, BENTLEY. I MEAN YOU NOT BEING A DOG ANYMORE.
NOT AS LUCKY AS YOU. I ONLY GOT *CURED*--ONE IN FIVE.
YOU, MY FRIEND, HAVE *POWERS*. YOU--
--CAN MAKE US *RICH*.
I'M JUST TAKIN' WHAT I NEED, AND TO PAY FOR MY SISTER'S--
HEY!

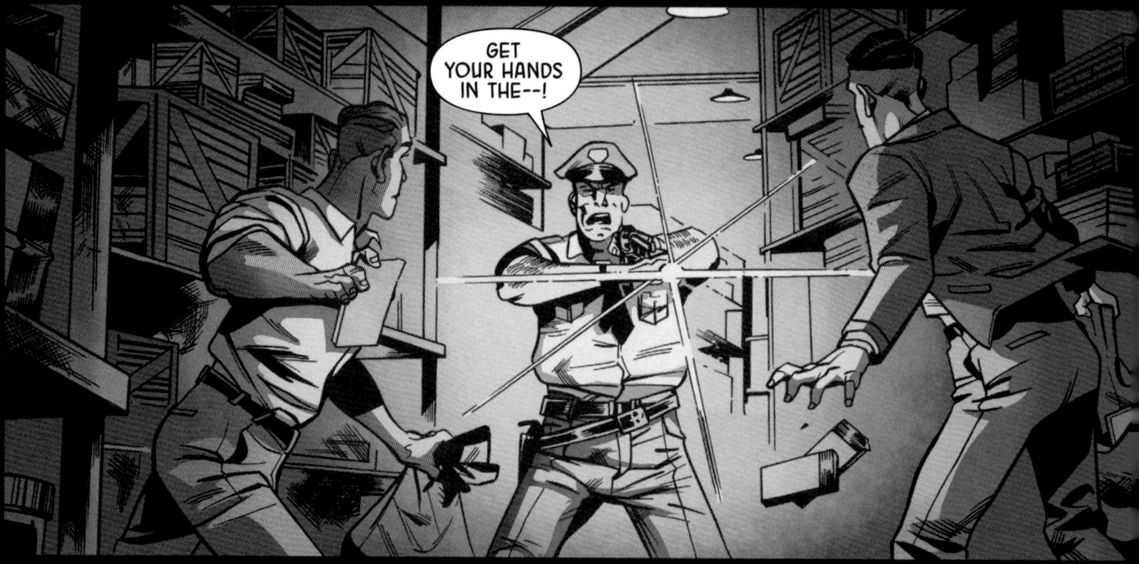
GET YOUR HANDS IN THE--!

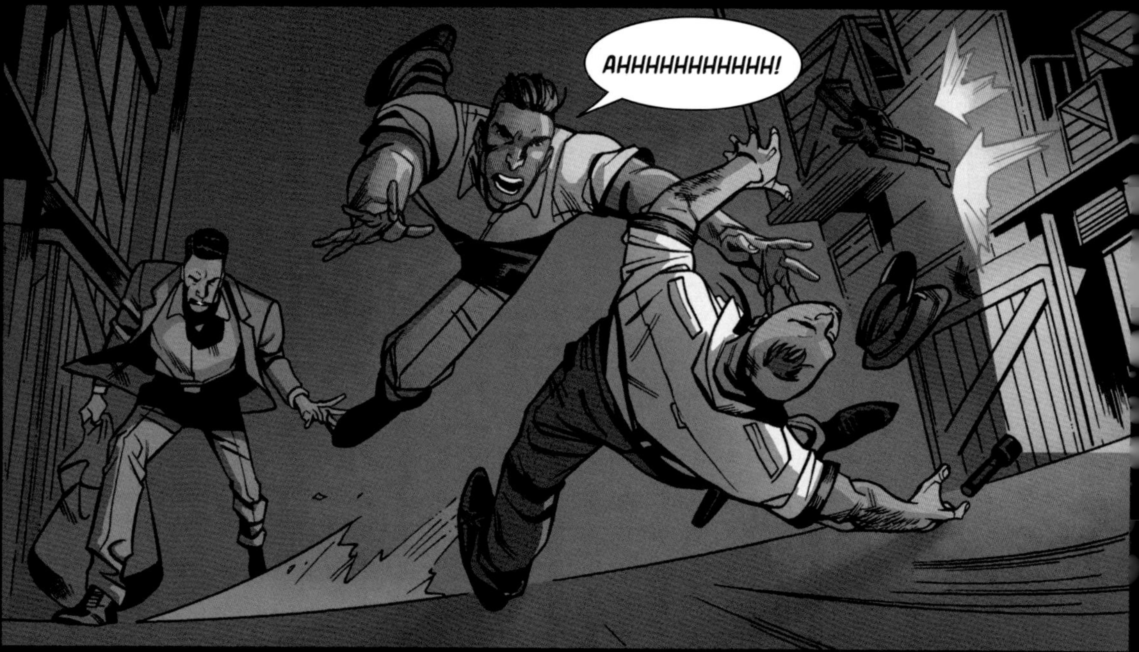
AHHHHHHHHHHH!

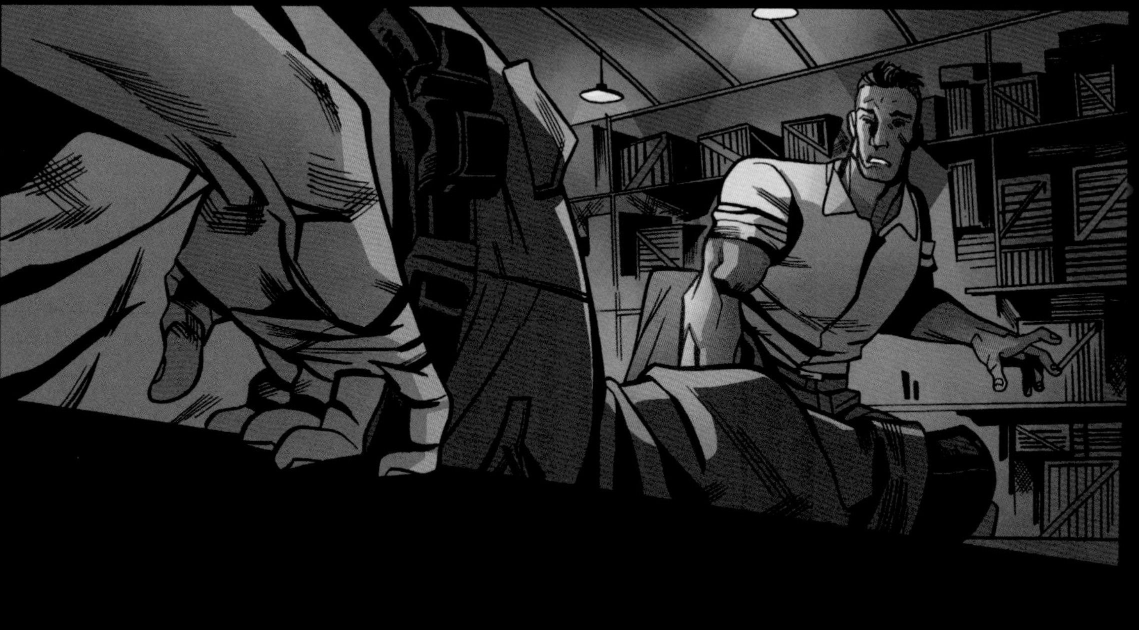

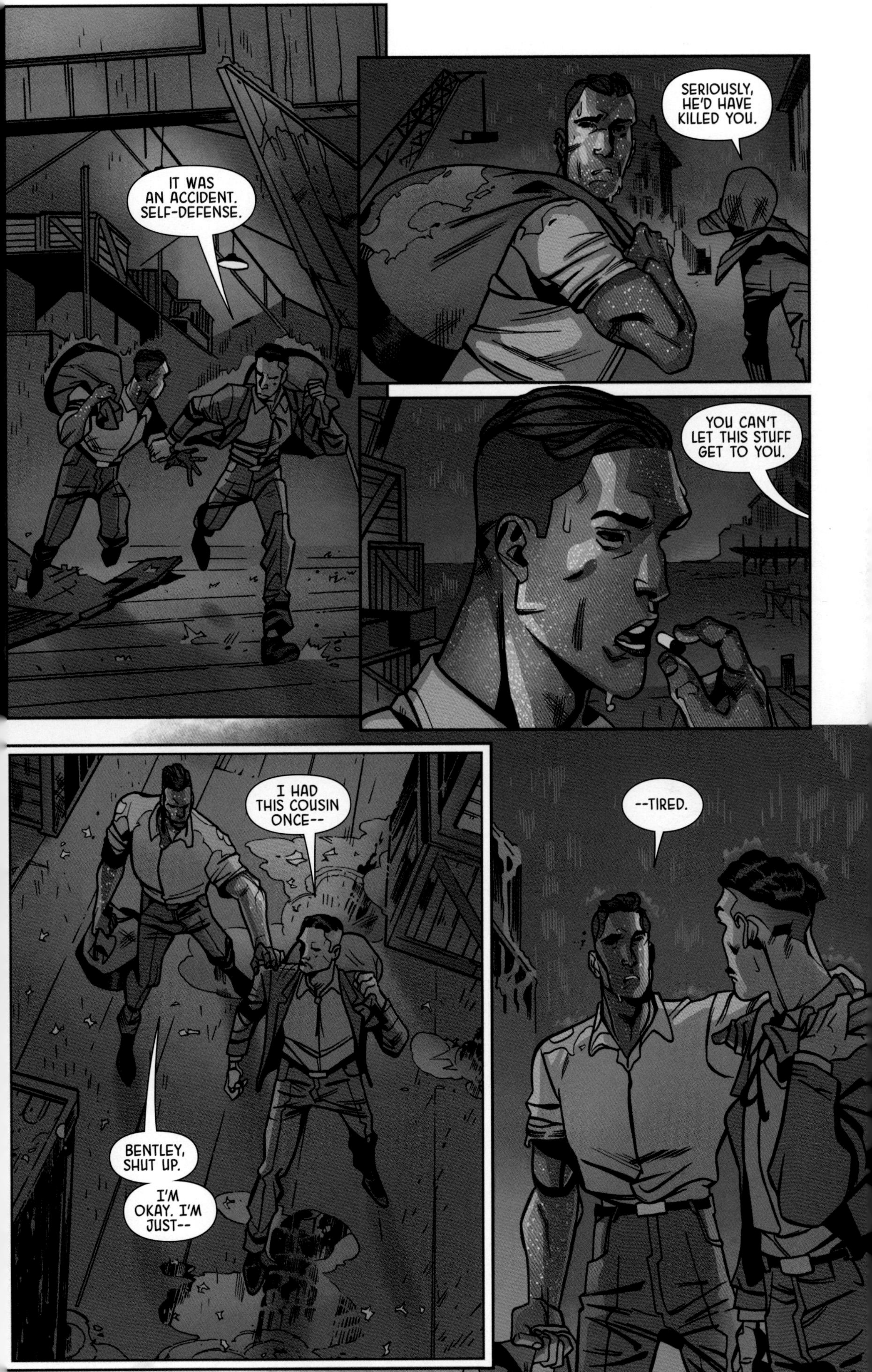
IT WAS AN ACCIDENT. SELF-DEFENSE.
SERIOUSLY, HE'D HAVE KILLED YOU.
YOU CAN'T LET THIS STUFF GET TO YOU.
I HAD THIS COUSIN ONCE--
BENTLEY, SHUT UP.
I'M OKAY. I'M JUST--
--TIRED.

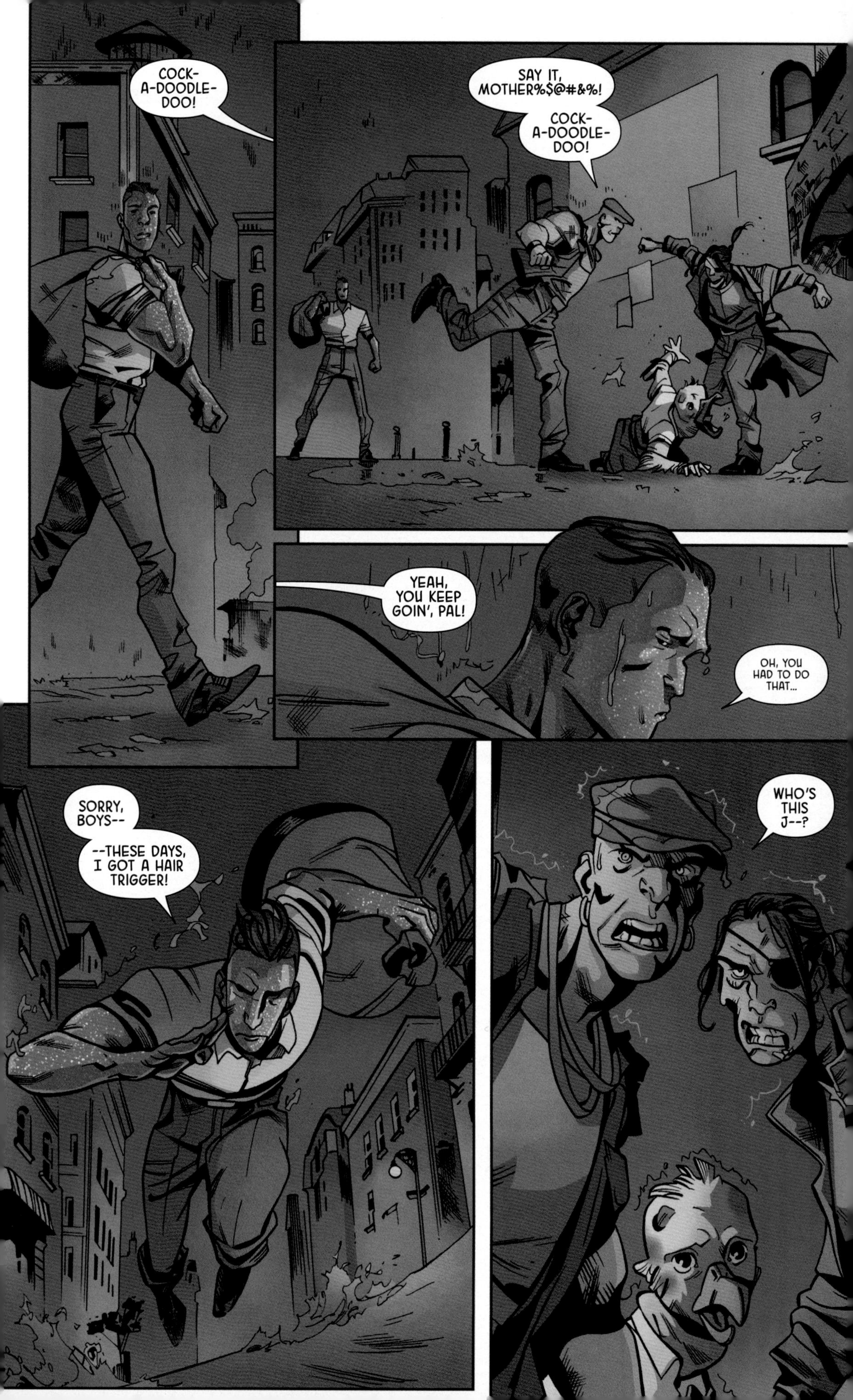
COCK-A-DOODLE-DOO!
SAY IT, MOTHER%$@#&%!
COCK-A-DOODLE-DOO!
YEAH, YOU KEEP GOIN', PAL!
OH, YOU HAD TO DO THAT...
SORRY, BOYS--
--THESE DAYS, I GOT A HAIR TRIGGER!
WHO'S THIS J--?

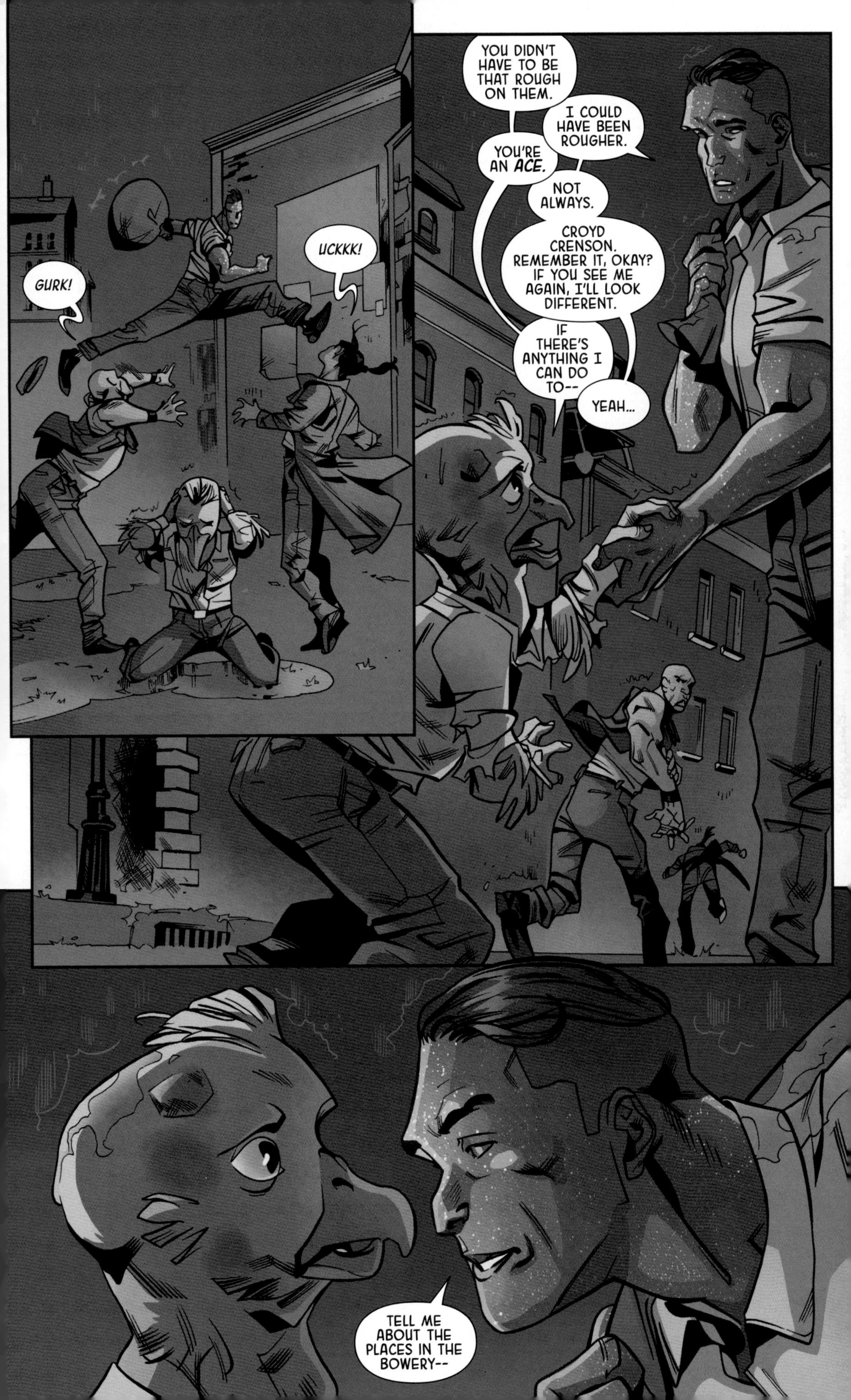
GURK!
UCKKK!
YOU DIDN'T HAVE TO BE THAT ROUGH ON THEM.
I COULD HAVE BEEN ROUGHER.
YOU'RE AN ACE.
NOT ALWAYS.
CROYD CRENSON. REMEMBER IT, OKAY? IF YOU SEE ME AGAIN, I'LL LOOK DIFFERENT.
IF THERE'S ANYTHING I CAN DO TO--
YEAH...
TELL ME ABOUT THE PLACES IN THE BOWERY--

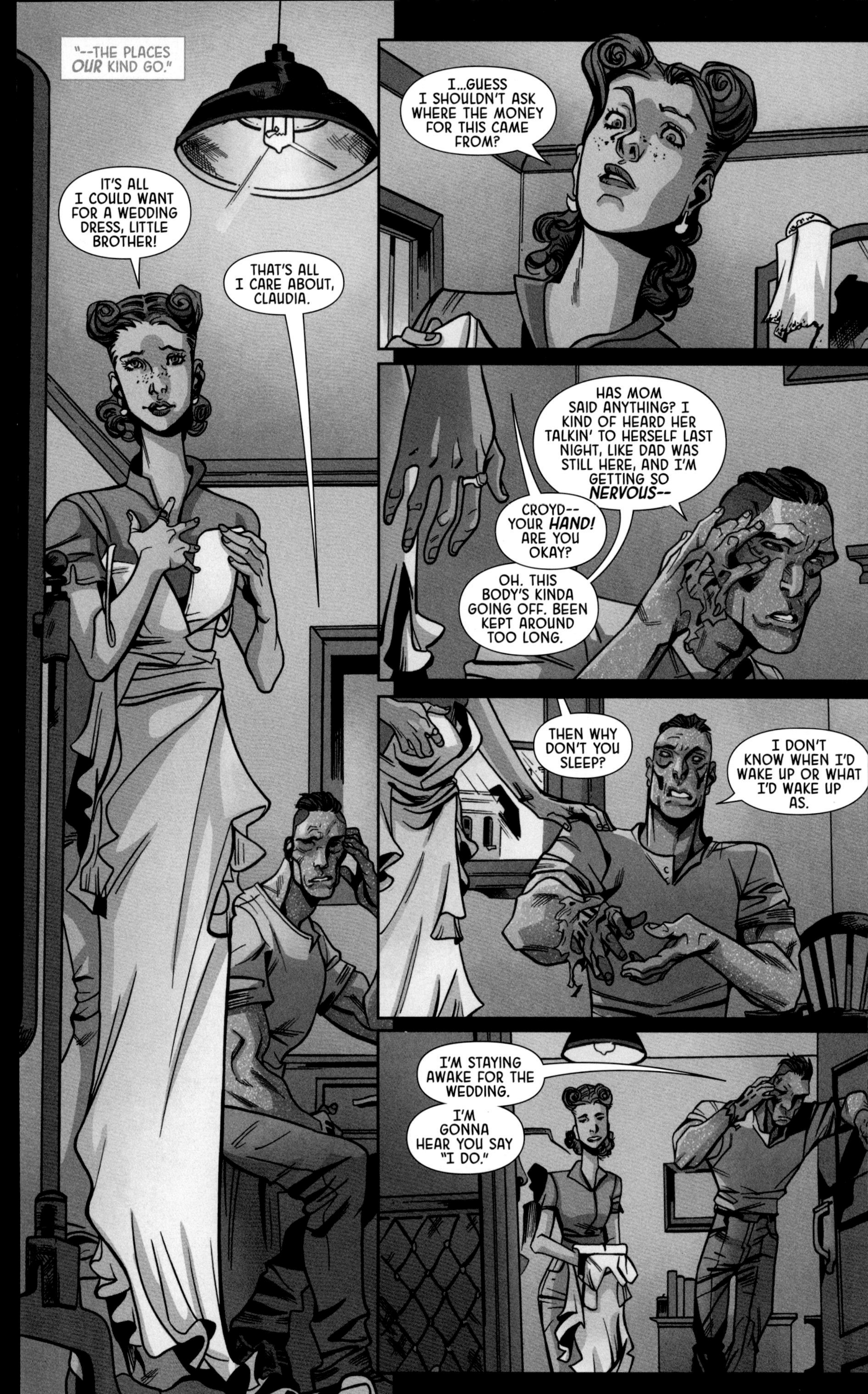
"--THE PLACES OUR KIND GO."
IT'S ALL I COULD WANT FOR A WEDDING DRESS, LITTLE BROTHER!
THAT'S ALL I CARE ABOUT, CLAUDIA.
I...GUESS I SHOULDN'T ASK WHERE THE MONEY FOR THIS CAME FROM?
HAS MOM SAID ANYTHING? I KIND OF HEARD HER TALKIN' TO HERSELF LAST NIGHT, LIKE DAD WAS STILL HERE, AND I'M GETTING SO NERVOUS--
CROYD-- YOUR HAND! ARE YOU OKAY?
OH. THIS BODY'S KINDA GOING OFF. BEEN KEPT AROUND TOO LONG.
THEN WHY DON'T YOU SLEEP?
I DON'T KNOW WHEN I'D WAKE UP OR WHAT I'D WAKE UP AS.
I'M STAYING AWAKE FOR THE WEDDING.
I'M GONNA HEAR YOU SAY "I DO."

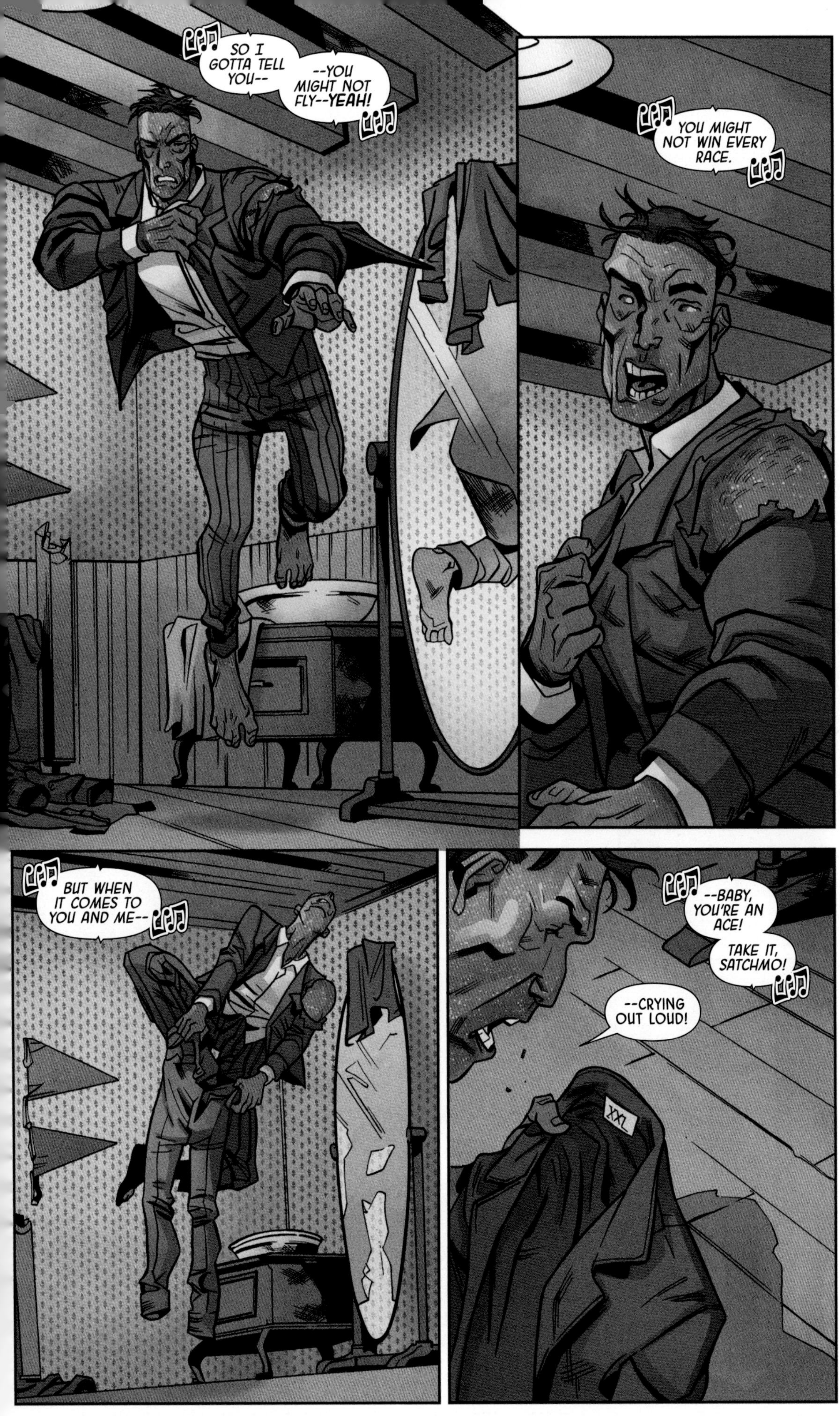
SO I GOTTA TELL YOU--
--YOU MIGHT NOT FLY--YEAH!
YOU MIGHT NOT WIN EVERY RACE.
BUT WHEN IT COMES TO YOU AND ME--
--BABY, YOU'RE AN ACE!
TAKE IT, SATCHMO!
--CRYING OUT LOUD!
XXL

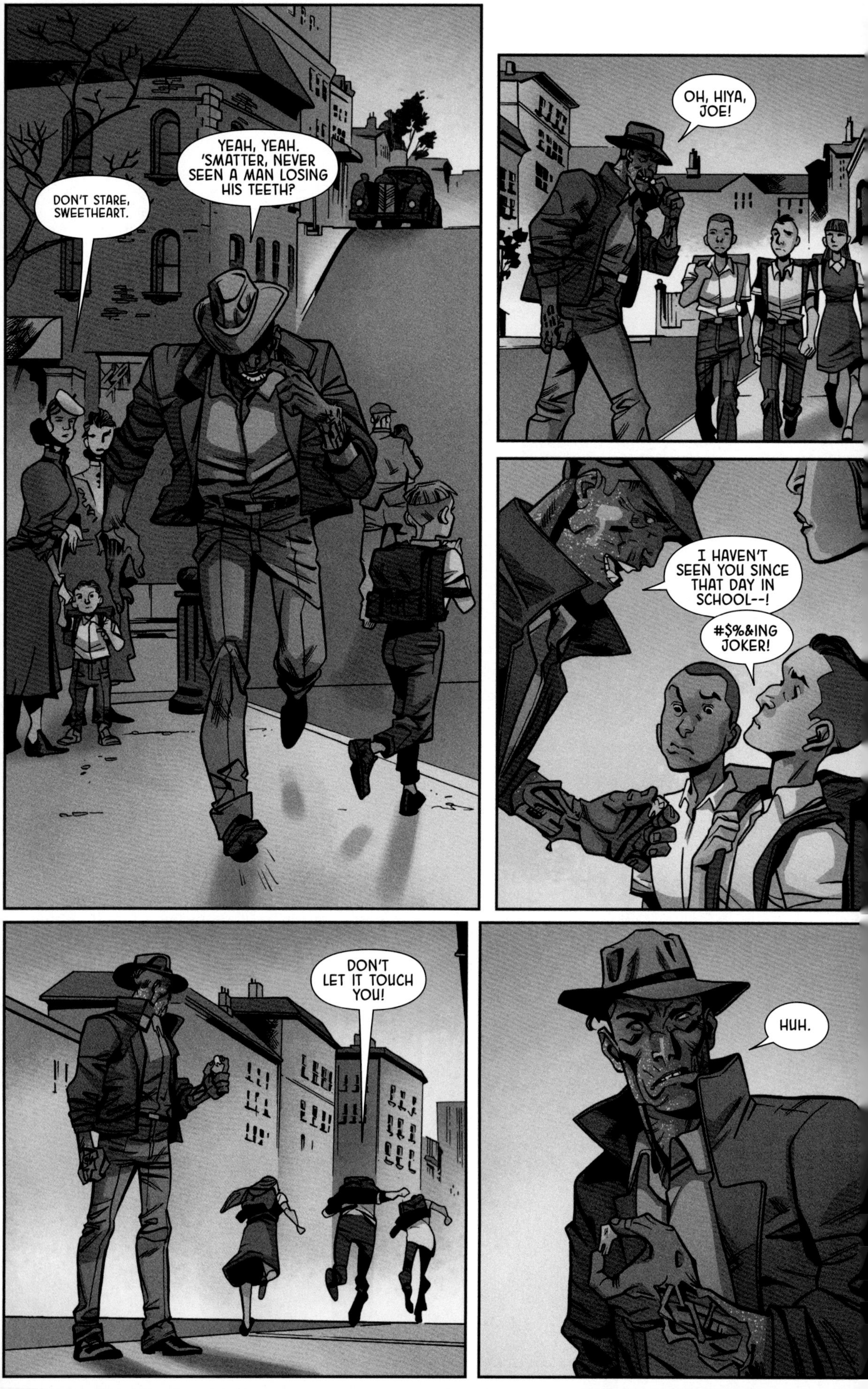
DON'T STARE, SWEETHEART.
YEAH, YEAH. 'SMATTER, NEVER SEEN A MAN LOSING HIS TEETH?
OH, HIYA, JOE!
I HAVEN'T SEEN YOU SINCE THAT DAY IN SCHOOL--!
#$%&ING JOKER!
DON'T LET IT TOUCH YOU!
HUH.

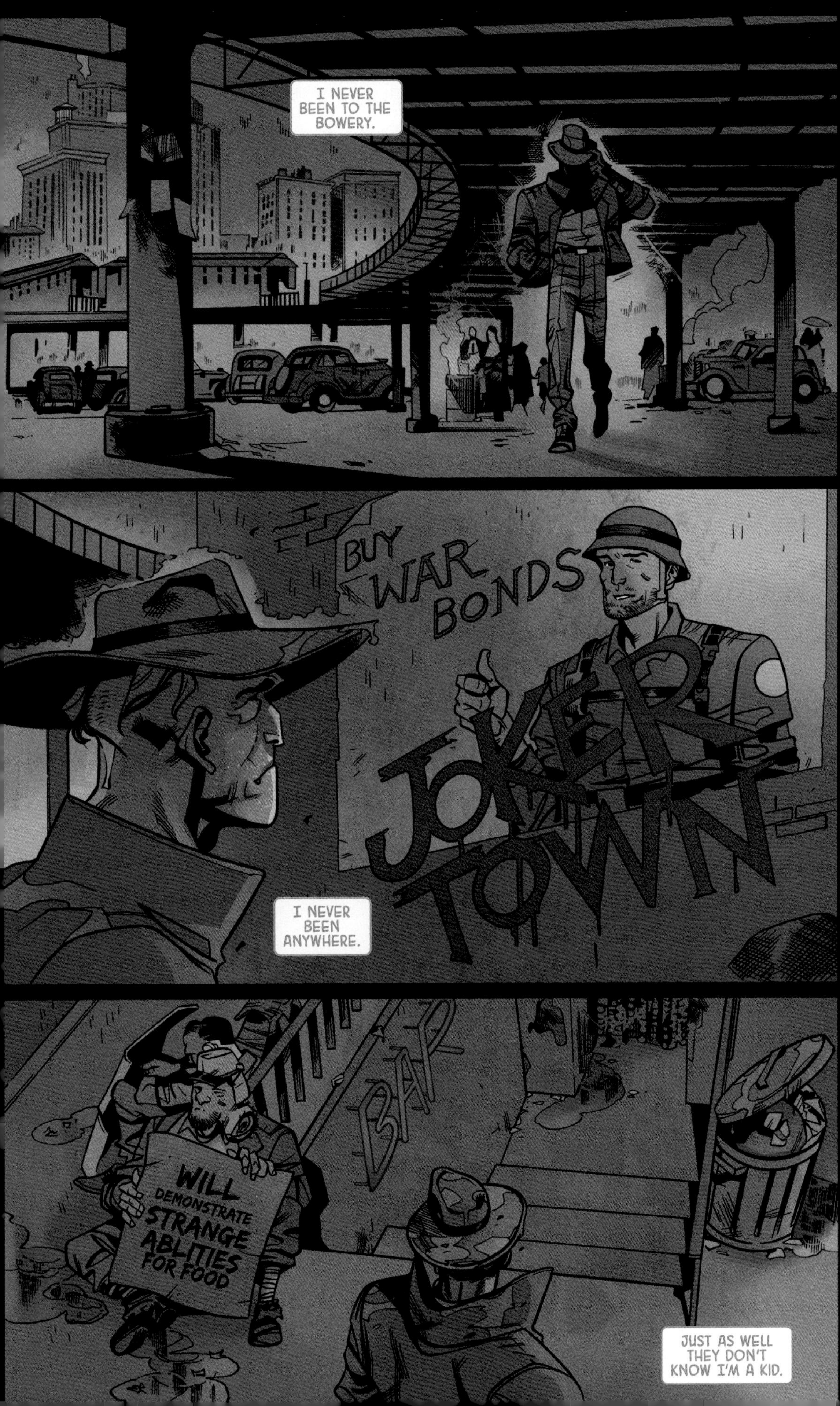

I NEVER BEEN TO THE BOWERY.
BUY WAR BONDS
JOKER TOWN
I NEVER BEEN ANYWHERE.
BAR
WILL DEMONSTRATE STRANGE ABLITIES FOR FOOD
JUST AS WELL THEY DON'T KNOW I'M A KID.

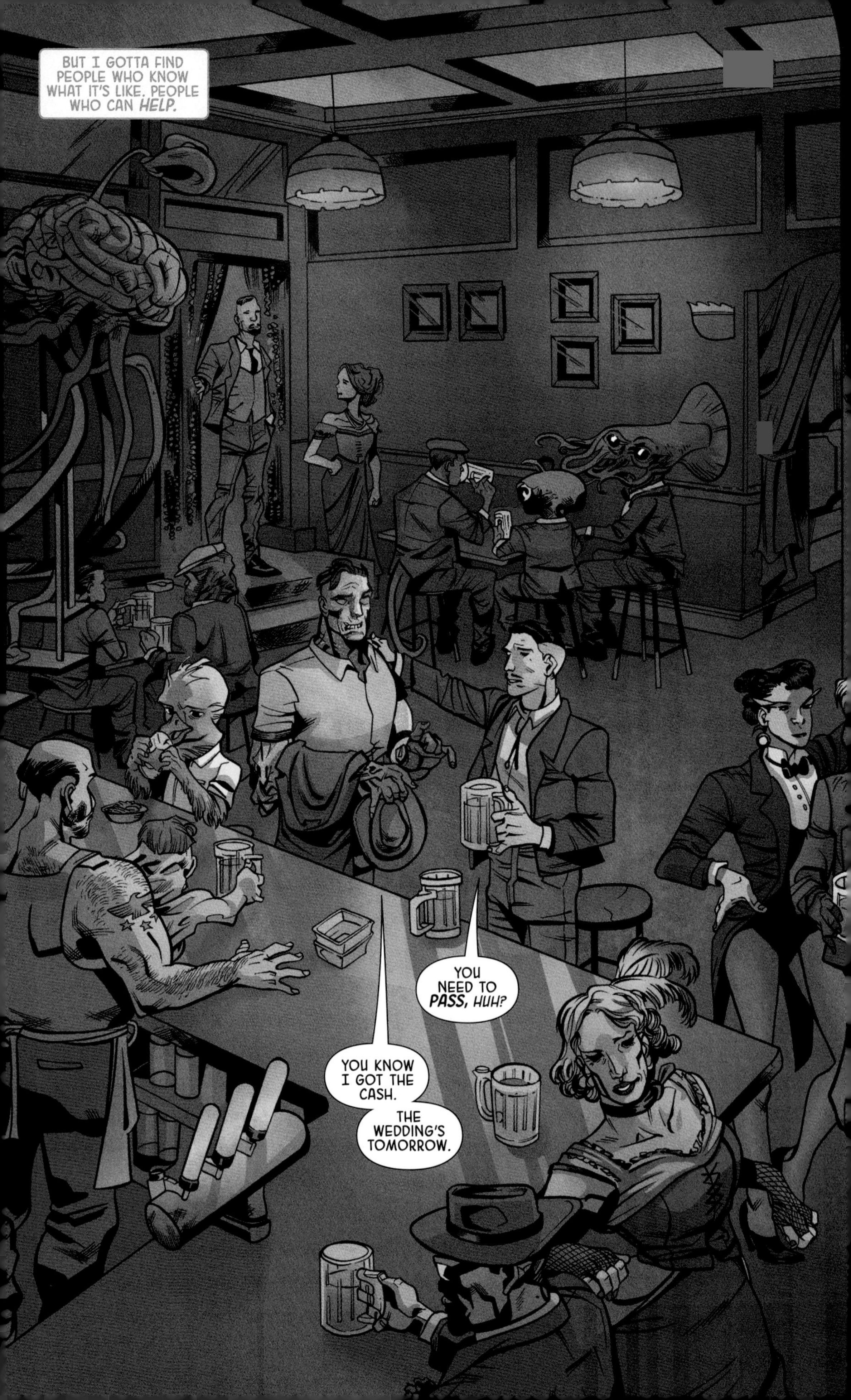
BUT I GOTTA FIND PEOPLE WHO KNOW WHAT IT'S LIKE. PEOPLE WHO CAN *HELP.*
YOU NEED TO *PASS,* HUH?
YOU KNOW I GOT THE CASH.
THE WEDDING'S TOMORROW.

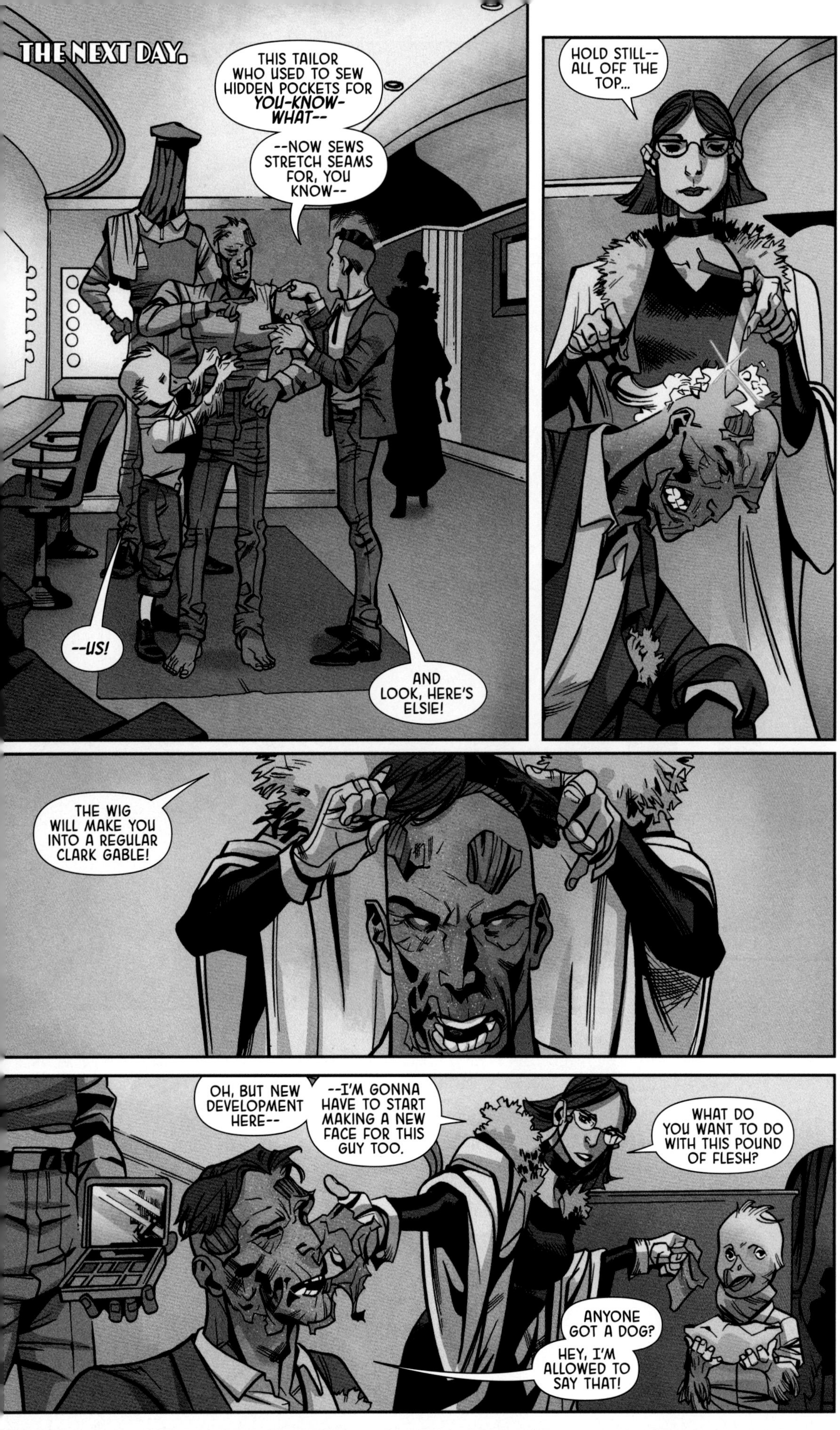
THE NEXT DAY.
THIS TAILOR WHO USED TO SEW HIDDEN POCKETS FOR *YOU-KNOW-WHAT--*
--NOW SEWS STRETCH SEAMS FOR, YOU KNOW--
--US!
AND LOOK, HERE'S ELSIE!
HOLD STILL-- ALL OFF THE TOP...
THE WIG WILL MAKE YOU INTO A REGULAR CLARK GABLE!
OH, BUT NEW DEVELOPMENT HERE--
--I'M GONNA HAVE TO START MAKING A NEW FACE FOR THIS GUY TOO.
WHAT DO YOU WANT TO DO WITH THIS POUND OF FLESH?
ANYONE GOT A DOG?
HEY, I'M ALLOWED TO SAY THAT!

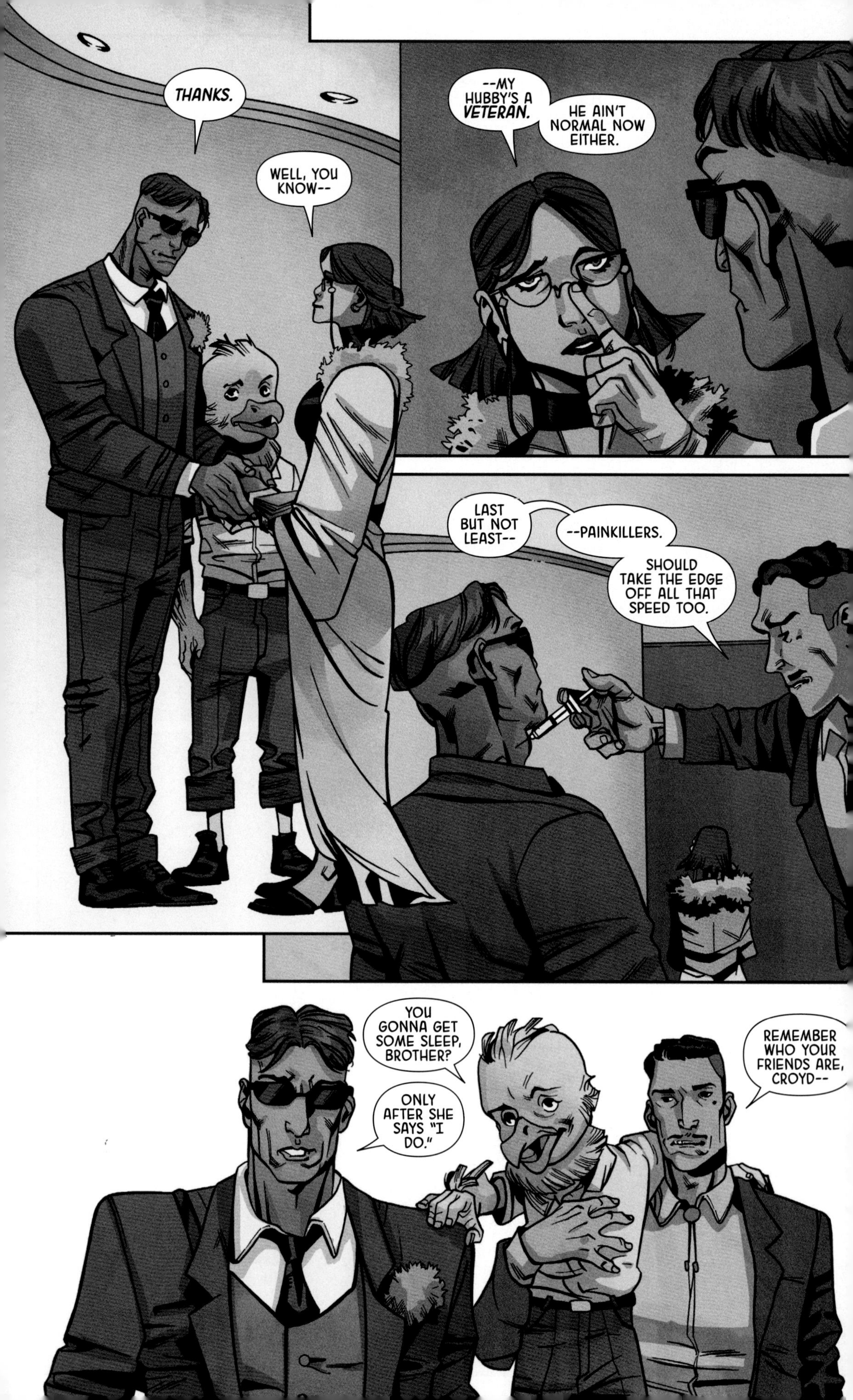
THANKS.
WELL, YOU KNOW--
--MY HUBBY'S A VETERAN.
HE AIN'T NORMAL NOW EITHER.
LAST BUT NOT LEAST--
--PAINKILLERS.
SHOULD TAKE THE EDGE OFF ALL THAT SPEED TOO.
YOU GONNA GET SOME SLEEP, BROTHER?
ONLY AFTER SHE SAYS "I DO."
REMEMBER WHO YOUR FRIENDS ARE, CROYD--

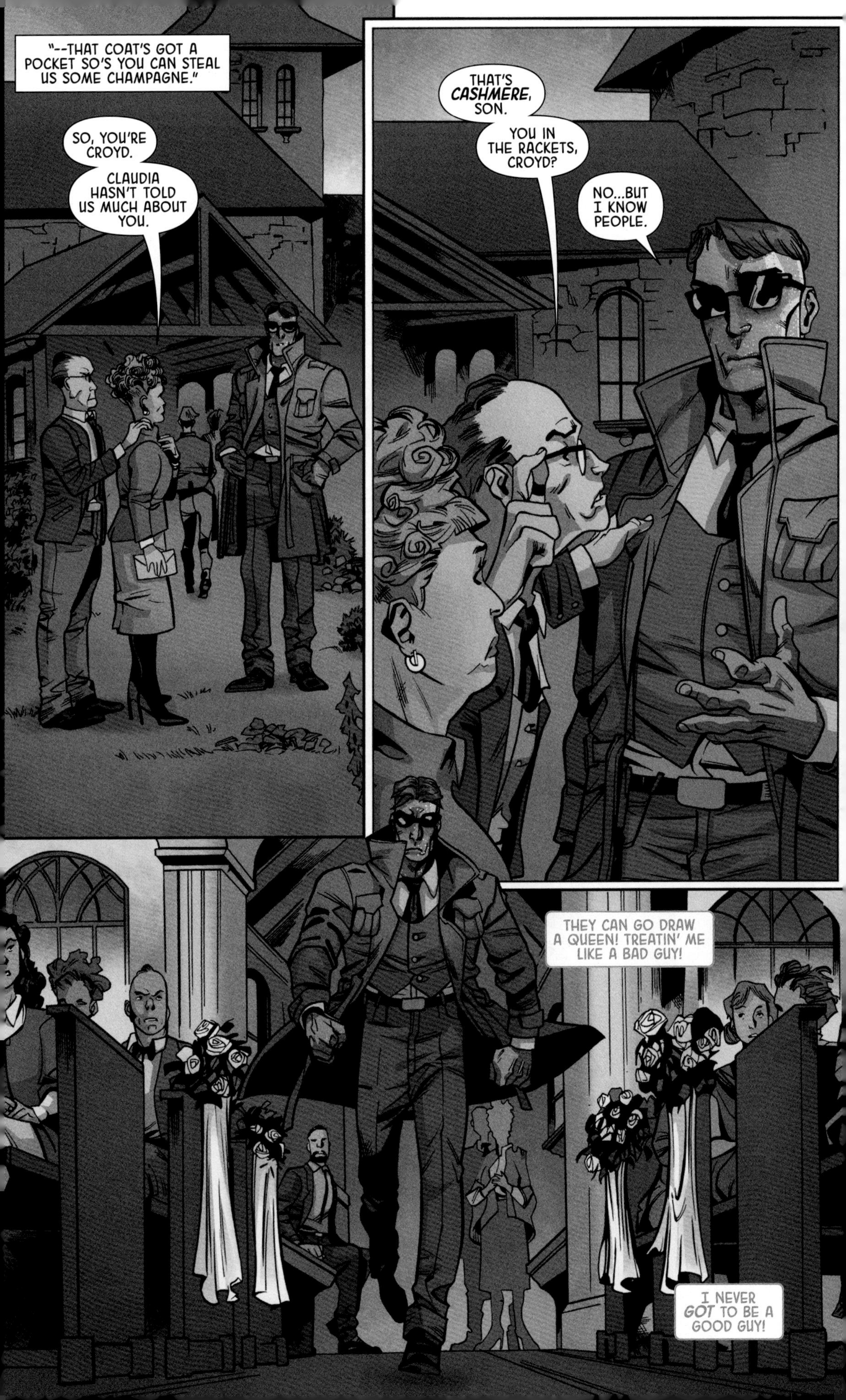
"--THAT COAT'S GOT A POCKET SO'S YOU CAN STEAL US SOME CHAMPAGNE."
SO, YOU'RE CROYD.
CLAUDIA HASN'T TOLD US MUCH ABOUT YOU.
THAT'S CASHMERE, SON.
YOU IN THE RACKETS, CROYD?
NO...BUT I KNOW PEOPLE.
THEY CAN GO DRAW A QUEEN! TREATIN' ME LIKE A BAD GUY!
I NEVER GOT TO BE A GOOD GUY!

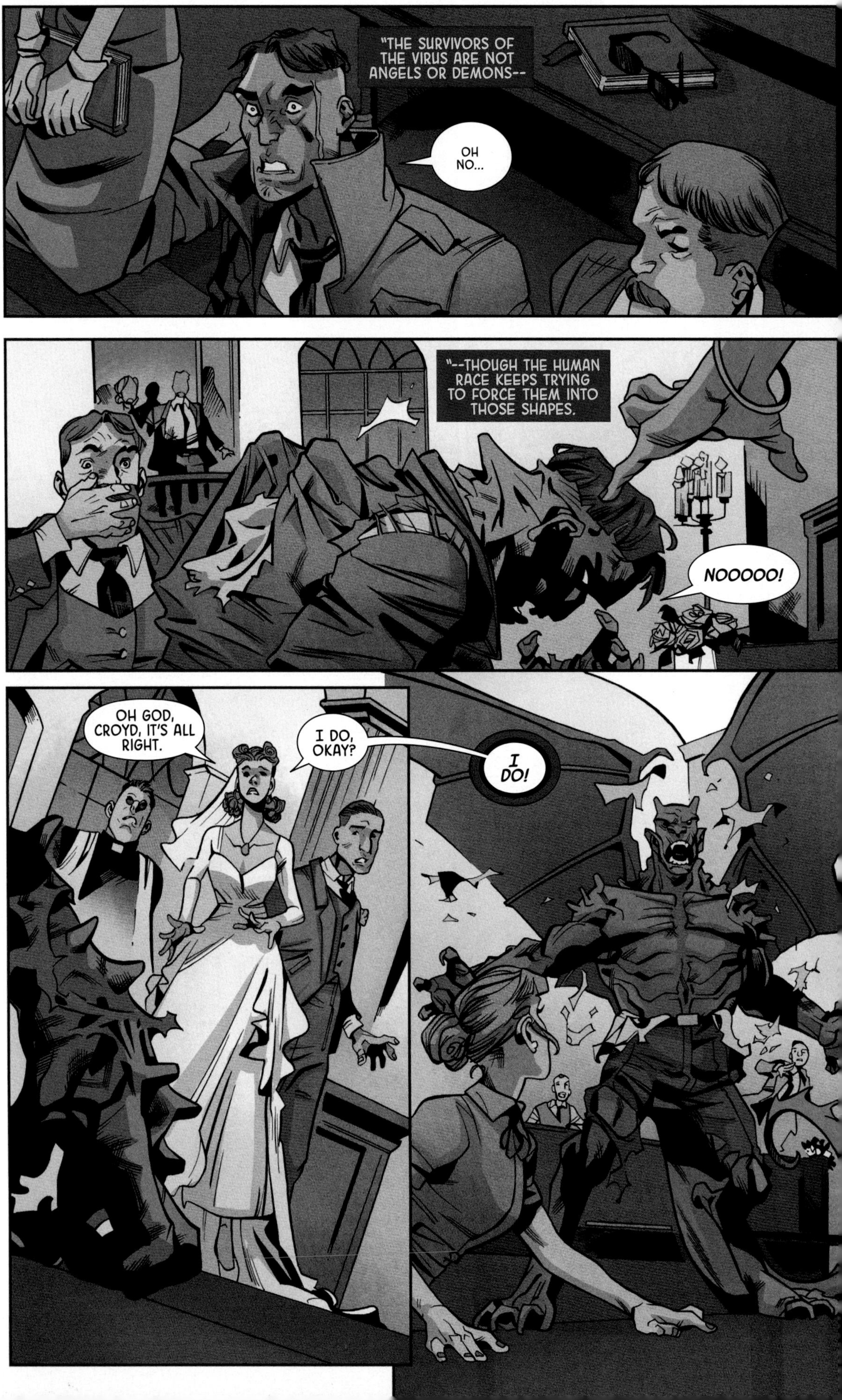
"THE SURVIVORS OF THE VIRUS ARE NOT ANGELS OR DEMONS--
OH NO...
"--THOUGH THE HUMAN RACE KEEPS TRYING TO FORCE THEM INTO THOSE SHAPES.
NOOOOO!
OH GOD, CROYD, IT'S ALL RIGHT.
I DO, OKAY?
I DO!

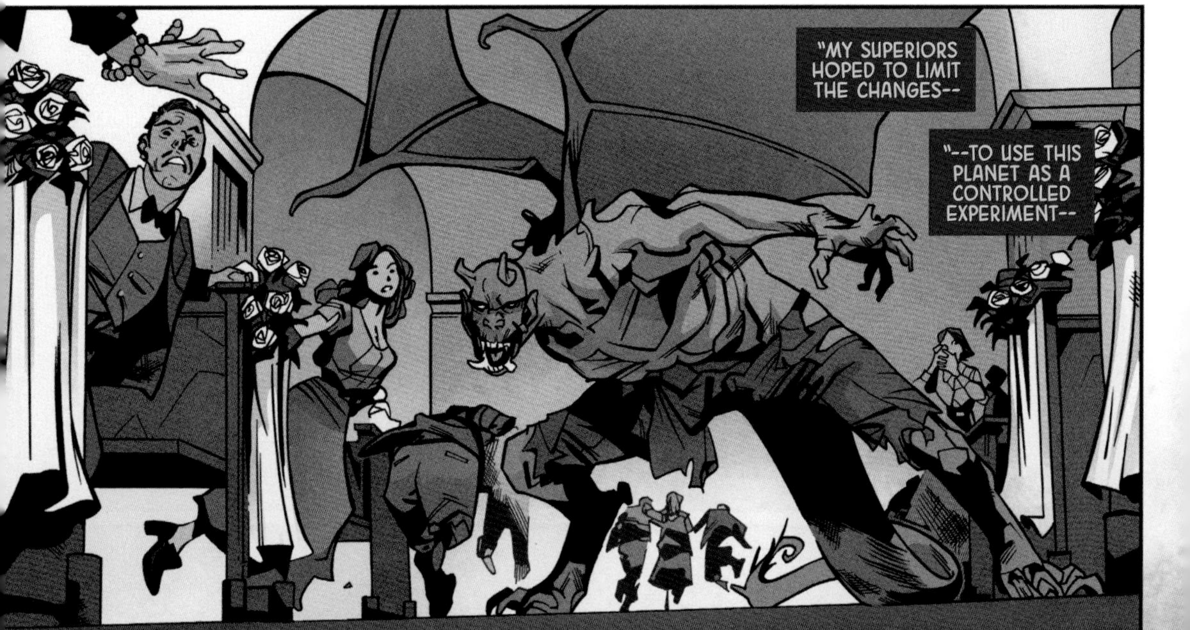
"MY SUPERIORS HOPED TO LIMIT THE CHANGES--
"--TO USE THIS PLANET AS A CONTROLLED EXPERIMENT--

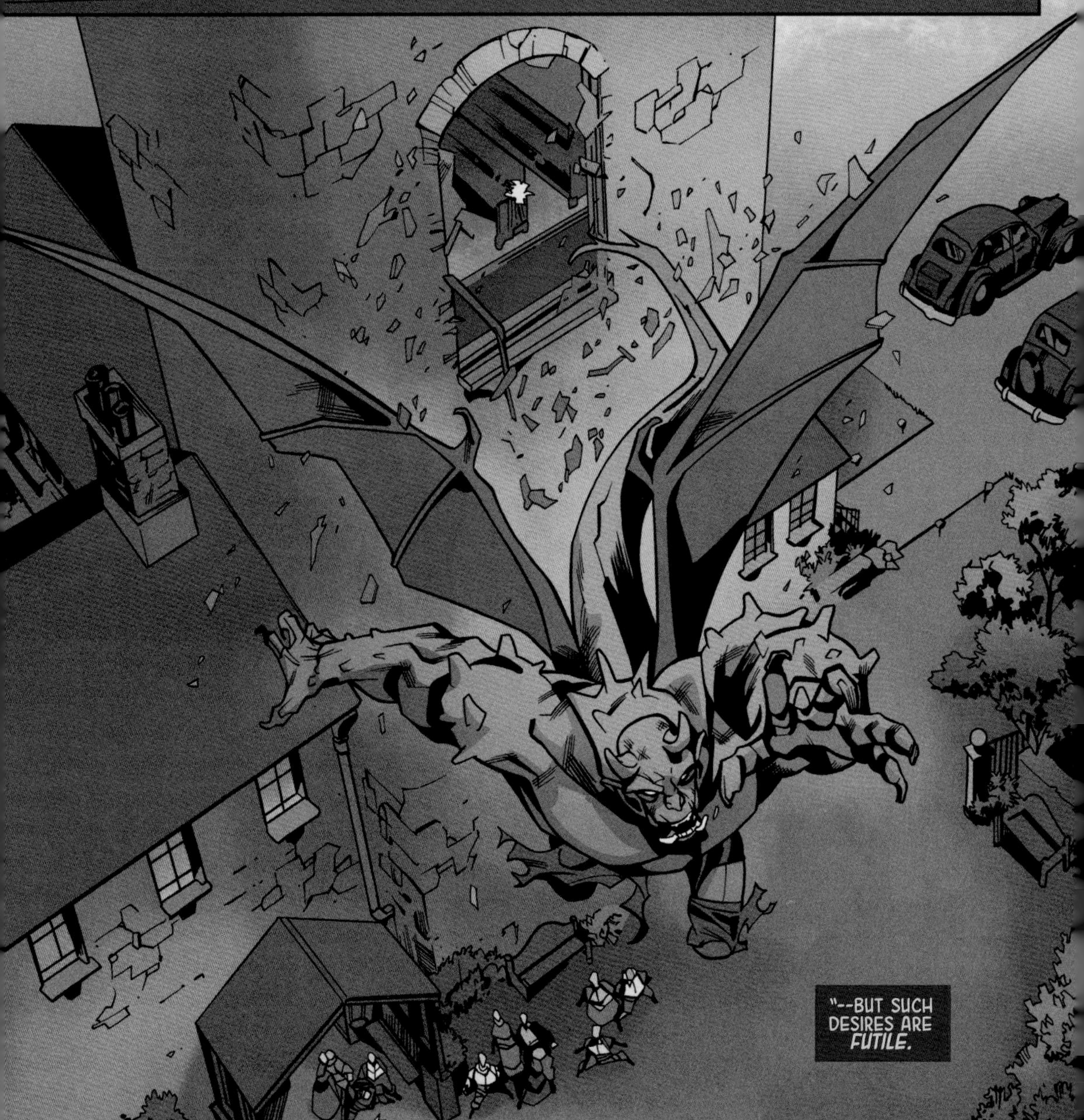
"--BUT SUCH DESIRES ARE *FUTILE*.

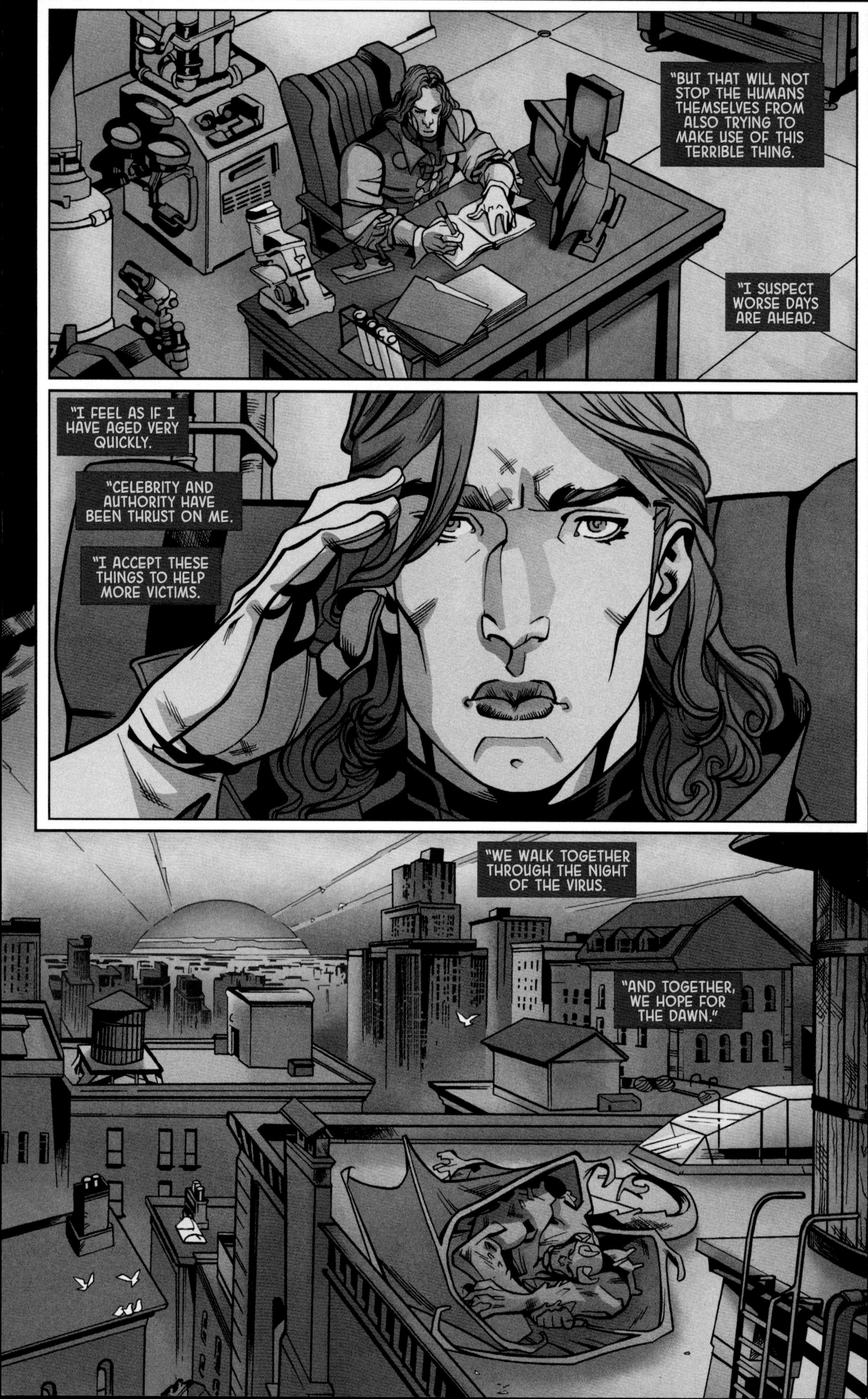
"BUT THAT WILL NOT STOP THE HUMANS THEMSELVES FROM ALSO TRYING TO MAKE USE OF THIS TERRIBLE THING.
"I SUSPECT WORSE DAYS ARE AHEAD.
"I FEEL AS IF I HAVE AGED VERY QUICKLY.
"CELEBRITY AND AUTHORITY HAVE BEEN THRUST ON ME.
"I ACCEPT THESE THINGS TO HELP MORE VICTIMS.
"WE WALK TOGETHER THROUGH THE NIGHT OF THE VIRUS.
"AND TOGETHER, WE HOPE FOR THE DAWN."

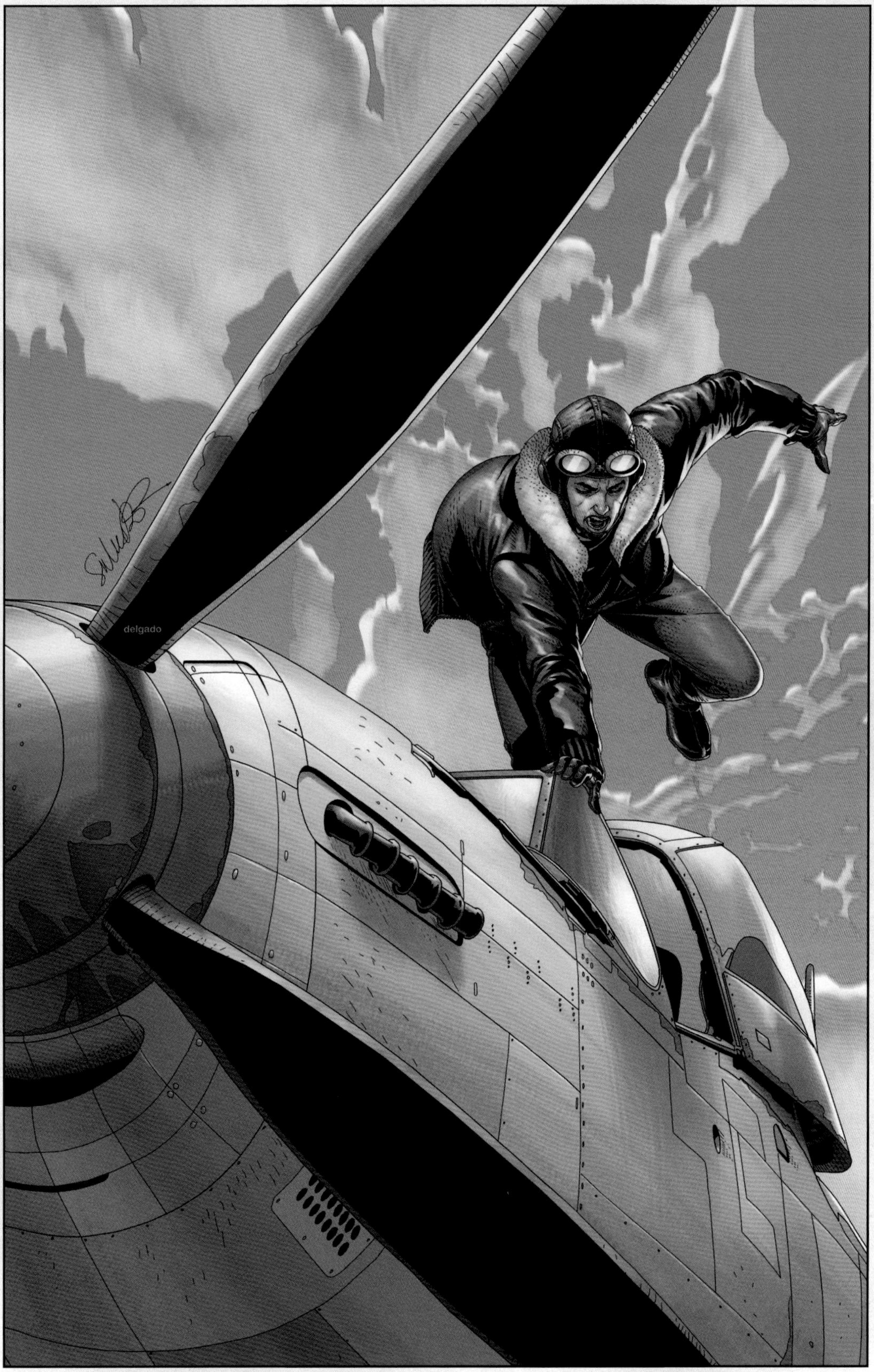
delgado

#1 VARIANT BY ***Salvador Larroca*** & ***Edgar Delgado***

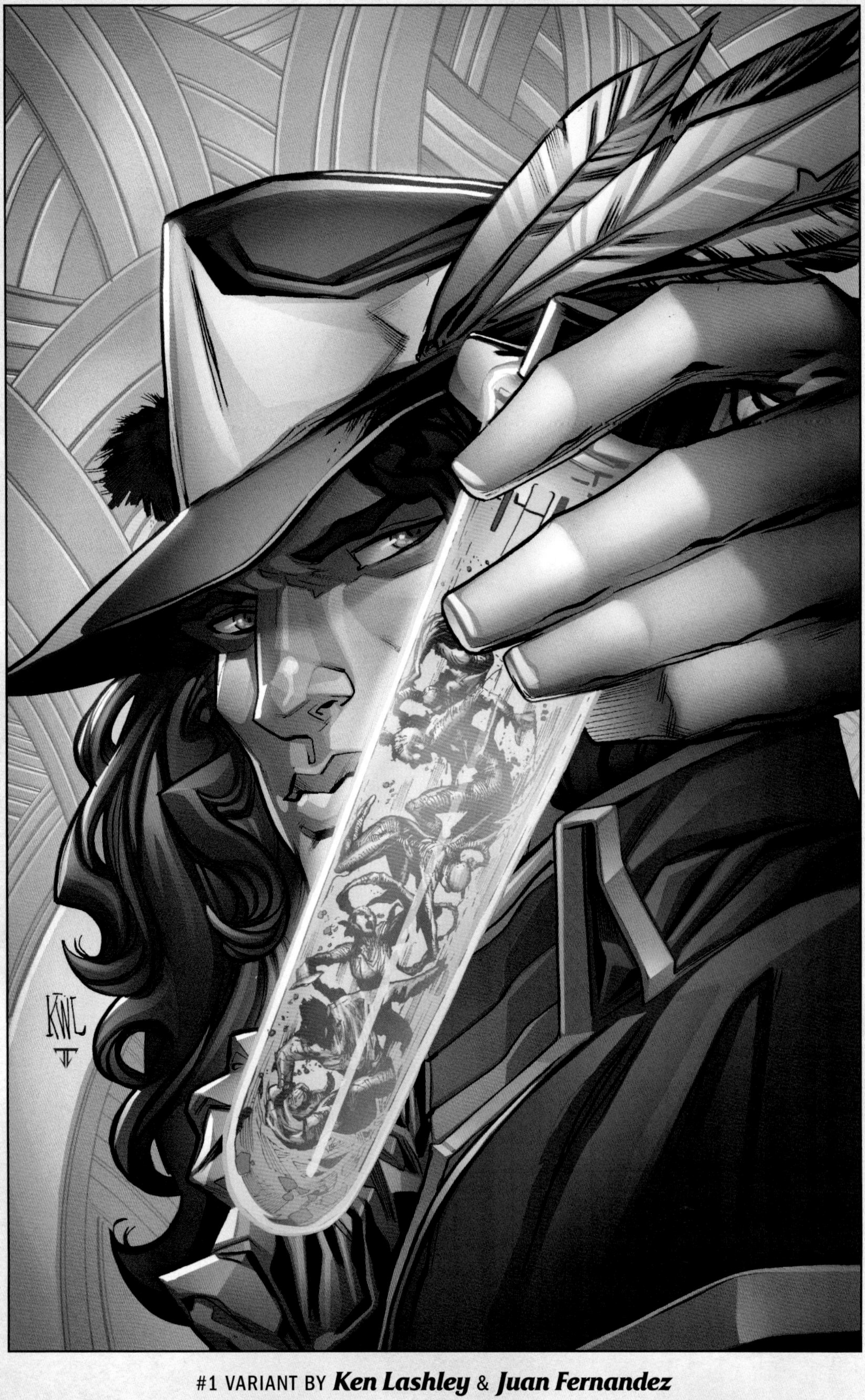

#1 VARIANT BY ***Ken Lashley*** & ***Juan Fernandez***

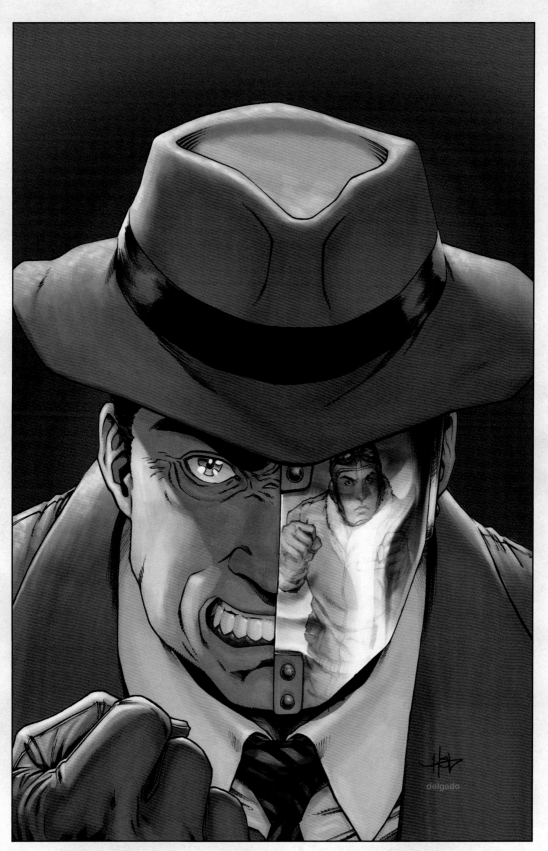

#2 VARIANT BY *Creees Lee* & *Edgar Delgado*

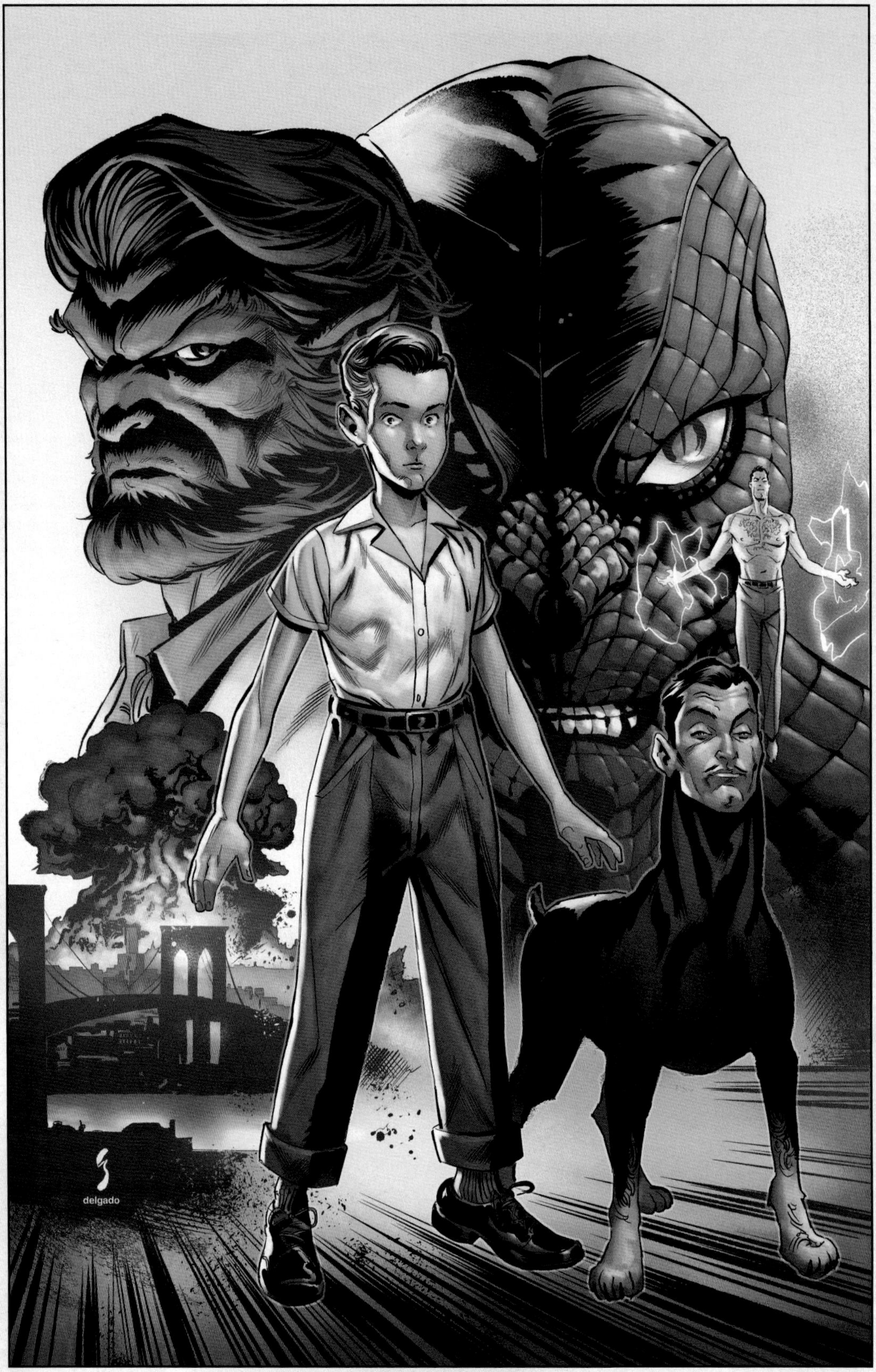
delgado

#3 VARIANT BY ***Geoff Shaw*** & ***Edgar Delgado***

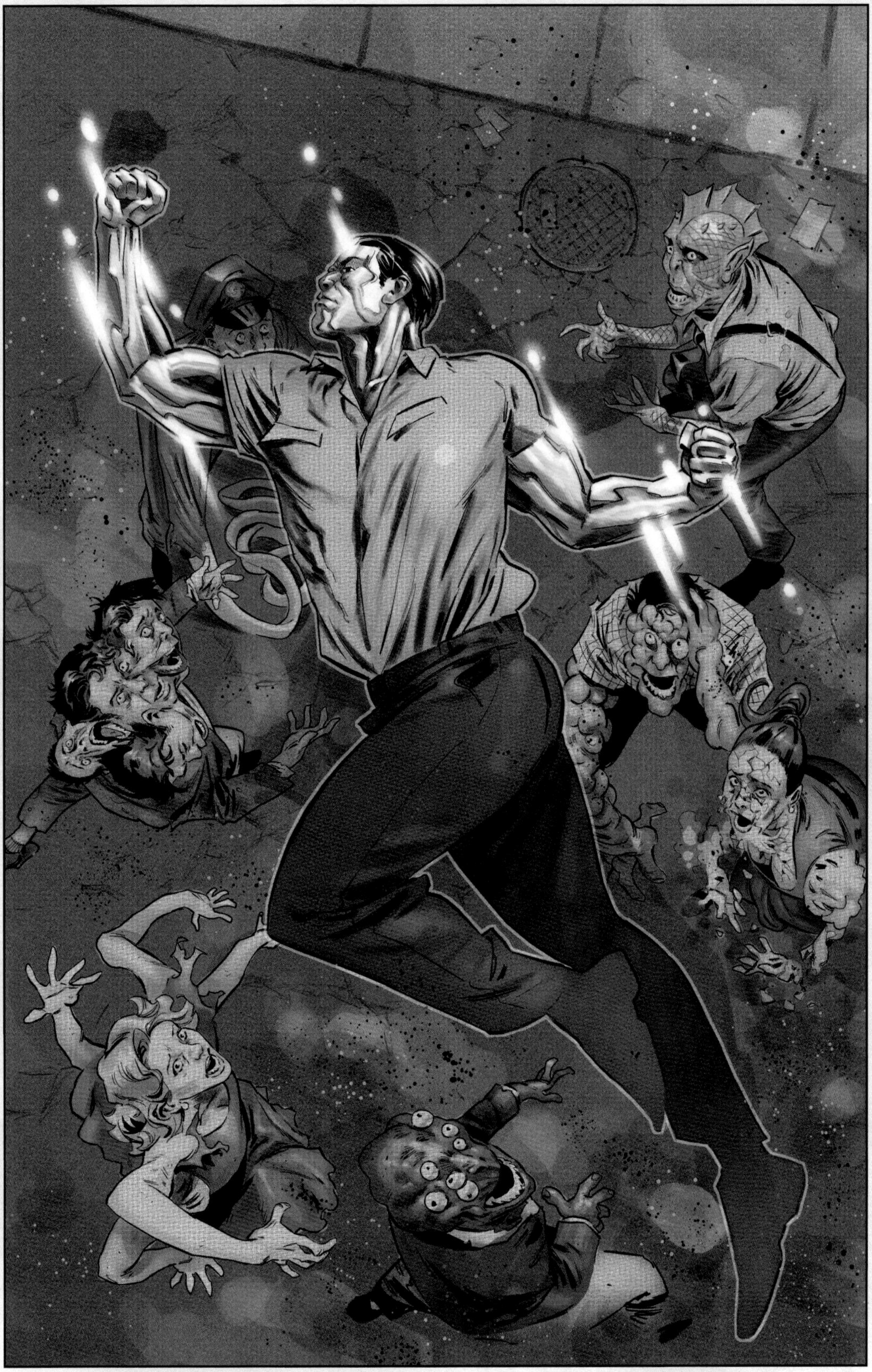

#4 VARIANT BY ***Francesco Mobili*** & ***Edgar Delgado***

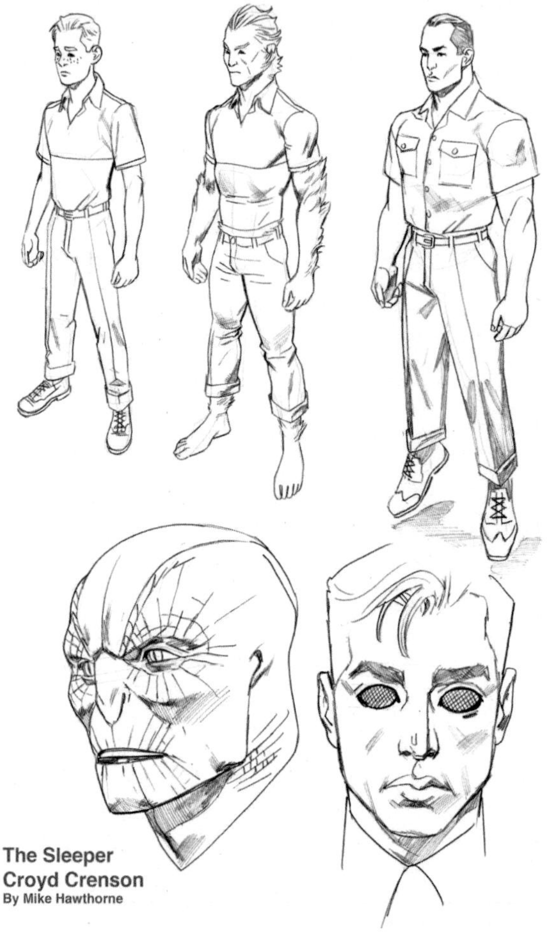

The Sleeper
Croyd Crenson
By Mike Hawthorne

Dr. Tachyon
By Mike Hawthorne

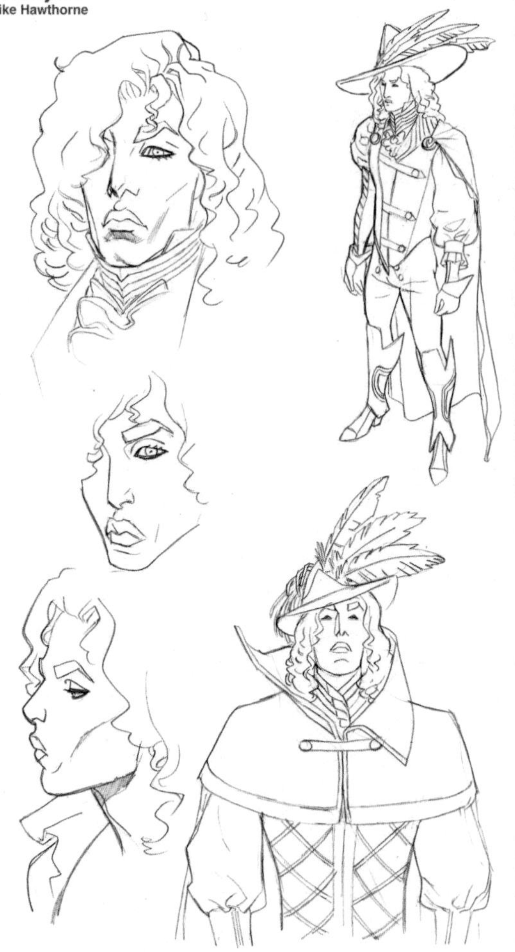

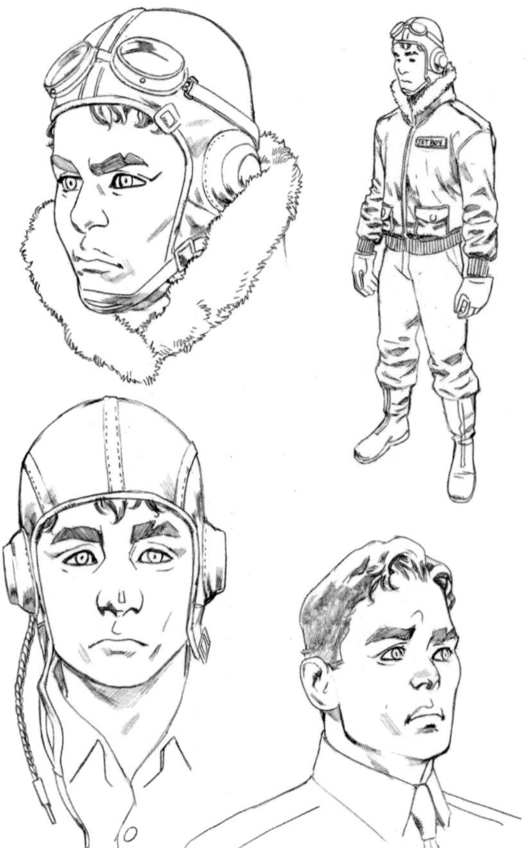

Jetboy
Robert Tomlin
By Mike Hawthorne

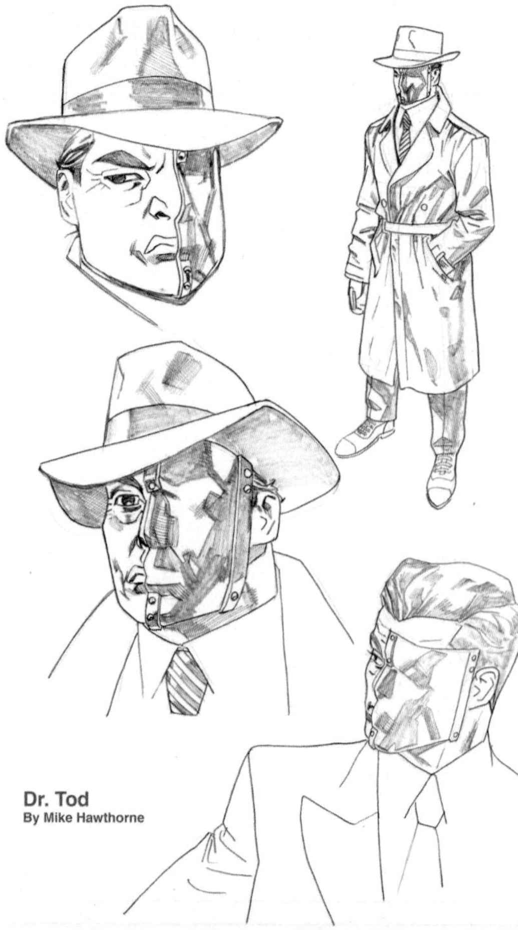

Dr. Tod
By Mike Hawthorne

Be sure not to miss these two

ORIGINAL

WILD CARDS GRAPHIC NOVELS

from Bantam Books

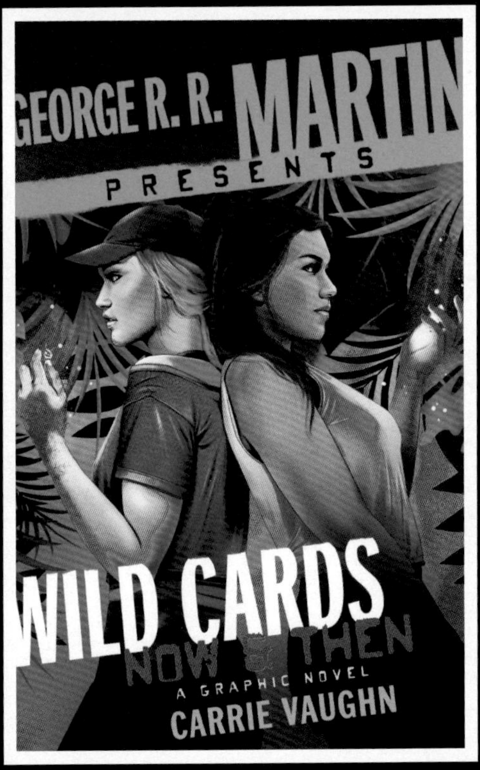
GEORGE R. R. MARTIN
PRESENTS
WILD CARDS
NOW & THEN
A GRAPHIC NOVEL
CARRIE VAUGHN

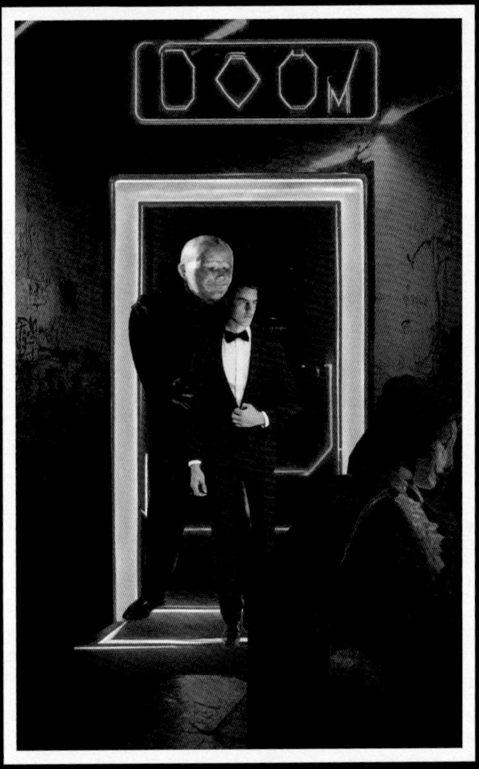

NOW AND THEN
BY CARRIE VAUGHN

COMING JULY 2023

SINS OF THE FATHER
BY MELINDA M. SNODGRASS

COMING OCTOBER 2023

Read on for a special preview of both titles.

GEORGE R. R. MARTIN

PRESENTS

NOW & THEN

BY CARRIE VAUGHN

AN ORIGINAL

WILD CARDS

GRAPHIC NOVEL

ART BY RENAE DE LIZ

INK AND COLORS BY RAY DILLON

LETTERING BY THOMAS NAPOLITANO

BANTAM

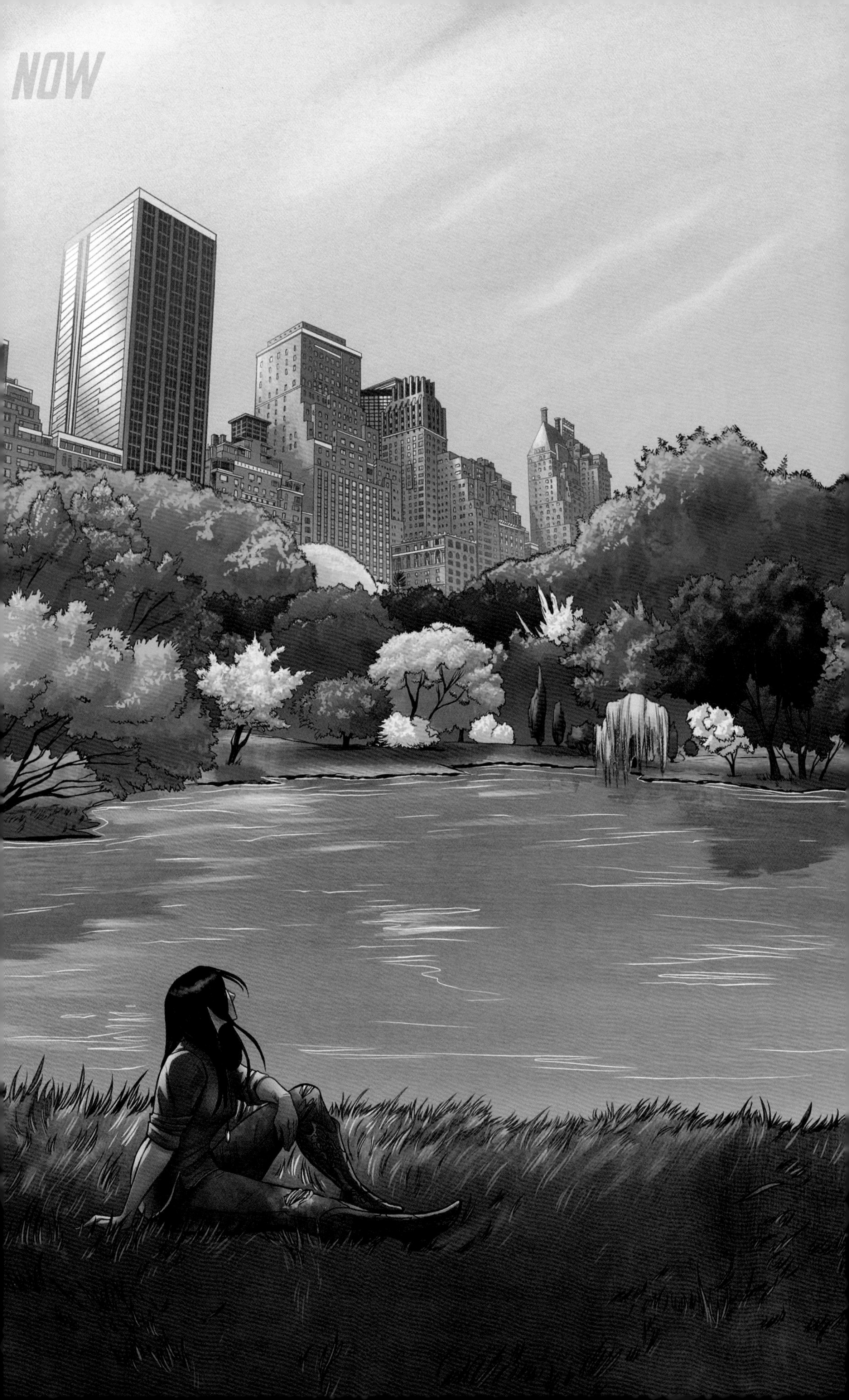
NOW

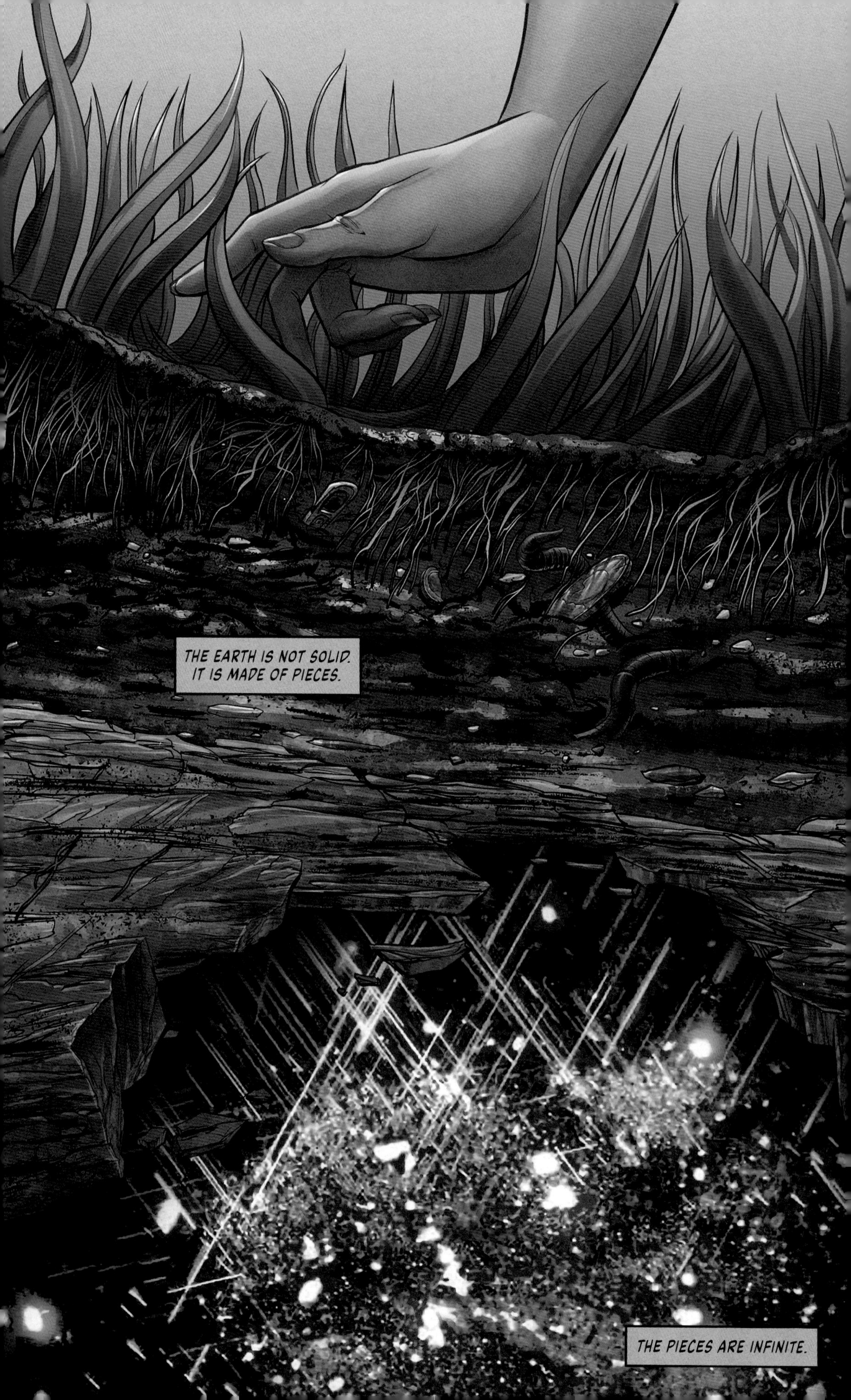
THE EARTH IS NOT SOLID. IT IS MADE OF PIECES.
THE PIECES ARE INFINITE.

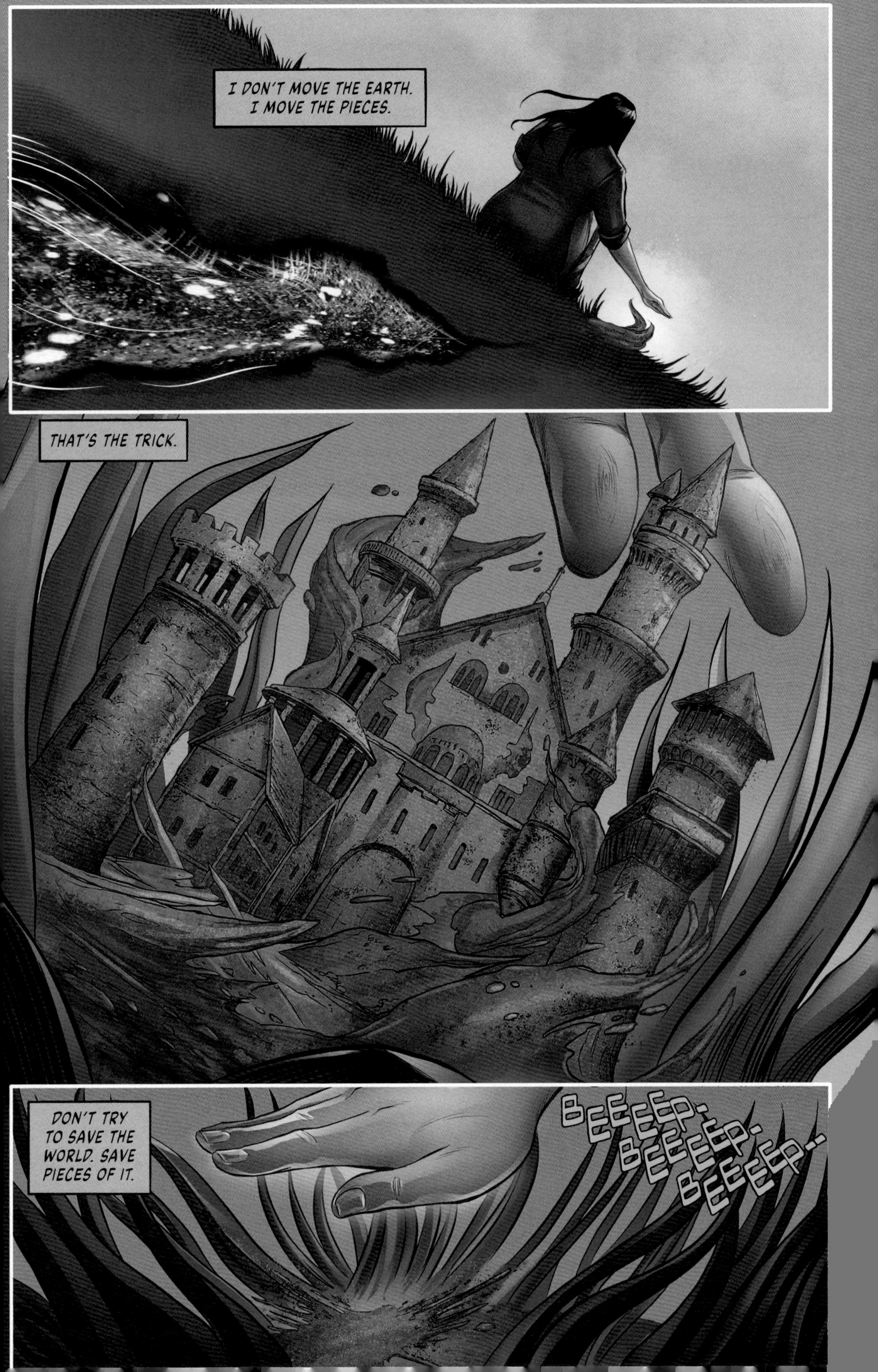
I DON'T MOVE THE EARTH. I MOVE THE PIECES.
THAT'S THE TRICK.
DON'T TRY TO SAVE THE WORLD. SAVE PIECES OF IT.
BEEEEP- BEEEEP- BEEEEP-

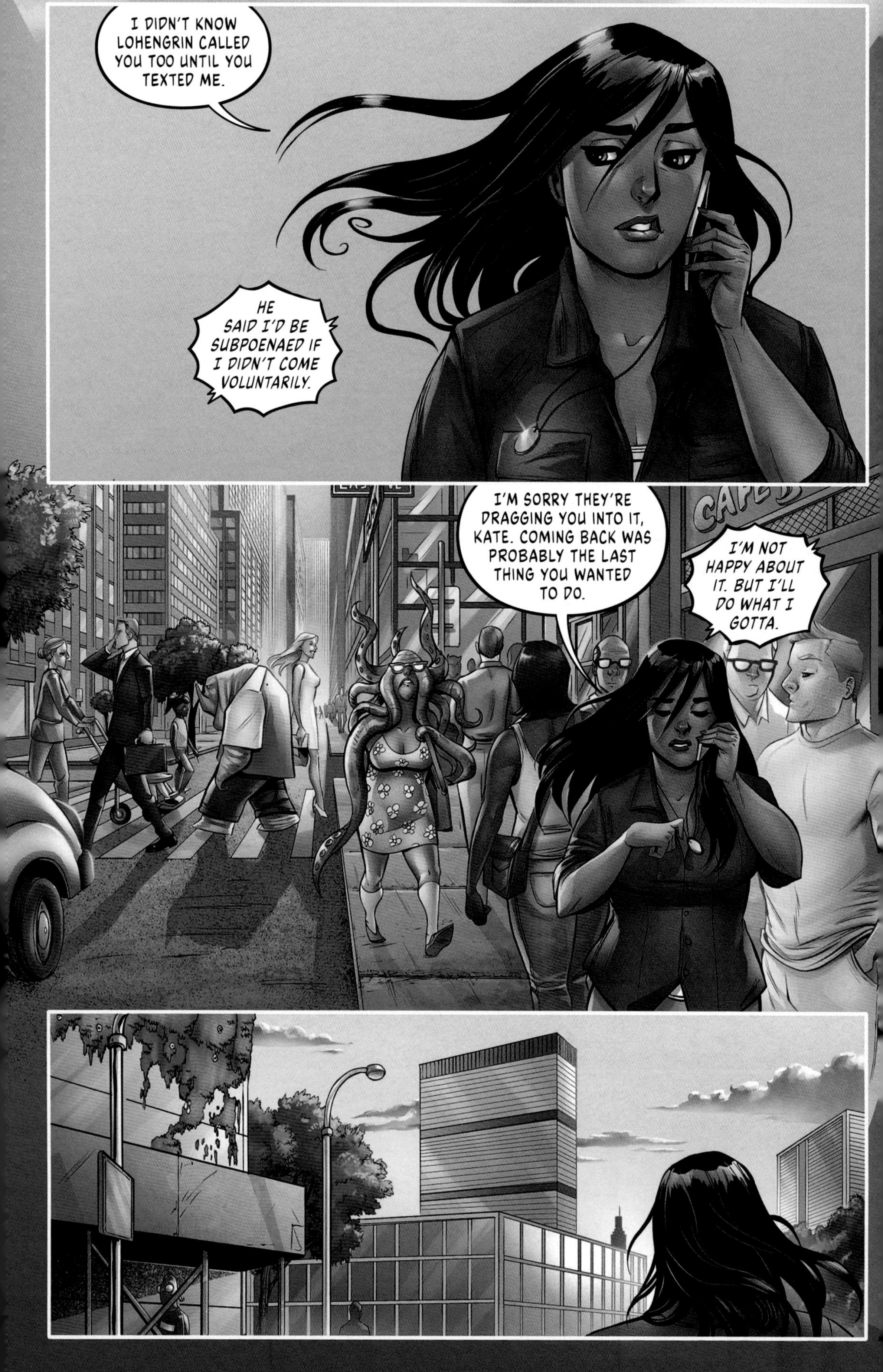
I DIDN'T KNOW LOHENGRIN CALLED YOU TOO UNTIL YOU TEXTED ME.
HE SAID I'D BE SUBPOENAED IF I DIDN'T COME VOLUNTARILY.
I'M SORRY THEY'RE DRAGGING YOU INTO IT, KATE. COMING BACK WAS PROBABLY THE LAST THING YOU WANTED TO DO.
I'M NOT HAPPY ABOUT IT. BUT I'LL DO WHAT I GOTTA.

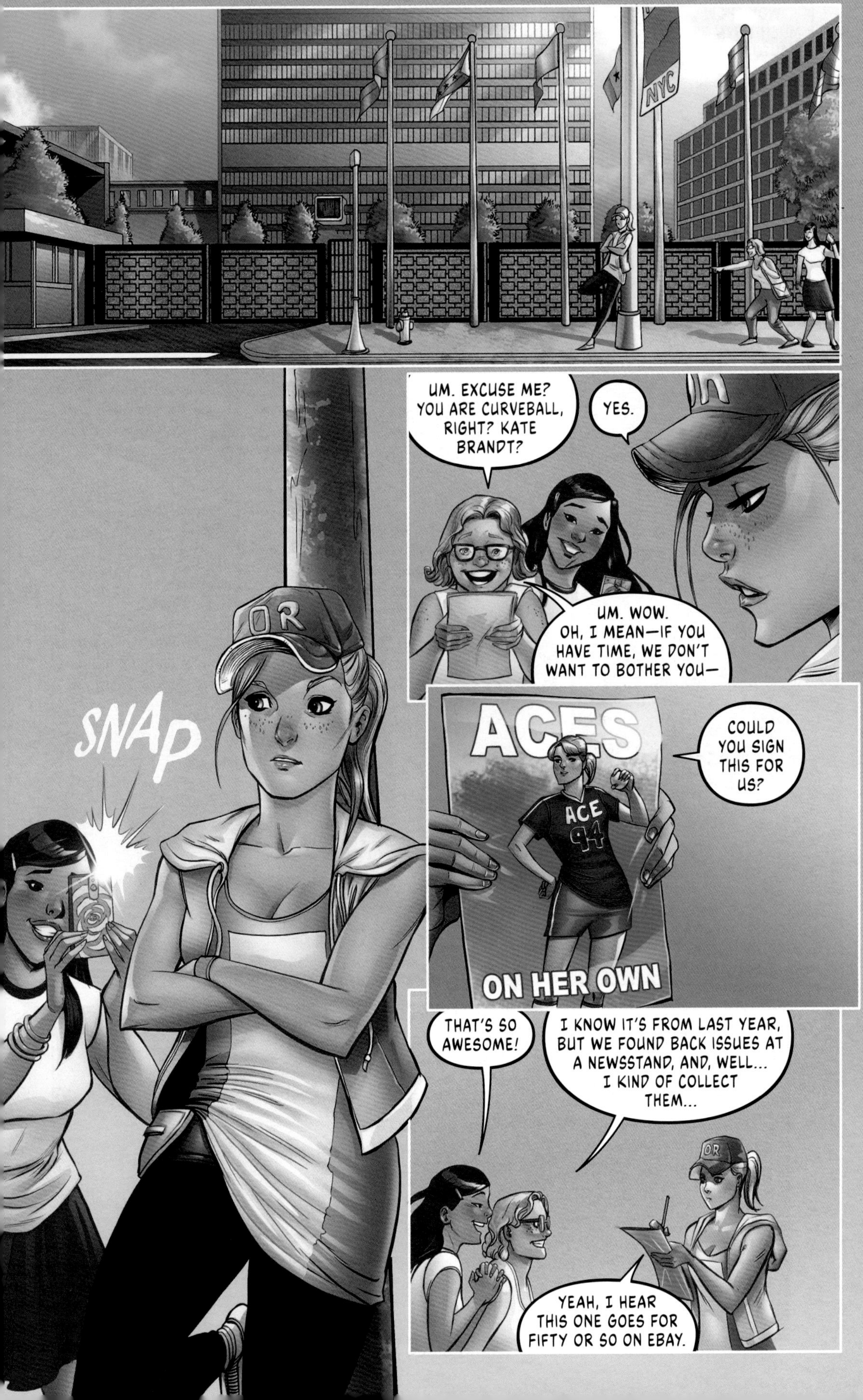
NYC
UM. EXCUSE ME? YOU ARE CURVEBALL, RIGHT? KATE BRANDT?
YES.
SNAP
UM. WOW. OH, I MEAN—IF YOU HAVE TIME, WE DON'T WANT TO BOTHER YOU—
ACES
ACE 94
ON HER OWN
COULD YOU SIGN THIS FOR US?
THAT'S SO AWESOME!
I KNOW IT'S FROM LAST YEAR, BUT WE FOUND BACK ISSUES AT A NEWSSTAND, AND, WELL... I KIND OF COLLECT THEM...
YEAH, I HEAR THIS ONE GOES FOR FIFTY OR SO ON EBAY.

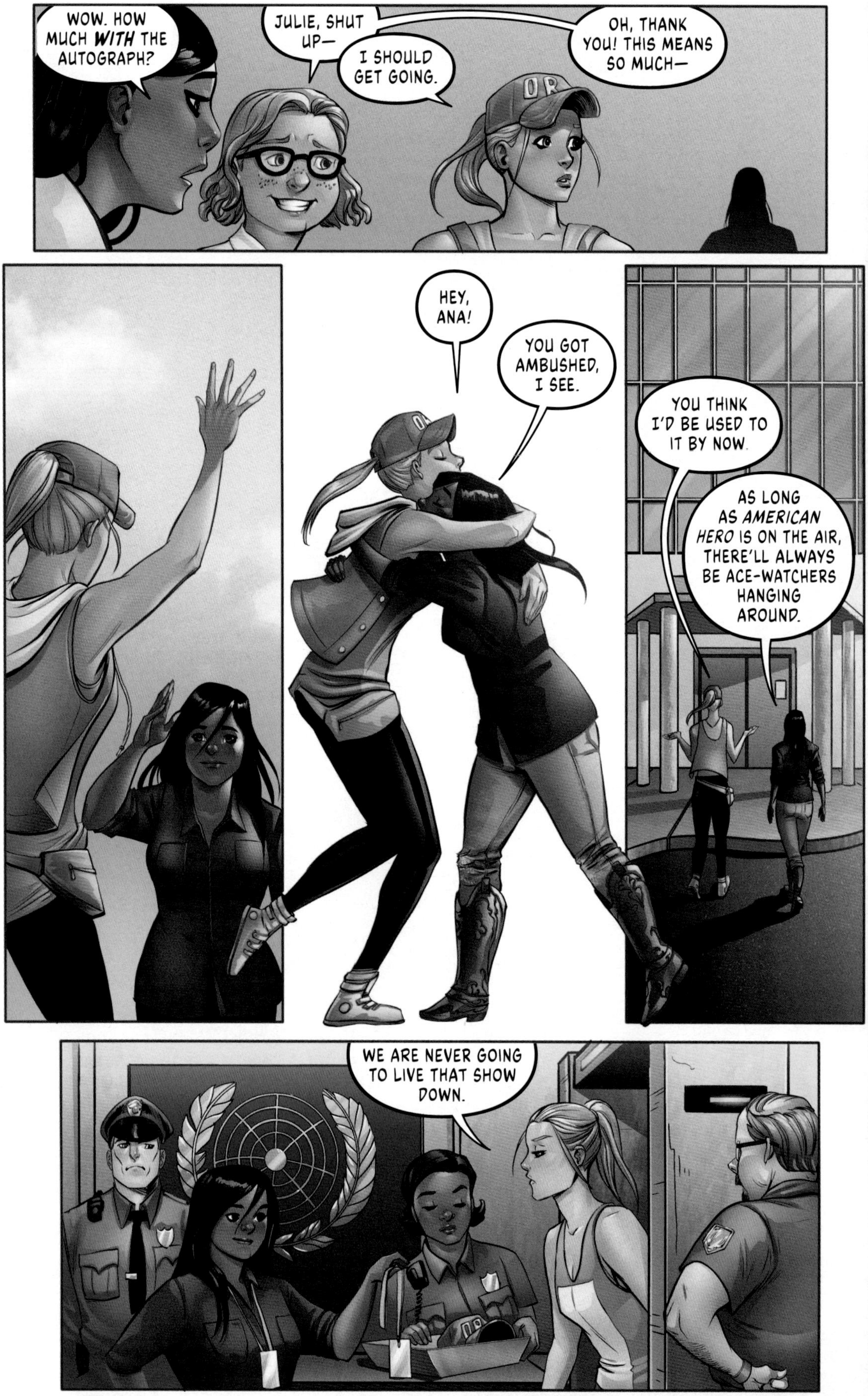
WOW. HOW MUCH WITH THE AUTOGRAPH?
JULIE, SHUT UP—
I SHOULD GET GOING.
OH, THANK YOU! THIS MEANS SO MUCH—
HEY, ANA!
YOU GOT AMBUSHED, I SEE.
YOU THINK I'D BE USED TO IT BY NOW.
AS LONG AS AMERICAN HERO IS ON THE AIR, THERE'LL ALWAYS BE ACE-WATCHERS HANGING AROUND.
WE ARE NEVER GOING TO LIVE THAT SHOW DOWN.

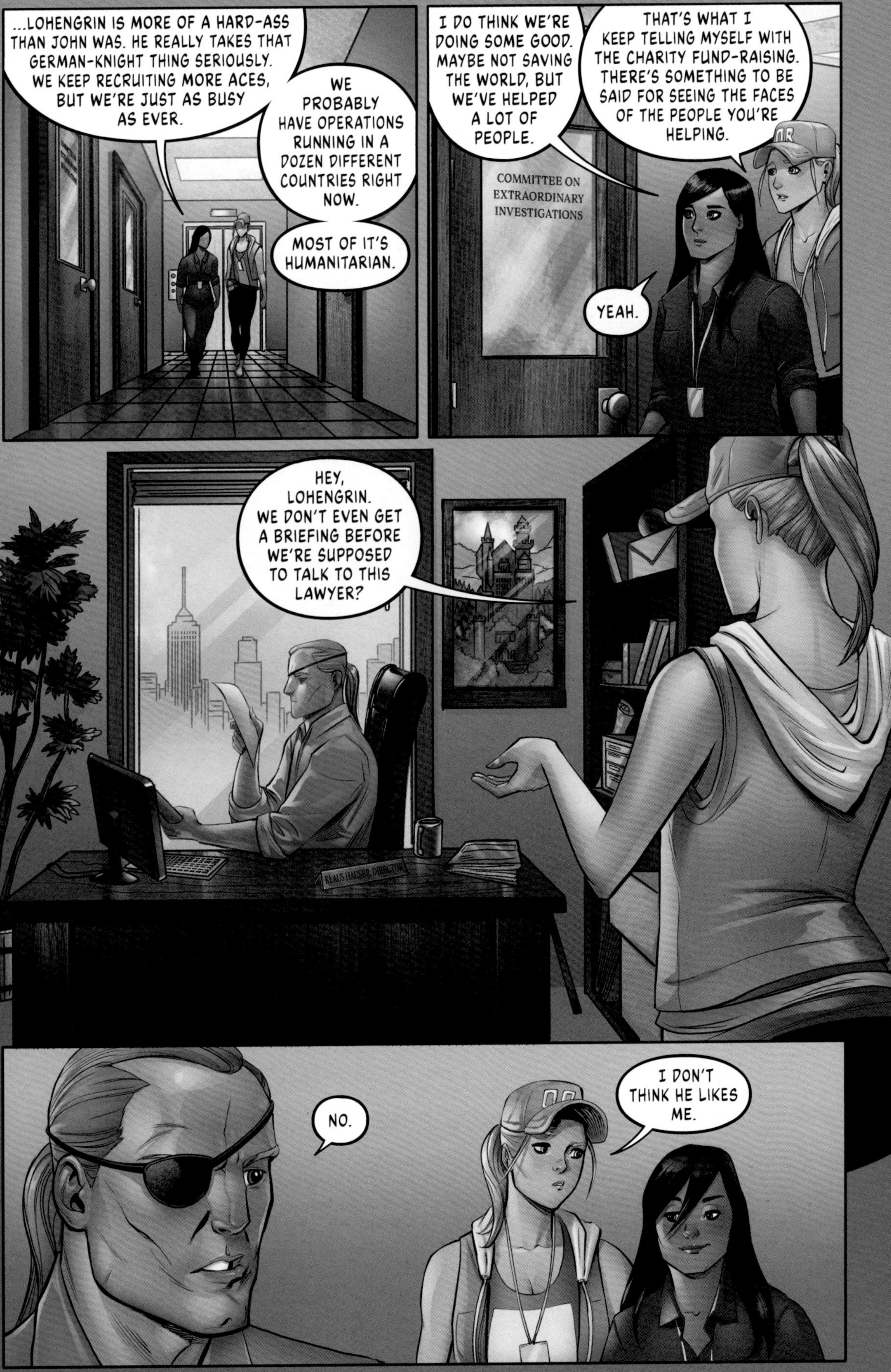
...LOHENGRIN IS MORE OF A HARD-ASS THAN JOHN WAS. HE REALLY TAKES THAT GERMAN-KNIGHT THING SERIOUSLY. WE KEEP RECRUITING MORE ACES, BUT WE'RE JUST AS BUSY AS EVER.
WE PROBABLY HAVE OPERATIONS RUNNING IN A DOZEN DIFFERENT COUNTRIES RIGHT NOW.
MOST OF IT'S HUMANITARIAN.
I DO THINK WE'RE DOING SOME GOOD. MAYBE NOT SAVING THE WORLD, BUT WE'VE HELPED A LOT OF PEOPLE.
THAT'S WHAT I KEEP TELLING MYSELF WITH THE CHARITY FUND-RAISING. THERE'S SOMETHING TO BE SAID FOR SEEING THE FACES OF THE PEOPLE YOU'RE HELPING.
COMMITTEE ON EXTRAORDINARY INVESTIGATIONS
YEAH.
HEY, LOHENGRIN. WE DON'T EVEN GET A BRIEFING BEFORE WE'RE SUPPOSED TO TALK TO THIS LAWYER?
NO.
I DON'T THINK HE LIKES ME.

GEORGE R. R. MARTIN

PRESENTS

SINS OF THE FATHER

BY MELINDA M. SNODGRASS

AN ORIGINAL WILD CARDS GRAPHIC NOVEL

ART BY MICHAEL KOMARCK AND ELIZABETH LEGGETT

LETTERING BY THOMAS NAPOLITANO

BANTAM

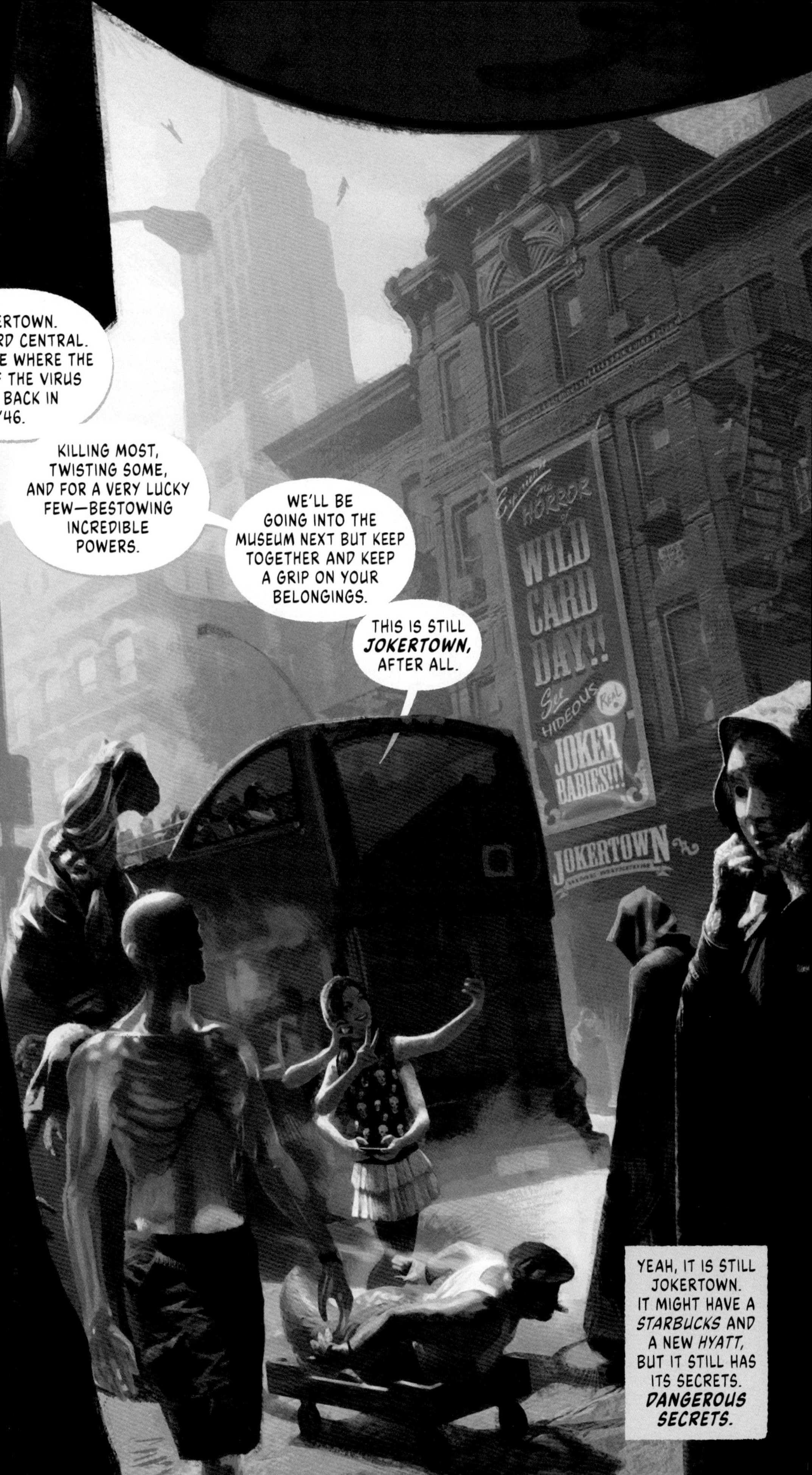
JOKERTOWN. WILD CARD CENTRAL. THE PLACE WHERE THE BULK OF THE VIRUS FELL BACK IN '46.
KILLING MOST, TWISTING SOME, AND FOR A VERY LUCKY FEW—BESTOWING INCREDIBLE POWERS.
WE'LL BE GOING INTO THE MUSEUM NEXT BUT KEEP TOGETHER AND KEEP A GRIP ON YOUR BELONGINGS.
THIS IS STILL ***JOKERTOWN,*** AFTER ALL.
HORROR
WILD CARD DAY!!
HIDEOUS
JOKER BABIES!!!
JOKERTOWN
YEAH, IT IS STILL JOKERTOWN. IT MIGHT HAVE A *STARBUCKS* AND A NEW *HYATT,* BUT IT STILL HAS ITS SECRETS. ***DANGEROUS SECRETS.***

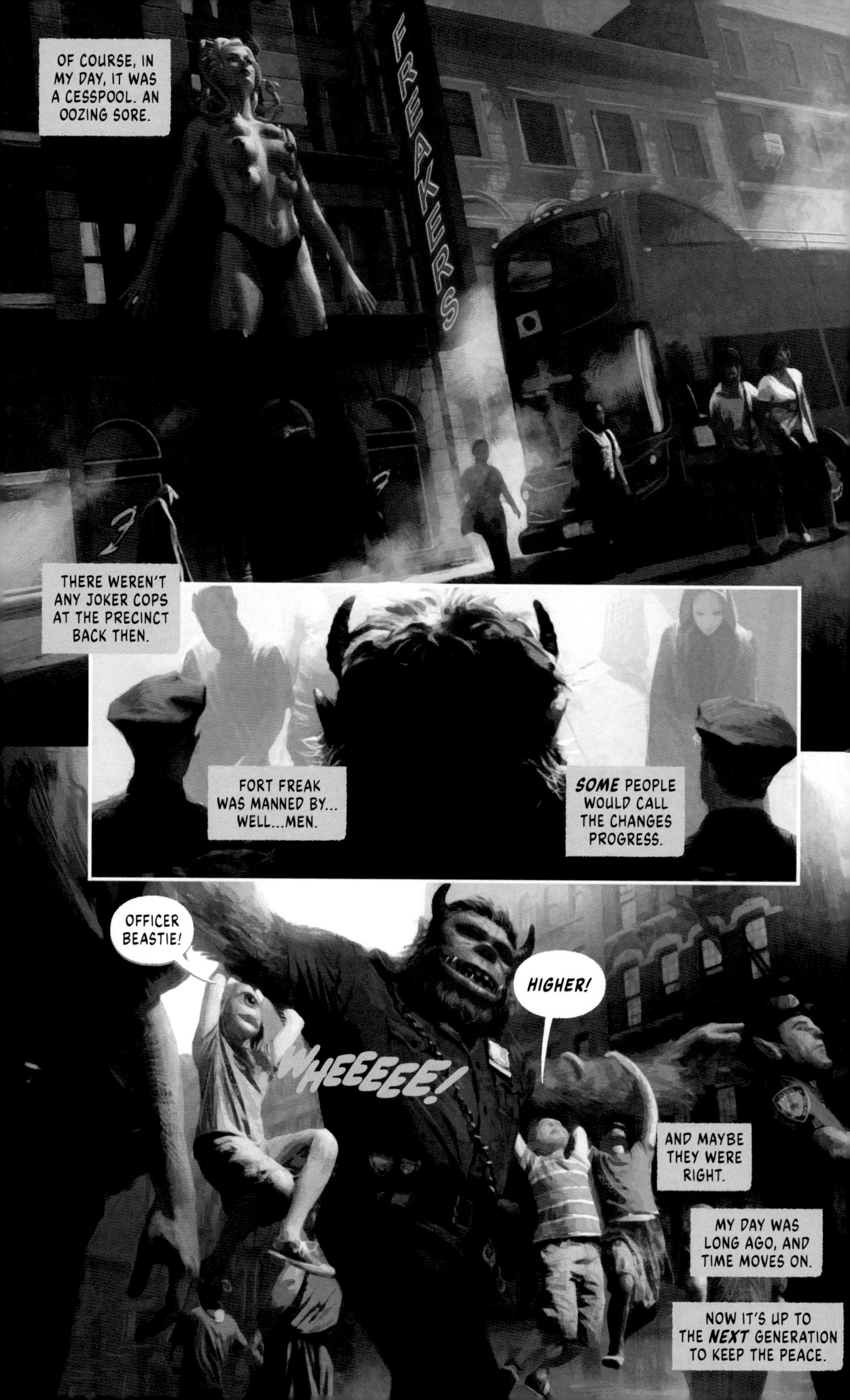
OF COURSE, IN MY DAY, IT WAS A CESSPOOL. AN OOZING SORE.
FREAKERS
THERE WEREN'T ANY JOKER COPS AT THE PRECINCT BACK THEN.
FORT FREAK WAS MANNED BY... WELL...MEN.
SOME PEOPLE WOULD CALL THE CHANGES PROGRESS.
OFFICER BEASTIE!
WHEEEEE!
HIGHER!
AND MAYBE THEY WERE RIGHT.
MY DAY WAS LONG AGO, AND TIME MOVES ON.
NOW IT'S UP TO THE NEXT GENERATION TO KEEP THE PEACE.

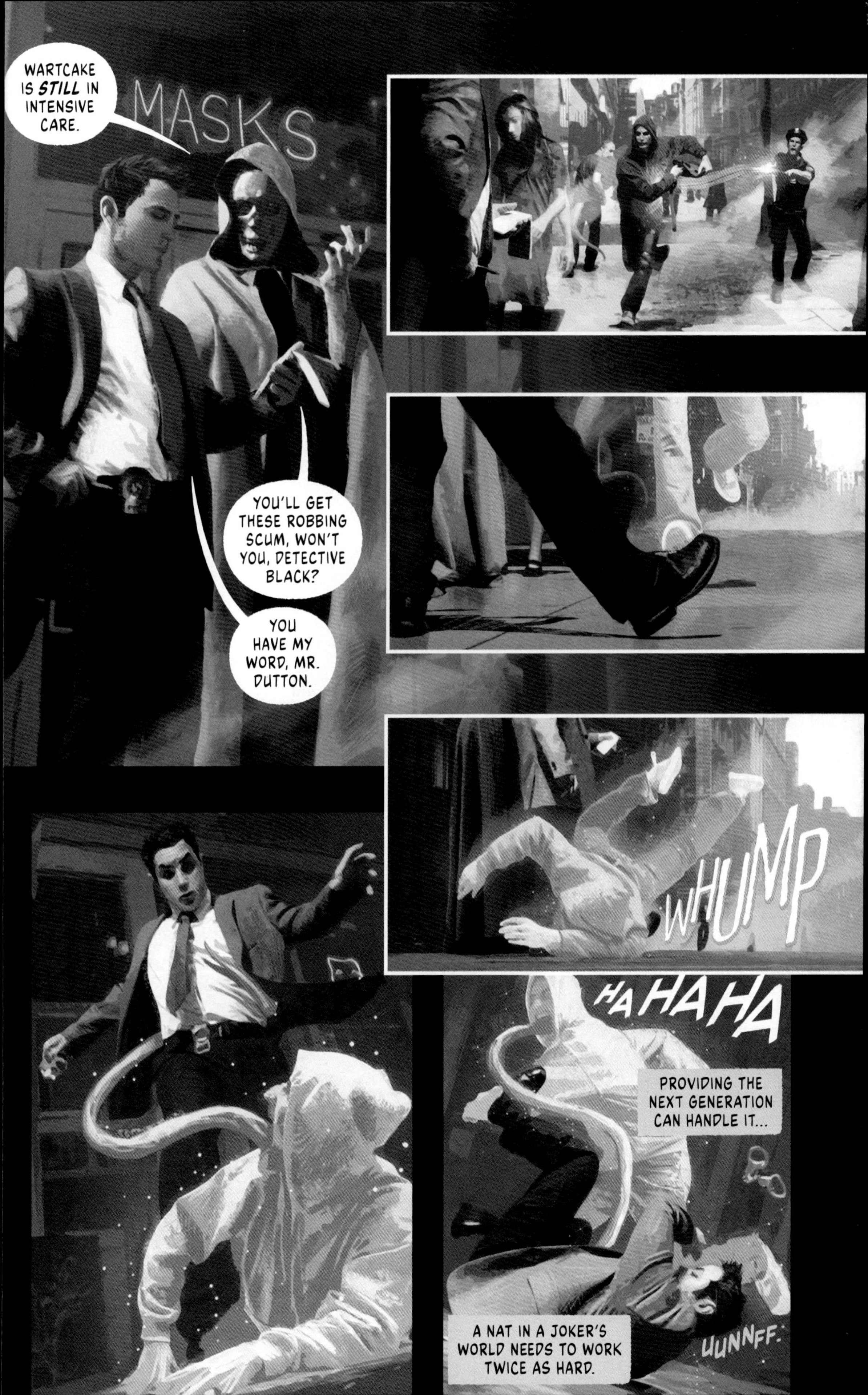
MASKS
WARTCAKE IS STILL IN INTENSIVE CARE.
YOU'LL GET THESE ROBBING SCUM, WON'T YOU, DETECTIVE BLACK?
YOU HAVE MY WORD, MR. DUTTON.
WHUMP
HAHAHA
PROVIDING THE NEXT GENERATION CAN HANDLE IT...
A NAT IN A JOKER'S WORLD NEEDS TO WORK TWICE AS HARD.
UUNNFF.

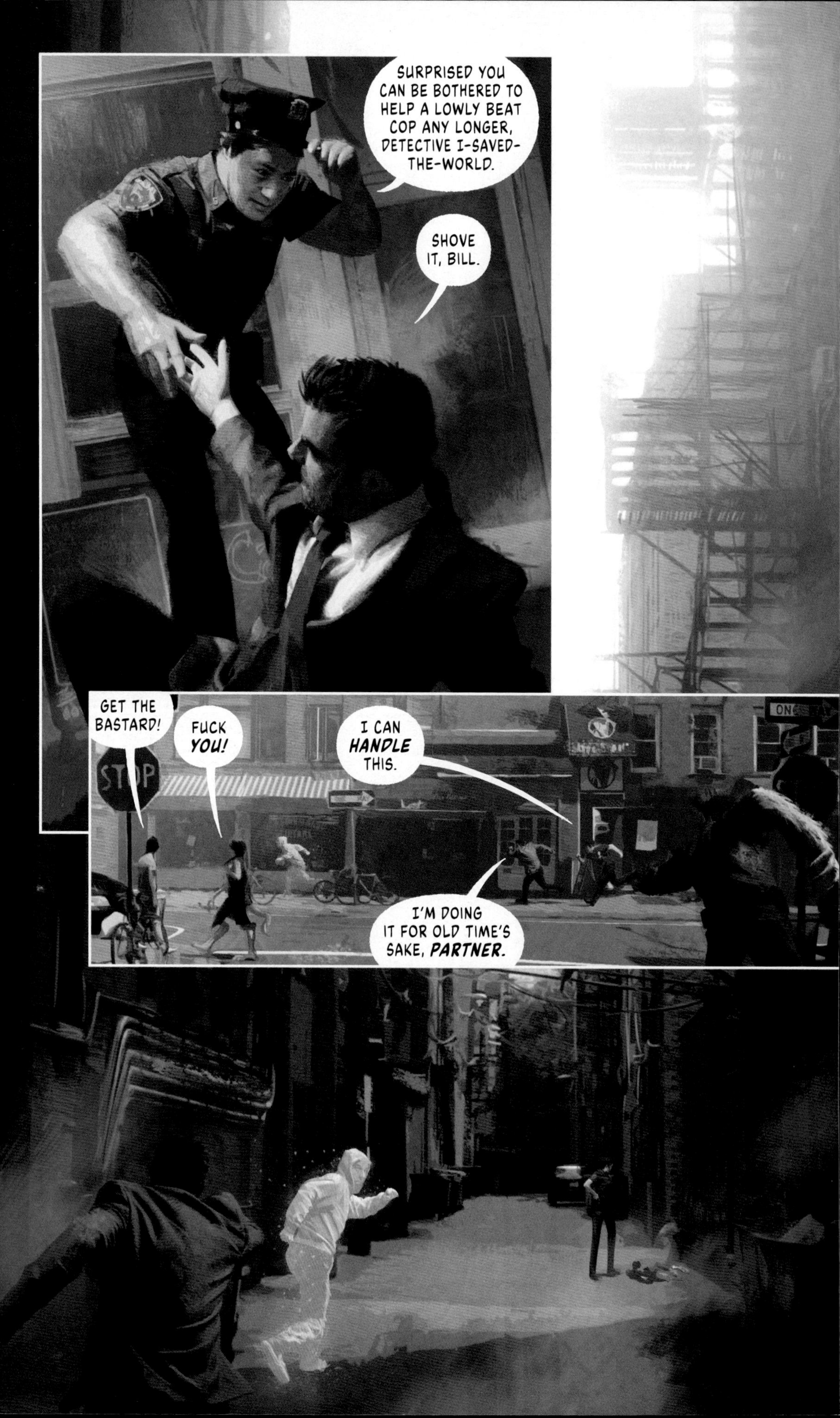
SURPRISED YOU CAN BE BOTHERED TO HELP A LOWLY BEAT COP ANY LONGER, DETECTIVE I-SAVED-THE-WORLD.
SHOVE IT, BILL.
GET THE BASTARD!
FUCK *YOU!*
I CAN ***HANDLE*** THIS.
I'M DOING IT FOR OLD TIME'S SAKE, ***PARTNER.***
STOP
ONE WAY

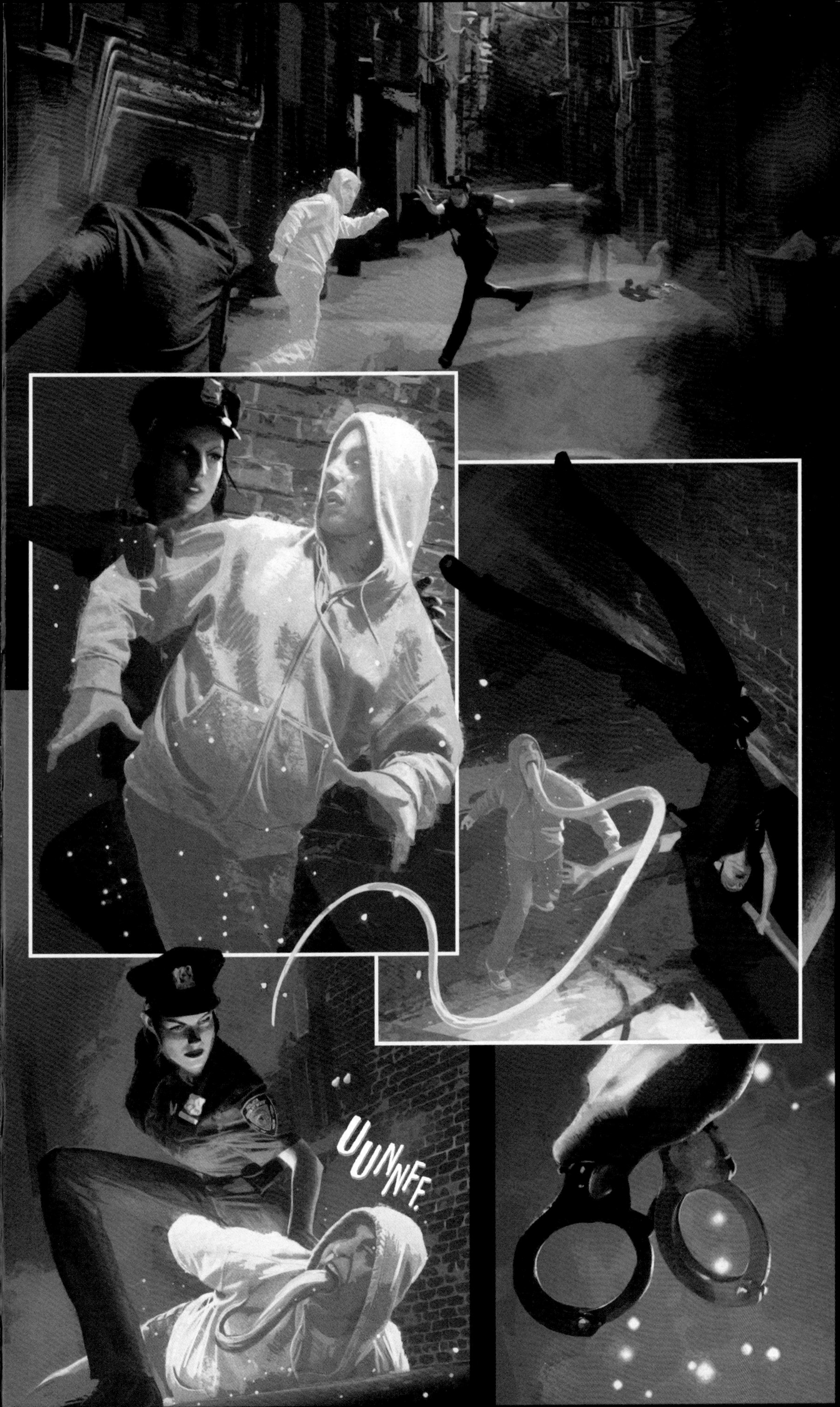
UUNNFF.

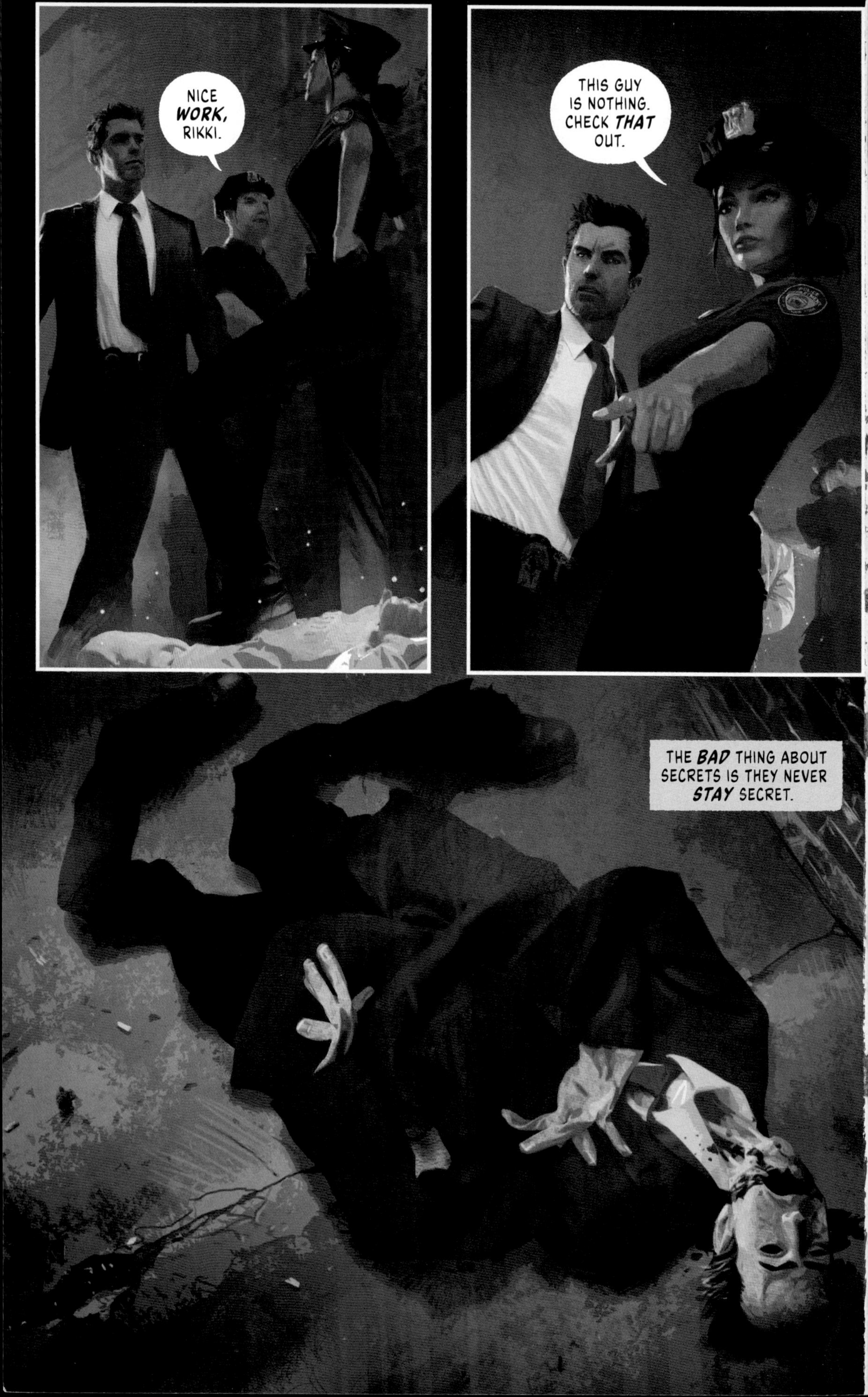
NICE WORK, RIKKI.
THIS GUY IS NOTHING. CHECK THAT OUT.
THE BAD THING ABOUT SECRETS IS THEY NEVER STAY SECRET.